Academic Work and Educational Excellence

THE NATIONAL SOCIETY
FOR THE STUDY OF EDUCATION

Series on Contemporary Educational Issues
Kenneth J. Rehage, Series Editor

The 1986 Titles:
Academic Work and Educational Excellence: Raising Student Productivity,
Tommy M. Tomlinson and Herbert J. Walberg, editors
The Contributions of the Social Sciences to Educational Policy and Practice:
1965–1985, Jane Hannaway and Marlaine E. Lockheed, editors

The National Society for the Study of Education also publishes
Yearbooks which are distributed by the University of Chicago Press.
Inquiries regarding all publications of the Society, as well as inquiries
about membership in the Society, may be addressed to the Secretary-
Treasurer, 5835 Kimbark Avenue, Chicago, IL 60637. Membership
in the Society is open to any who are interested in promoting the
investigation and discussion of educational programs.

Academic Work and Educational Excellence

RAISING STUDENT PRODUCTIVITY

Edited by

Tommy M. Tomlinson

National Institute of Education

and

Herbert J. Walberg

University of Illinois at Chicago Circle

McCutchan Publishing Corporation

2526 Martin Luther King Jr. Way
Berkeley, California 94704

ISBN 0-8211-1908-7
Library of Congress Catalog Card Number 85-62682

Printed in the United States of America

Contents

Contributors

Joseph Adelson, University of Michigan
Philip A. Cusick, Michigan State University
Walter Doyle, University of Arizona
Thomas L. Good, University of Missouri, Columbia
William F. Neumann, Educational Consultant
C. Robert Pace, University of California, Los Angeles
Robert J. Sternberg, Yale University
Deborah J. Stipek, University of California, Los Angeles
Tommy M. Tomlinson, National Institute of Education
Richard K. Wagner, Yale University
Herbert J. Walberg, University of Illinois, Chicago
Beatrice A. Ward, Center for Interactive Research and Development
Herbert Zimiles, Bank Street College of Education

Preface

History will probably show that the National Commission on Excellence in Education's *A Nation At Risk* ranks among the most important educational reports of this century. Although it was intended to address American problems, it was translated into many languages, most recently Arabic, Greek, and Japanese. Even though it was published only a few years ago, it appears to be the country's most often reprinted educational report (see Tomlinson's chapter in this book); and it was followed by much debate, additional reports, and the beginning of a large wave of educational reform.

The chapters in this book were among the many papers prepared for the commission. These chapters, however, are a select few that concentrate, as the title of this book implies, on academic work, excellence, and student productivity. These are perhaps the main themes of *A Nation At Risk*, which argues that excellence is important for the future of our nation, and that educators and students must work more effortfully and intelligently to achieve greater academic productivity. What may have been neglected in the report (short as it was), in many other reports, and in debates and reforms is the scholarly basis for such assertions about the role of the student. Many of the recent reports have focused on the curriculum, methods of teaching, ways of reorganizing schools, and the like. But students are the central actors in education; how and to what extent they pursue academic work are crucial to educational effectiveness. Hence this collection of papers.

The commission placed no constraints on the authors of papers that were commissioned. They were to write freely and persuasively on their assigned topics, and a great deal of debate about the commission's report has ensued. When we selected some of the papers for publication in this volume, we invited the authors to update and revise their manuscripts in the light of subsequent research and discussion, while remaining faithful to their original papers.

We hope these papers will inform educators and the public, as they have informed the commission, about students and their academic work.

Tommy M. Tomlinson
Herbert J. Walberg

PART I

Introduction

1

A Nation At Risk: Background for a Working Paper

Tommy M. Tomlinson

With notable vision, members of the National Commission on Excellence in Education (NCEE) decided that their report, *A Nation At Risk* (hereinafter also called the Report), should be short. They meant it to be read by people who would not ordinarily read such a thing—the public at large—and they composed it accordingly: ten thousand words of text on thirty-one pamphlet-size pages unimpeded by footnotes and references. Together with some introductory ma-

An earlier version of this chapter was presented on October 15, 1983, at the New York Academy of Sciences in New York City. In preparing this document I have tried with writing style to distinguish between material developed by and for the National Commission on Excellence in Education and information from other sources that I have used to compose the analysis and develop the narrative. The distinctions are not always clear and it would impede the reader to make them so in every instance. Therefore a caveat: This account is the product of my own experience and perspective, and while it involves the commission, the analysis is mine alone and in no way is to be understood as an official account of the commission's deliberations and thinking or the process by which it came to its conclusions. I would like to thank Peter Gerber, Milton Goldberg, and Ramsey Selden for their critical assistance in the preparation of this paper.

terial and a twenty-five page appendix, the result was a seven-inch by nine-inch educational blockbuster set off on April 26, 1983. The reverberations from its explosion continue to this day.

Initially 40,000 copies were printed for distribution by the Department of Education and 2,000 more were produced for sale by the U.S. Government Printing Office—but this printing fell far short of the demand for the Report. Just ten months later the Report was in its fifth printing and over 150,000 copies had been distributed. It was the U.S. Government Printing Office's fastest seller in recent years; over 70,000 copies had been sold through the mail or from their bookstores, and demand remained heavy.

But the demand experienced by the U.S. Government Printing Office was only a fraction of the overall demand for the Report. Indeed, it was the smallest of the circulation statistics. Over 500,000 copies of the Report were duplicated and distributed by various organizations. For example, the American Association of School Administrators sent copies to its entire membership of 18,000. The Association for Computing Machinery blanketed its 63,000 members with copies, and the Iowa State Department of Education distributed copies to 60,000 state residents. The trade press, the *Congressional Record*, and daily newspapers across the land have printed the piece in its entirety. A conservative calculation is that the text of the Report reached the hands of at least four million citizens, and there is no estimating how many more people shared the same copy or read the same newspaper.

The report has sparked a degree of debate and discussion of educational matters unsurpassed since Sputnik. Within a few months after the release of the report, the *New York Times* had run almost fifty articles in which the name of the commission was specifically cited; the *Washington Post* printed over forty. *Time, Newsweek, U.S. News and World Report,* and *Better Homes and Gardens,* among many other magazines, in company with myriad newspapers, news broadcasts, columnists, and pundits had described, discussed, and debated the conclusions and implications of the Report.

The Report was not the only call for educational reform. Several other major statements on the status of schooling in America followed the Report's release. In addition, well over a hundred state task forces and an incalculable number of local ones were established throughout the nation. It was a rare state that was not intensively engaged in reform activity based on an educational status report and plan for action of its own devising. While much of this activity was started before the publication of the Report, there is no doubt that the activity intensified after its publication. Taken together, the events of 1983 and 1984 represent a professional and popular review of American public education unprecedented in scope.[1]

CONSENSUS AND CONTROVERSY

From the beginning, *A Nation At Risk* has received more comment—pro and con—than any of the other statements. Not only was it first and federal, but, possibly unique in the annals of government reports, it was also written with rhetorical flair and a minimum of technical jargon. It was a report to the public, and it captured the public's ear as well as its mood. In short, it focused the attention of the nation and thereby became the lightning rod as well as the rallying point for school reform interests throughout the United States.

Moreover, by generating debate and interest in the state of the nation's schools, *A Nation At Risk* not only produced a windfall of publicity for education in general but also increased the prospects for the consideration of the subsequent longer and more complex treatments of secondary schooling, including, for example, those by Boyer (1983), Goodlad (1984), and Sizer (1984). Ordinarily, reports of this kind are prized by educators and academics for their rich detail, but for the very reasons of their length and complexity they are of limited appeal to the general public and policymakers. *A Nation At Risk*, however, enlarged the readership of the subsequent reports, presumably because it led to higher levels of debate and greater sophistication of the public and of policymakers in educational matters.

Perhaps more startling than the sheer number of statements was their consensus. Indeed, whether national or local in perspective, whether supported and prepared by state government or by private foundations, the conclusions of the various organizations, commissions, task forces, and study groups about the status of secondary schools and the recommendations for their improvement were much more alike than they were different (Congressional Research Service 1983; Griesemer and Butler 1983). These statements differed more in their emphasis and in their analytic and contextual detail than they did

---

1. The reader is referred to "The Nation Responds: Recent Efforts to Improve Education," a compendium of state and local education reforms compiled by the staff of the National Commission on Excellence in Education and published in May 1984 by the U. S. Department of Education.

in their evidence, conclusions, and recommendations. Although some critics have treated these differences as though they were examples of serious substantive conflict, the fact remains that the many independent studies on curriculum, students, standards, teachers, textbooks, and leadership were all based on essentially the same evidence, came to essentially the same indictment of the current status of public education, and steered essentially the same course of reform. Thus, in just thirty-one pages *A Nation At Risk* covered the essentials, sparked the interest of readers outside the profession, and successfully challenged the nation to reform its schools; no other report can make these claims.

About the Evidence

The impact of *A Nation At Risk* was a measure of its style as well as its substance. Short, pungent, and free of distractions, its claims implied evidence and experience; but its style forbade references, citations, and footnotes as well as the usual "scholarly" discussion of the issues. As a consequence, some critics have challenged the currency and timeliness of some of the Report's evidence and conclusions and, consequently, its recommendations (for example, see Stedman and Smith 1983). As it has turned out, however, the evidence on which the Report was based has stood up well to criticism. For example, Walberg in chapter 12 of this volume and others (Rohlen 1983; Stevenson 1983) offered more up-to-date comparisons of Japanese and American students showing differences that were larger than those noted in the ten-year-old, allegedly "obsolete" data that were available to the commission.

While the durability of the evidence was reassuring, the critics' observation that shortcomings in the nation's educational research and statistical efforts forced the commission to employ information that may have been out of date or of uncertain validity was a fair assessment. Although the commission had anticipated this situation and sought the advice of experts in areas of uncertainty—for example, no fewer than ten papers and the testimony at two meetings buttressed the commission's assertions that American education compared unfavorably with education in other countries—the fact remains that the quality and kind of educational research and statistics necessary to assess the status of education were not up to standard. The controversy about the quality of the evidence, however, may have produced yet another windfall for education. The urgent need for a larger and an up-to-date effort to document the status of learning and education in the nation was established, and a substantial effort to design indicators and collect the appropriate statistics has emerged at both the federal and state levels.

Although the quality of some of the available data was suboptimum, over forty separate papers covering every major facet of secondary and postsecondary education were commissioned and submitted for the commission's consideration. The menu for this feast of information is substantial; almost half of the Report is given to a list of the scope of the research and the sources of evidence considered by the commission (NCEE 1983, pp. 39–61). From these papers the commission compiled a body of evidence and developed a working conceptualization of the process and substance of schooling and learning.

In this chapter I will try to illustrate how these papers and other evidence compiled by the commission's staff served to inform the commission's work; how a conceptual framework that emphasized time, content, and expectations was developed; and, finally, as a case in point, how academic work emerged as an important, probably decisive, but poorly understood and little-used dimension of schooling and learning.

TIME, CONTENT, AND EXPECTATIONS: DEVELOPING A CONCEPTUAL FRAMEWORK

The description of schooling and achievement developed by the commission was strongly influenced by the thought and work of John Carroll and Benjamin Bloom. Carroll's (1963) short and powerful paper, "A Model of School Learning," emphasizes the learning task and hence the conditions that promote effective academic work rather than the mechanics of learning or the role of student ability. When Carroll's work is combined with propositions about time and learning (Bloom 1976) and the role of alterable variables in school reform (Bloom 1980), clues to school improvement emerged that were straightforward and expedient.

What Is Alterable

Borrowing liberally from John Carroll's (1963) work, the commission pictured a generally positive relationship between the kind and quality of the time, content, and expectations that go into the academic task and consequent learning. Alterations in the amount or quality of any of the three can presumably affect the quantity or quality of learning that results. To illustrate, consider the familiar distinctions drawn between "power tests" and "speed tests." Power tests provide unlimited time to perform a limited task and aim to measure competence by assessing how well the student performed the completed task. Speed tests provide limited time to perform a typically unlimited task and assess competence according to the amount of the task correctly completed (the rate of performance). Time, content, and expectations (standards) all play an obvious role in the two methods of assessment in differentiating between students who have and have not learned. For example, in a power test slow performers may achieve as much as fast ones; it just takes them longer. Similarly, if students with content deficiencies have time to recoup the missing content, they may learn as quickly and as much as students who are initially more knowledgeable. In both instances, time is a proxy for effort and for opportunity to learn, and, as such, may substitute for ability and prior experience, thereby serving to equalize the otherwise unequal results owing to prior advantage. On the other hand, if time is limited—as is the case with speed tests—so is the opportunity to learn; the duration but not the intensity of effort is decreased. Differences that result from unequal ability and prior experience are thus emphasized, and slow or knowledge-deficient learners may do poorly or fail because they run out of time.

Viewed from this perspective, the relationship of time, content, and expectations to student achievement depends on a number of factors. For example, consider the following list of variables, all of which to varying degrss have been associated with the quantity and quality of student achievement, and, if they were alterable, would be the focuses of school improvement reform efforts:

1. student ability
2. teacher ability (quality of instruction)
3. quality of academic work ('study skills')
4. quantity of academic work ('time-on-task'; effort)
5. previous learning (background)
6. student, parent, and teacher expectations
7. graduation requirements
8. textbook content
9. nature of the subject matter (English, mathematics, science, and the like)

10. length of school day and year (allocated time)

Intuitively, some of these variables seem to influence learning directly (for example, the quality and quantity of academic work), and some indirectly (for example, teacher expectations). Some appear easy to manipulate (for example, academic requirements), while others seem more difficult (for example, student ability). Would evidence support intuition? What is the nature of the relationship between these factors and learning? How many of them can be altered as a matter of educational policy and practice? Which of them most affect learning, and how can they be systematically moved toward that end?

For example, there is a commonsense appeal to the idea that the quantity and the quality of student effort are directly and causally related to achievement. The notion is so obvious that one would think that the nature of academic work and methods of learning would have been closely studied and developed. Yet little is known about the effects of homework or study methods on learning. In fact, we discovered that most students and their teachers knew very little about effective and efficient study methods (Griffin and Ridgway 1983; MacVicar 1982), and we found that most educators know almost nothing at all about recent developments in cognitive science that promise to improve the quality of the teacher's instruction and the student's academic work.

Thus we quickly concluded that one of the most obvious causes of learning—studying—is among the least well understood dimensions of education. Indeed, when it comes to the role of the student in learning, what is true of studying is true generally: We know startlingly little about the students' role in learning or how to improve on their "naturally" developed approaches to schoolwork. In the literature, students are typically treated as passive recipients of instruction who depend entirely on the teacher for learning, as if learning and instruction are the same thing. Yet we found in the literature conceptions of the academic task and strategies for learning that suggest that how students learn is at least as important as the content and instruction in determining academic achievement. Can students be taught how to learn? If so, will it make any difference in achievement? Can students at risk of failure for want of enough time be enabled to learn more—enough to pass—in that limited amount of time? Can trained and expert learners master a school task in less time than those whose skills are informed only by intuition and habit? Is learning a more rewarding task for trained learners than for novices? And do these trained learners thus have a motivation to study that they may not otherwise have if they were not trained.?

Thus it is apparent that this line of thinking directs attention to multiple factors in the schooling experience, especially those that may influence the quality and quantity of students' academic work effort. Some of these factors have been studied or given substantial thought, and we found a sizable body of instructive literature has been published, which often aided the fact-finding process. To reach conclusions in areas where little was known or the material was of uncertain validity, the commission used informed guesswork. In such cases, the commission sought advice from experts who reviewed the evidence and, depending on its quality, drew conclusions or made expert guesses. From these resources as well as from the testimony at many hearings and symposia on special topics, substance was given to the framework of time, content, and expectations. A summary of the evidence follows.

I. TIME

A. School Time

The quantity of school time—the amount of time spent at school—is fixed by arbitrary rules and dates; there are so many hours in a class day and so many days in a school year. Accordingly the allocation of school time is a zero-sum game in which numerous elements compete for a share, and for every winner there must be a loser. Among these elements are courses of study, some with academic content but with an increasing minority of students enrolled in them (NCES 1982). With few exceptions, the number of academic courses required for graduation or college admission has declined, and furthermore, since most courses count equally toward graduation, there are few incentives for students to volunteer for the hard work and uncertain grades of unimposed rigorous academics. The net result is that students spend less time on academics than is necessary to maintain the standards of achievement that the commission believed necessary to the welfare of the society and of the students.

B. Personal Time

Personal time—the time students spend out of school—is viewed as a discretionary resource, equally available for schoolwork, making money, or playing. As homework, it can be added to the time of the school day and, to the extent that time-on-task contributes to learning, it can to varying degress compensate for scholastic inadequacy or enhance scholastic advantage. Many attractions compete for discretionary time, almost all of which seem to exceed schoolwork in appeal. In the head-to-head competition with, for example, playing or a job for the use of leisure time, homework is a natural loser; homework is more difficult than course work to require, and teachers find it almost impossible to make students do it. To paraphrase an old metaphor, you can lead students to the trough of knowledge but they may not drink enough to pass, especially when the thirst for education is merely another elective.

So it was reckoned that if the amount of school time is limited and if capable students are failing to choose important but difficult academic courses or academic work, then the task of raising the level of academic achievement is straightforward: enlarge the proportion of the school day allocated to academic pursuits, and increase the advantage of spending time on schoolwork over the competing alternatives. Specific policies responsive to these conclusions can be found in a number of recommendations in the Report, including reduced social promotions, more required academic courses, improved learning skills, more homework, more efficient classroom management, longer school day or year, and higher college entrance requirements.

C. Time-on-Task

Once school time is allocated, the task is to fill it with schoolwork that most effectively and efficiently achieves the goal of learning. However, the role of time in schoolwork, that is, in studying and learning, is hardly straightforward and does not easily lend itself to reform. For example, the evidence about the relationship between learning and what has by now become a cliché in education, time-on-task, is well established (Caldwell, Huitt, and Graeber 1982), but it is by no means a clear or particularly robust relationship (Karweit 1982). The quantity of work that students can do in any unit of time varies according to the limits of their endurance (motivation) and performance rate (ability). Standards of quality will also affect the level of effort as well as the role of talent or experience in meeting expectations. It goes without saying—or ought to—that how the time is used for learning is the critical issue in achievement, and that these factors will determine the returns per unit of gross time. This view undergirds the eight recommendations the commission made about time, seven of which emphasized more effective and efficient use of time by improving the student's learning skills and the teacher's instructional skills.

II. CONTENT: CURRICULUM AND INSTRUCTION

A. Curriculum: Optional Learning

The evidence reviewed by the commission indicated that the typical curriculum is deficient on a number of counts:

1. Across the nation curricula vary substantially in the subjects that are offered or required; in many instances science and one or more of its constituent disciplines are missing entirely, especially at the elementary level. Even when they are offered, too few substantive courses are required in the areas of science and mathematics (Adelman 1983; Astin 1982; Hurd 1982; NCEE 1982a).
2. Electives are credited from a wide variety of nonacademic topics and often compose most of the official curriculum; most graduation requirements permit at least one year of electives in high school—usually the last year—and to the exclusion of advanced academic courses, with the consequence of a wasted senior year; middle school curricula often repeat previous course work or are irrelevant to academic goals (Cusick 1982; Farrar, Neufeld, and Miles 1982; Resnick and Resnick 1982; Ward, Mergendoller, and Mitman 1982).
3. The substantive quality of textbooks and teachers has declined in company with standardized achievement test scores: texts have been "written down" and mathematics and science teachers are insufficient in quality and quantity (NCEE 1982a; NCEE 1982b).

In short, from school to school and from state to state the content of the curriculum is unacceptably variable and too often weak, insubstantial, and academically debased. While an academic curriculum is offered in most large high schools, it is optional and apparently unpopular with many students. The commission's conclusion is irresistible: If achievement is to improve, especially in the areas most acutely deficient in content, the schools must require or add courses in the weak areas, improve the quality of the textbooks, and increase the knowledge and number of those who teach the subjects.

B. Instruction: What Do Teachers Do?

The first concern of the commission about teaching was why it appeared to take more schoolpeople to get less learning out of fewer students than it did twenty years ago. The line of evidence appeared to be uncomplicated: Over the past twenty years, while the scores on standardized tests and the number of students enrolled in school have decreased, the number of school personnel, teachers, and administrators has increased (NCES 1983). Since it is popularly held that teachers are responsible for learning, and since the teachers themselves claim that the "student-teacher ratio" has a significant, perhaps decisive, influence on their ability to help their students learn, it is understandable that as the number of students declines and the number of teachers increases, the public would expect student achievement to improve; instead, it has diminished. From this perspective, the taxpayers are getting ever less for their money and have been fully justified in turning down bond issues and otherwise expressing their displeasure with the apparent decline in the productivity of the schools and especially of the teachers.

Other facts were found to bolster the argument that the effectiveness of teachers has decreased. Teachers have been overrepresented at the low end of the distribution of SAT scores; they are exposed to training that has been considered by many to be intellectually bankrupt; they are trapped in a dead-end occupation of their own design since they refuse to accept differential pay; and while claiming to be singularly important to learning are nonetheless at pains to disclaim responsibility for the steady decline in the indicators of academic achievement.

On the other hand, it remains that teachers are very important to learning. They are the purveyors of content, the managers of the media through which information flows to the students. We expect that teachers should not only be masters of their subject but be effective in its communication. Other things equal, we should also expect that the more teachers know of their subject and the better they communicate it, the more students should learn. In short, there should be an identifiable connection between the teacher's knowledge of the subject matter and instructional competence and consequent student achievement.

.Alas, the commission found very little reliable information that explains, much less proves, a causal relationship between these features of instructional skill and student achievement. Research that describes and demonstrates how teachers' behavior influences learning has been largely confined to the beginning stages of formal schooling, and it describes an instructional context that is found only at the elementary level (Rosenshine 1983). Despite the burgeoning literature on the characteristics of so-called "effective schools," there simply is not much in it about life and learning in American high schools (Tomlinson 1981a; Farrar et al. 1982; Purkey and Smith 1983).

So far as educational research has found, instructional skills and pedagogical methods are only indirectly and unclearly related to learning but should not be taken as evidence of incompetent or weak instruction. After all, learning is not caused by teachers; at best they only aid and abet it. Students do the learning, and although they might like it otherwise, it is they who must perform the academic work. Teachers, of course, know this; it is not exactly a secret, although it is not talked about much in public. It is, however, a problem. Managing learning and persuading and instructing distracted and disinterested students to the view that they should learn even if it is hard and boring and apparently irrelevant is not easy. But there are ways to do it.

Some teachers inspire work in their students, others make it impossible to avoid. The instructional key to learning will be found in the management of students' behavior toward more effective and efficient academic work, which is a responsibility shared by the teacher and the student. To this end, teachers, as classroom managers, exert their effect through their own efficient management of time and instruction in the classroom and by enabling and demanding similar qualities in the academic labor of their students.

In this light, we sought to discover how to keep students working effectively and efficiently at school, both at the hands of their teachers and when they study on their own time. A substantial factor in this process will be reflected in the expectations that are imposed on the students by "management" (the classroom teacher), the quality or skill level required by their academic tasks, and the outcome of the negotiations between the students and the teachers that Doyle (1982) tells us determines the amount of academic work they will perform to achieve the reward they seek.

III. EXPECTATIONS: DECLINE AND RENEWAL

Forty or fifty years ago it was convenient to assume that all students were equally exposed to a common academic core, even students who pursued a vocational curriculum, and that the grades they received were a fair measure of the time and talent they spent in meeting the teacher's standard of achievement. Prior to the 1960s, students who could not or would not meet the standard were understood to be incompetent, customarily failed, and, if they could, usually left school before graduation. Their failure was seldom taken to reflect the incompetence of either teacher or school. In view of the close association between academic success and social background, the net effect was to turn schooling into a class-related academic competition in which poor children and slow learners were usually excused early from the exercise (some were never admitted), and the schools were largely held harmless from responsibility.

With the changes in our society and its students during the 1960s and 1970s (described by Adelson in chapter 2 and contrasted with the 1980s by Zimiles in chapter 3 of this volume), the competitive system gave way under a mandate to educate all children. Ineluctably the standard of merit based on variable mastery of a common academic core, but which accepted failure and dropouts as a matter of course, was replaced by a social imperative to pass and to graduate. So that everyone could graduate, the standards of achievement or the content of the standard curriculum or both were necessarily weakened (Resnick and Resnick 1982). Beginning in the 1960s, the evidence of academic erosion in the nation's schools was plain to see: declining test scores, grade inflation, reduced academic enrollments, less homework, endemic disinterest in learning, curricular tracks for "nonacademics" and disinterested learners, and, finally, individually tailored curricula. In the 1970s three curriculum tracks were fully developed where only two had been before: to the traditional academic and vocational education curricula had been added the once inchoate general course of study (Adelman 1983). Each was suited to different students depending on their aptitude and effort, and each promised a diploma indistinguishable from the other two.

The effects of these developments at all levels of schooling are described in part 3 of this volume. The sense of these effects is captured in a single statistic: By 1982 barely one-third of high school seniors were enrolled in the academic track. The art of effortless matriculation reached its peak as student discretion and elective choice replaced required courses in each track. Students could tailor their own curriculum according to their tastes and plans, which, for many, did not include academic learning. Expectations had become a personal matter. Standards were in a shambles. Learning suffered.

So that everyone could graduate—the appearance of equal outcomes—a system of certification had been devised that obviated talent or competence, required the same amount of time for all (homework was often optional), and led to a diploma for everyone who stayed the course. It also carried the pernicious side effect of debasing the diploma while providing most students (not just the poor) with an inferior academic experience. The multiple and elective curriculum system not only defeated the goals of equity and equal opportunity but also corrupted the fragile integrity of academic standards and reduced the justification for effort on behalf of learning.

EQUITY AND EXCELLENCE

The road to equality is neither smooth nor easily followed. Which way lies equity: making school easy by routing students around academic courses, especially the hard ones, or insisting that all children encounter the academic core even if some of them have a difficult time of it? There ought not be a problem here. Our society had long ago settled on its definition of quality and no group adheres to that definition more closely than those minorities that see education as a way to social and economic equality (for example, see McCarthy 1983 and Wharton 1984).

The need for a quality education is not a rhetorical matter. Citizens from every walk of life ought to be able to understand the effects of pollution and pesticides, should understand the politics of ecology, should be able to make informed decisions about nuclear energy, and must know how to cope with life in a society shaped and changed by high technology; with such knowledge they can select their representatives and leadership. In this society who could ask for less, and who, knowing this, would settle for less?

Quality education is an academic education. It is America's educational grail. Anything else is treated as inferior, and any person with less is considered to that degree less educated. We all know this, and most of us, with good reason, believe it. From *Brown* v. *Board of Education* to basic skills, from direct instruction to mastery learning and effective schools, the theme has been constant: A quality academic education is necessary and possible for all children. The efforts of the past twenty-five years have virtually without exception been directed to providing children with the basics, that is, the fundamental academic core. As elementary school curricula have emphasized basic academic learning and as instruction has rigorously inculcated these skills, the standardized achievement scores of minority children in these subjects in the early grades have steadily improved. The time has come to extend these gains into middle and secondary schools. The efforts expended in elementary schools are wasted if middle and secondary schools offer only "make-work" and theater because of the belief that many students cannot or will not learn but must at any cost be kept coming to school.

On behalf of returning quality to the high school experience of all students, the commission recommended that, at minimum, all students seeking a high school diploma be "required to lay the foundations in the Five New Basics by taking the following curriculum during their four years of high school: (a) four years of English; (b) three years of mathematics; (c) three years of science; (d) three years of social studies; and (e) one-half year of computer science" (p. 24).

The new basics not only set a new and higher standard of academic requirements but asks that many more students be expected to study the same content and meet a higher standard of learning. Obviously, this is a troublesome area. Can all students meet this expectation at a level that deserves or justifies the belief that some acceptable level of mastery of some intellectually acceptable quantity and quality of content has taken place?

Success in the venture may require a reconception of schooling, certainly a reconception of our goals in view of the current methods of structuring the work. We will want to retain the benefits of specialized instruction for slow learners; the new basics do not and must not depend on sheer talent for mastery. At the same time, content must not be thinned to vanishing to compensate for differential learning rates or initial disadvantage within fixed-time frameworks. It will, however, take longer for slow learners or language-burdened students to meet an acceptable criterion of achievement than it will take their more facile peers.

Accordingly, it is perhaps time to stop acting as though burdened students can or must learn at the same rate or in the same amount of time to the same criterion as those who start free of impairment. It is clear that they do not and that the consequence is unnecessary failure. The distinction among students need not be invidious. For example, children who do not speak English when they enter school have the extra burden of mastering the three R's and English too. It may take them a year just to learn English well enough to meet the academic requirements of first grade. Given the priority of English over other academic content, the language-burdened children might require a year longer to graduate than those without the burden.

In taking the position that all students can learn and that time is the only limiting factor, it follows that schooling must be structured to take account of and promote those features. The goal is mastery of a common curriculum by all graduates—a power test—not sorting students according to their speed of acquisition. Therefore, the time available for learning must equal the time required, adjusted for the rate at which the students learn. So instead of using curriculum tracks based on content or ability and structured according to a fixed time framework, why not use a common (academic) track structured within a flexible time framework according to the student's learning rate or initial burden? Facile students will be given or may be expected to complete the course in eleven years, average students in twelve and slow or burdened students in thirteen. The academic goal is not unique—we have been talking about it since the inception of public schooling, and the time format is merely a working and realistic version of mastery learning that Bloom (1976) and his colleagues have been advocating for years.

THE ROLE OF WORK

Withal, concerns about the nature and magnitude of revising education through the implementation of the new basics are not misplaced. Some critics and not a few students have begun to think of this Report as the "hard work" report, and there is little question that if the provisions of the Report are seriously addressed, students and teachers will both be burning the midnight oil.

Armed with faith and fact, the Report assumed that all children can learn, but also that children vary greatly in the quality of their academic performance. The commissioners were not persuaded that an index of mental ability should determine access to the new basics, any more than they believed that the limits of achievement are defined by social and economic background. On the contrary, because re-duced expectations and their corollary, underachievement, have been endemic, the commissioners saw a large reservoir of untapped effort available for academic use. Thus, they believed that while it would be practicable to raise standards for everyone, achievement would not likely improve if reform began by setting arbitrary limits on the number of learners eligible for the new basics.

Thus, while acknowledging a relationship between achievement and academic talent, the evidence of erosion, especially the decline of standardized test scores, was ascribed more to deficits in the (alter-able) quantity and quality of academic work that result from reduced expectations than to a (fixed) decline in or absence of intellect. It follows, then, that an academic education is within the intellectual range of a majority of students, certainly far more than the fraction currently enrolled in the academic curriculum. Furthermore, the interests of educational equity—opportunity and outcome—and the full realization of talent will be met only if all students can validly claim exposure to and opportunity to learn from a quality academic curriculum. Because of this and because the prospects for altering talent are unpromising—although some think it possible to train intelligence (Sternberg 1984)—attention was turned to other causes of learning, most prominently those reported by Doyle (chapter 8 in this volume), Stipek (chapter 9), Sternberg and Wagner (chapter 10), and Pace (chapter 11) concerning the nature of the academic task and the kind and quantity of work necessary for its effective and efficient performance.

ACADEMIC WORK

Just as there is more to learning than time alone, there is more to raising student productivity than just hard work. Nonetheless, there is plenty of room for work, especially if it is combined with methods and intellectual tools that will increase the returns of the labor. Thus, for example, B. F. Skinner, when asked about the commission's recommendation that the school day and year be lengthened, ob-served that, "There's no need to lengthen the school day, lengthen the school year, and add more homework, as the commission recom-mended. What we need to do is to arrange matters so students can now learn twice as much in the same time, with the same amount of effort, if they're properly taught. Look into any classroom. At any

given time, how many students are working hard? Usually very few"
(Hall, 1983, p. 26).

Skinner sells short the value of additional school time, and,
consistent with his observation, the public thinks that more and better
work will help. For example, the 1984 Gallup poll about education
found that 67 percent of the sampled population believes that high
school students are not worked hard enough by the schools and 59
percent believes that elementary school children are underworked
(Gallup 1984). Either the public believes that since 1975 schools have
become lax in their work standards or that schoolchildren have
become more lazy (or both), because the percentages in 1975 were 49
percent and 54 percent respectively.

However, the public, like Skinner, does not look favorably on
extending the school day or year as a method to increase learning.
Just 42 percent favor lengthening the day by one hour and 44 percent
favor lengthening the year by thirty days. This is an understandable
position for a public who believes that shortages of effort should be
made up before it invests in more schooling. Thus, because of the
public's strong sentiment for working harder, the absence of support
for more school time suggests that either the students (and teachers
too?) will have to work more "unpaid overtime" (homework) or they
will have to learn faster to meet the standards set by higher graduation requirements and the new basics.

Fortunately some things can be done to improve the quality of
students' work and enable them to "learn faster." There are promising methods of increasing productivity, methods that directly affect
the students' performance of academic work. This approach understands the student to be the locus of learning and assumes that
improvements in students' work capability and efficiency will have
commensurate and direct effects on the product of their labor, learning. The problem is to improve the returns—the learning—per unit of
student time and effort expended on the learning task. A discussion of
the dimensions to the process follows.

A. The Quantity of Work

Although the scientific evidence is limited, both intuitive/
empirical and statistical evidence exists to support the association
between the amount of time a student spends on a learning task and
the amount and quality of learning that results (see for example,

Bloom's [1976, 1982] and Walberg's [1984] work with gifted persons and the review of the evidence by Caldwell et al. [1982]).

Perhaps one reason the research evidence is so limited is that most of it is gathered in situations (elementary school classrooms) and under circumstances (low-achieving learners and criterion-referenced tasks) that permit little room for the expression of differences in ability or learning rate. Learning-to-criterion says little about how much more content could be learned by bright students within the time available, or how much more time would be required by slow students if the criterion were raised. Indeed, even Bloom, that most ardent advocate of equal outcomes, observes that inexperienced and slow learners take as much as five times longer than fast learners to reach mastery, and even then skilled slow students still need twice as much time to learn as do fast students (Bloom 1976).

Most of us who went to high school or beyond remember that the serious work of learning did not result from our listening and note taking during the class period itself but was a result of the work we did out of class—the homework. To be sure, many of us may also remember that we learned enough to pass even if our homework involved little more than taking our books home every day. But we all knew that when serious learning was required, of the kind, say, that was expected for final exams, then we "burned the midnight oil." Though formal proof is seldom required, and although educational research has thus far failed to make much of a case for it, most students come to believe that the quality of their academic performance is closely associated with the amount of work they give to their studies (Frieze 1980). Indeed, depending on the conditions, academic work serves most students as both a complement to and a substitute for academic ability. Although science paints a more complex picture of the relationship, it remains that studying is one of the more productive things that students can do to learn.

It is a commonsense axiom that any factor or event that adds to or subtracts from the effectiveness or the efficiency of the academic work will influence the quantity or quality of the subsequent learning. The factors that influence the amount of time spent in academic work are many and variable in their effects, but from the standpoint of raising achievement, we must consider means to expand the time spent doing academic work. For example, schools could increase the production requirements (standards, course requirements, and the like), assign more homework, reduce nonacademic school time (cut out frills, drop football, eliminate "redshirting" athletes in the seventh grade, and so forth), reduce distractions (lock the entrance doors, turn off the squawk box, patrol the halls), or lengthen the school day. In theory, all of these serve the interests of increasing academic time by making more of it available or by preempting competing interests.

B. The Quality of Work

Academic work is not exactly a natural process (Sherman 1983). Students are not innately effective, much less efficient, learners. Left to their own devices, bright learners appear to develop intuitively learning strategies that are reasonably effective but seldom optimal. Slower learners, if they grasp the requirements of the task at all, typically use brute-force (rote and repetitive) methods, and the extent to which they can be trained in more effective and efficient work skills remains uncertain (Sternberg and Wagner 1982). Furthermore, most teachers, when students themselves, were not taught how to study, and since teachers are seldom among the intuitively expert academic workers, they can provide little instruction and few examples of effective or efficient work skills. Further, even when they grasp and can describe the relationship between academic work and learning, they are seldom interested in teaching their students how to do it themselves. Some teachers believe that teaching study skills is boring and time-consuming—another encroachment on the time available for "real learning" (Griffin and Ridgway 1983; MacVicar 1982).

Unskilled, brute-force methods (most notably rote memorization), are labor intensive and hence slow and inefficient; these methods require an inordinate and, for slow learners, ultimately disastrous amount of time (Tomlinson 1981b). As the content of schooling becomes more and more complex and as the learning task shifts from memorization to understanding and comprehending, brute-force learning strategies become ever less effective and ultimately worthless. Somewhere along the way, usually around the fifth or sixth grade, academic learning virtually stops for many students, especially the poor ones who can no longer keep up. In this light, Jencks's (1978) observation that the "learning problem" is not in the (memorized) basics but in the complex skills, may be understood, at least in part, as the result of a failure to advance from primitive to complex methods of academic work.

In this circumstance slow learners are at a double disadvantage. They neither absorb nor process information as rapidly or as easily as their quicker peers, nor do they spontaneously and independently develop more efficient and effective work methods as they encounter more complex tasks. Slow students risk failure because their methods either take more time than is available or are irrelevant to learning complex tasks. In both cases time is wasted, and when time runs out and learning is incomplete, failure occurs.

Finally, since homework has been suggested as a method of increasing the length of the school day, any improvement in students' ability to learn outside the classroom not only provides for independent work and self-teaching but also husbands the time officially allocated for teaching and supervised study. This is clearly a windfall for both teacher and student and maybe even the taxpayer, although its success may require explicit attention to students' capability to manage and perform independent study.

Turning naive and dependent pupils into skilled and sophisticated independent learners is or ought to be a principal task of high school. The activity looks ahead to life as well as to college; in both instances the vast majority of learning takes place outside class, on the students' own time and according to their own self-imposed criteria of mastery. That the schools have work to do in this regard, especially for marginal students, is documented by the testimony that 25 percent of entering college freshmen quite literally do not know how to do college work (Hechinger 1982).

Mundane as it seems, old-fashioned as it sounds, there is no doubt that academic work is the key to raising achievement. As we observe American high school students studying less (NCES 1982) and the influence of their parents declining, we are overwhelmed with stories about the long hours of hard work that Japanese students spend on their studies and how much pressure their parents and teachers place on them to work to excel. For example, Garfinkel (1983), in an article titled "The Best 'Jewish Mother' in the World," provides an amusing but sobering version of the role of work and maternal pressure in the education of Japanese children. School has become life in Japan; there is no time for anything else (Fiske 1983; Rohlen 1983).

Japanese education may not be a model for America. Indeed, many Japanese are beginning to complain about the rigors of their routine, and some even look wistfully to the "humane" aspects of the more "relaxed" American system. However, the Japanese show us what is possible with hard work, and they provide us with an example and a justification for asking more from our own typically far less industrious students. Expecting our students to work hard on behalf of learning is neither unfair nor irrelevant. Hardworking students learn more regardless of their talent, even if talented hard workers learn the most. In his studies of gifted children, Bloom (1982) observes over and over and in many ways how hard the children worked and how devoted they were to the development of their gift, whether it was physical or mental.

While not impervious to poor teaching, independent and hardworking students can be prodigious learners regardless of the quality of instruction. Sizer (1983) is instructive: "The way one learns to teach oneself is to practice doing it and to have that practice critiqued. This absolutely requires serious independent work (homework) and time available both for teachers to challenge students' efforts and for students to struggle with this process of learning to learn" (p. 682). The best compensation, then, for the uncertainties and irregularities of teaching are students who can teach themselves and who work hard at it.

Recent survey data indicate, however, that the point may be moot. In choosing among a variety of methods for improving academic achievement, both schoolteachers and administrators are strikingly ambivalent about homework (NCES 1983). Only 7 percent of the high school administrators surveyed thought homework was a very important means of improving achievement, and less than 20 percent of them have taken steps to raise homework requirements (although an additional 19 percent intended to increase homework requirements by the 1984–85 school year). One cannot tell whether these educators do not believe homework affects student achievement or whether for one reason or another they see little potential in it for raising test scores.

There are many opportunities for homework to fail, including poorly designed assignments that add little to the regular instruction, teachers who themselves are incompetent learners and cannot teach students what they do not know themselves, teachers' inability to enforce the assignments for students who are indifferent in school and are worse outside class, and the excessive burden on teachers who review the homework (of course, homework unreviewed is a waste of students' time). While these problems must be solved before students are given more homework, most of them may be answered through better design of the homework lesson, improving the performance of teachers, and creating incentives to motivate students.

While homework does not require students to have special aspirations and abilities, there is no reason to delay enabling all students to

become as good at learning as they can be. Learning how to learn is a
key to successful academic performance and successful lifelong learning. In this respect there are no distinctions among learners. Slow
learners are at risk of failure when left to use their own methods to
learn, which simply consume too much time with too little return.
While no students need fail because they lack skills, the greatest gains
to training, gains now being missed, will likely accrue to the most
facile learners. High ability multiplies the results of academic labor,
especially the results of the complex but powerful study skills being
discovered and developed by cognitive science.

ON THE ROAD TO TECHNOLOGY

An appropriate conclusion to this discussion is another quotation
from B. F. Skinner:

First of all, we need to be clear about the importance of teaching basic skills. Then we
must tackle the problem that is at the heart of the greatest source of failure in
American education: the effort to get the whole class to move at the same rate. That is
absolutely impossible, and everybody knows it. No teacher can arrange proper
learning conditions for thirty or forty students. In the typical classroom, students who
could go much faster are held back, and students who need more time don't get it and
fall further and further behind. The only solution is to make use of devices of one kind
or another, call them what you will, computers, teaching machines, or even interactive systems. . . . (Hall 1983, p. 26)

We must heed Skinner and add technology to learning so that we
can move from unskilled and labor-intensive learning to skilled and
electronically aided learning. To this end the main purpose of computers and other electronic devices is to impove on the methods of
learning or to enhance the results of the labor of learning. Cognitive
science is making great progress in understanding the mental processes by which learning takes place and hence the nature of the work
that most efficiently produces learning (Bransford et al. forthcoming;
Brown, Campione, and Day 1980; Doyle 1983; Glaser and Pellegrino
1982; Sternberg 1984). Many educators believe that making human
cognitive processes and electronic information processing compatible
and productively interactive is the approach that learning demands.
But pending that development, I would settle for a good course in
study skills.

REFERENCES

Adelman, Clifford. "Devaluation, Diffusion, and the College Connection: A Study of High School Transcripts." Paper prepared for the National Commission on Excellence in Education, Washington, D.C., 1983.

Astin, Alexander W. "The American Freshman, 1966–1981: Some Implications for Educational Policy and Practice." Paper prepared for the National Commission on Excellence in Education, Washington, D.C., 1982.

Bloom, Benjamin S. *Human Characteristics and School Learning.* New York: McGraw-Hill, 1976.

Bloom, Benjamin S. "The New Direction in Educational Research: Alterable Variables." *Phi Delta Kappan* 61 (February 1980): 382–385.

Bloom, Benjamin S. "The Role of Gifts and Markers in the Development of Talent." *Exceptional Children* 48 (April 1982): 510–522.

Boyer, Ernest. *High School: A Report on Secondary Education in America.* New York: Harper and Row, 1983.

Bransford, John D.; Vye, Nancy; Adams, L. T.; and Perfetto, Greg A. "Learning Skills and the Acquisition of Knowledge." In *Handbook of Psychology and Education*, edited by Robert Glaser and Alan Lesgold. Hillsdale, N.J.: Lawrence Erlbaum Associates, forthcoming.

Brown, Ann L.; Campione, Joseph C.; and Day, Jeanne D. "Learning to Learn: On Training Students to Learn from Texts." *Educational Researcher* 10 (February 1981): 14–21.

Caldwell, Janet H.; Huitt, William G.; and Graeber, Anna O. "Time Spent in Learning: Implications from Research." *Elementary School Journal* 82 (May 1982): 471–480.

Carroll, John. "A Model of School Learning." *Teachers College Record* 64 (May 1963): 723–733.

Congressional Research Service. *Comparison of Recommendations from Selected Education Reform Reports.* Washington, D. C.: Library of Congress, 1983.

Cusick, Philip. "Secondary Public Schools in America." Paper prepared for the National Commission on Excellence in Education, Washington, D.C., 1982.

Doyle, Walter. "Academic Work." Paper Prepared for the National Commission on Excellence in Education, Washington, D.C., 1982.

Doyle, Walter. "Academic Work." *Review of Educational Research* 53 (Summer 1983): 159–199.

Farrar, Eleanor; Neufeld, Barbara; and Miles, Matthew W. "School Programs in High Schools: Implications for Policy, Practice, and Research." Paper prepared for the National Commission on Excellence in Education, Washington, D.C., 1982.

Fiske, Edward B. "Education in Japan: Lessons for America." *New York Times*, 10 July 1983.

Frieze, Irene H. "Beliefs about Success and Failure in the Classroom." In *The Social Psychology of School Learning*, edited by J. H. McMillan. New York: Academic Press, 1980.

Gallup, George. "Sixteenth Annual Gallup Poll of the Public's Attitude toward the Public Schools." *Phi Delta Kappan* 66 (September 1984): 33–47.

Garfinkel, Perry. "The Best 'Jewish Mother' in the World." *Psychology Today* 17 (September 1983): 56–60.

Glaser, Robert, and Pellegrino, James. "Improving the Skills of Learning." In *How and How Much Can Intelligence Be Increased?* edited by Douglas K. Detterman and Robert J. Sternberg. Norwood, N. J.: Ablex, 1982.

Goodlad, John I. *A Place Called School: Prospects for the Future.* New York: McGraw-Hill, 1984.

Griesemer, J. L., and Butler, C. *Education under Study.* 2d ed. Chelmsford, Mass.: Northeast Regional Exchange, 1983.

Griffin, C., and Ridgway, J. *Study Skills Instruction.* Final report of an inquiry into perceptions of school practices requested by the National Commission on Excellence in Education. Washington, D.C.: Service Delivery Assessment, Office of Management, U. S. Department of Education, 1983.

Hall, Elizabeth. "A Cure for American Education." *Psychology Today* 17 (September 1983): 26–27.

Hechinger, Fred. "About Education." *New York Times*, 9 September 1982.

Hurd, Paul D. "An Overview of Science Education in the United States and Selected Foreign Countries." Paper prepared for the National Commission on Excellence in Education, Washington, D.C., 1982.

Jencks, Christopher. "The *Wrong* Answer for Schools Is: (b) Back to Basics." *Washington Post*, 19 February 1978.

Karweit, Nancy. "Time on Task: A Research Review." Paper prepared for the National Commission on Excellence in Education, Washington, D. C., 1982.

MacVicar, Margaret. Testimony at the National Commission on Excellence in Education Public Symposium on College Admissions and the Transition to Postsecondary Education held at Roosevelt University, Chicago, 1982.

McCarthy, Colman. "Don't Lower the Standards." *Washington Post*, 17 September 1983.

National Center for Education Statistics. "High School Senior: A Comparative Study of the Classes of 1972 and 1980." Unpublished report from the Study of High School and Beyond. Washington, D.C.: National Center for Education Statistics, 1982.

National Center for Education Statistics. *School District Survey of Academic Requirements and Achievement.* Washington, D.C.: Fast Response Survey System, U. S. Department of Education, 1983.

National Commission on Excellence in Education. "Science, Mathematics, and Technology Education." Public hearing held at Stanford University, Stanford, California, 1982b. (a)

National Commission on Excellence in Education. "Teaching and Teacher Education." Public hearing held at Georgia State University, Atlanta, Georgia, 1982. (b)

National Commission on Excellence in Education. *A Nation At Risk.* Washington, D.C.: U. S. Department of Education, 1983.

Purkey, Stewart C., and Smith, Marshall S. "Effective Schools: A Review." *Elementary School Journal* 83 (March 1983): 427–452.

Resnick, Lauren, and Resnick, Daniel. "Standards, Curriculum, and Performance: A Historical and Comparative Perspective." Paper prepared for the National Commision on Excellence in Education, Washington, D.C., 1982.

Rohlen, Thomas P. *Japan's High Schools*. Berkeley: University of California Press, 1983.

Rosenshine, Barak. "Teaching Functions in Instructional Programs." *Elementary School Journal* 83 (March 1983): 335–351.

Sherman, Thomas M. "Is Schooling an Unnatural Act?" *Educational Technology* 23 (September 1983): 26–30.

Sizer, Theodore. "High School Reform: The Need for Engineering." *Phi Delta Kappan* 64 (June 1983): 679–683.

Sizer, Theodore. *Horace's Compromise: The Dilemma of the American High School*. Boston: Houghton Mifflin Co., 1984.

Stedman, Lawrence C., and Smith, Marshall S. "Recent Reform Proposals for American Education." *Contemporary Education Review* 2 (Fall 1983): 85–104.

Sternberg, Robert J. "How Can We Teach Intelligence?" *Educational Leadership* 42 (September 1984): 38–48.

Sternberg, Robert J., and Wagner, Richard. "Understanding Intelligence: What's in It for Educators?" Paper prepared for the National Commission on Excellence in Education, Washington, D. C., 1982.

Stevenson, Harold W. *Comparisons of Japanese, Taiwanese, and American Mathematics Achievement*. Stanford, Calif.: Center for Advanced Study in the Behavioral Sciences, 1983.

Tomlinson, Tommy M. "The Troubled Years: An Interpretative Analysis of Public Schooling Since 1950." *Phi Delta Kappan* 62 (January 1981): 373–376. (a)

Tomlinson, Tommy M. "Student Ability, Student Background, and Student Achievement: Another Look at Life in Effective Schools." In *The Minority Student in Public Schools: Fostering Academic Excellence*. Proceedings of an invitational conference, New York. Princeton, N. J.: Educational Testing Service, 1981. (b)

Walberg, Herbert J. "Quantification Reconsidered." In *Review of Research in Education*, Vol. II. Edited by Edmund Gordon. Washington, D. C.: American Educational Research Association, 1984.

Ward, Beatrice; Mergendoller, John R.; and Mitman, Alexis. "The Years between Elementary School and High School: What Schooling Experiences Do Students Have?" Paper prepared for the National Commission on Excellence in Education, Washington, D. C., 1982.

Wharton, Clifton R., Jr. "The Minority Student Challenge." *Science* 224 (June 1, 1984): 937.

PART II

The Social Context

2

Twenty-Five Years of American Education: An Interpretation

Joseph Adelson

Writing a full half-century ago, Walter Lippman (1925) pointed out that every optimistic book written on democracy concludes with a chapter on education. In the years since, we have seen no change in the avidness with which Americans—those consummate, ultimate democrats—pursue their optimistic, at times millennial, hopes for schooling. Even when we are gloomy, our sadness is that of the disappointed yet ever hopeful lover. A few months ago I participated in the taping of a series of programs for the National Humanities Center on the state of American secondary education. Of the five discussants, three were morose and two ambivalent. For nearly a full day the panel complained about the public schools: their mediocrity, their low standards, the loss of discipline, the flight to the private schools, legislative intrusion, the dearth of science and mathematics teachers, the prevalence of drug use, minimum competence testing (necessary but troubling), the low SAT scores of prospective teachers, and much, much more. Apparently overwhelmed by this catalog of woes, the moderator concluded by asking the group to comment on what it foresaw for the next ten years. Every face brightened as the discussants reported their consensus: Things would be far better;

demographic trends were favorable; there would be fewer students, and we already had in place a splendid educational plant; social pathology showed signs of ebbing; the legislators had at last learned their lessons and were beginning to butt out; SAT scores would soon begin to show a rise; school administrators were feeling more confident; and parents were making themselves heard. All in all we could look forward to a glorious decade.

That peculiar ambivalence has been noted by a number of thoughtful observers of American education. Diane Ravitch (1981) has pointed out the swings between utopian zeal on the one hand and a tendency to blame the schools for "failures" that are not genuinely their responsibility. Indeed, we can note that very ambivalence in Lippman himself. One thinks of him as a writer concerned almost exclusively with the large political issues—foreign policy, the philosophy of democratic government, public opinion—yet to a truly surprising degree he was preoccupied with education, which he saw as vital to a democratic nation and which he wrote about persistently throughout his long career. Much of the time his tone is elegiac as he looks back nostalgically to the past triumphs of public education and as he laments the increasing failure of the schools to teach the Western cultural tradition. And at other times he gives way to urgency, even passion, as in his stirring Phi Beta Kappa oration (1941), calling for the nation to resume its great tradition of excellence in education.

During the last quarter-century, American sentiments on the success of education have fallen and risen and fallen, as they so often do, though on the whole they have been more elated than depressed. In the heart of that period, from about 1960 to 1975, we witnessed what can only be called a frenzy of exalted expectations on the prospects of schooling. The present mood is despondent, and I suspect more so than ever before in our history; certainly more so than in the memory of most of us. A great many of us feel that we are not merely coming down from a high, but that the high is itself to be blamed for the depths in which we now find ourselves—that the reforms of the late 1960s, undertaken thoughtlessly, giddily, produced the shallowness of learning and ennui of spirit we find so commonly in the schools.

The degree of disaffection amounts almost to disgust. Here is a sampling of opinion compiled in just one recent week. The chancellor of a southern university comments to the *New York Times* that "the quality of secondary education is just awful." An eminent political philosopher begins a powerful essay on higher education by writing that "students in our best universities do not believe in anything, and those universities are doing nothing about it, nor can they" (Bloom 1982). A noted investment banker, being interviewed about our country's loss of economic competitiveness, mentions almost offhandedly that an important part of the problem is our educational system. One of our most distinguished academicians, in a new preface to a classic book on American education, says: "The once proud and efficient public school system of the United States—especially its unique free high school for all—has turned into a wasteland where violence and vice share the time with ignorance and idleness" (Barzun 1980).

Part of us wants to believe that this is rhetorical excess, reflecting the disappointment of those inflated hopes mentioned earlier. Yet the data we now have on the achievement of students in American schools tell us precisely the same thing. Barbara Lerner (1982) has written a masterful analysis of these findings, which will put to rest any surviving complacency about our nation's educational system. Her article concentrates on two types of comparisons: historical and international. As to the former, she marshals evidence from a number of studies showing a substantial decline in the competence of American students during the last quarter-century, especially at the high school level. The decline of SAT scores is by now so well known as to have become a journalistic cliché; but Lerner points out that this key finding is corroborated by almost every other reliable study of the performance of American students then and now. The international comparisons are equally dispiriting. Examining the massive research sponsored by the International Association for the Evaluation of Educational Achievement (1973—), Lerner concludes that our country compares quite poorly: "Out of nineteen tests, we were never ranked first or second; we came in last three times and, if comparisons are limited to other developed nations only, the United States ranked at the bottom seven times" (p. 64). In attempting to discount the poor performance of students in the United States, the argument is sometimes made that many more of our youngsters remain in school to the senior year than do children in other nations; hence we are comparing groups that differ considerably in academic selectiveness. Lerner examines this argument skeptically; she particularly stresses the fact that the two countries that retain their students at rates very close to our own—Japan and Sweden—both score extremely high on these comparisons.[1] The Japanese—to no one's surprise—outscore all others, and it may be worth noting that many observers credit Japan's superb and very demanding primary and secondary education for that nation's economic prowess.

Nor is the impression of widespread crime and violence in the schools without equally impressive empirical confirmation. The most recent large study we have was carried out by the National Institute of Education (some of its details are reported by Jackson Toby [1980]); it tells us that crime in the schools is substantial. For example, about 7 percent of all junior high school students report having been assaulted within the month before the survey was taken, and a slightly higher percentage report having been robbed. Well over 10 percent of teachers report being victims of theft during that period. We will return to this topic later in this essay; I mention these figures now to make the point that the widespread disaffection with American schools is neither hyperbolic nor hysterical nor based on fantasy, but rather that it is rooted in an accurate perception of what a great many schools are like.

How shall we understand this apparent decline in both civility and competence? Is there some fault in the national temper? Paul Samuelson believes we may be seeing a diminution of the American work ethic, as a response to more general economic changes in the country. A substantial body of opinion holds that the country "has had it," especially with respect to economic innovation and productivity, the corollary hypothesis being that the slackness often seen in the schools reflects a more general failure of will. We have caught the "English disease," so it is said, and are now experiencing that loss of energy that laid low Great Britain's economy. The good times of the post World War II years took some of the edge off. Economic enterprise, technical innovation, and intellectual drive must have behind them some stimulus to effort or to risk taking. For various reasons, these motives have declined in force during the last quarter-century, as an unwarranted self-satisfaction took over the national consciousness.

---

1. Lerner seems to believe, as I do, that the authors of these studies have gone out of their way to make it difficult to make comparisons, presumably to spare national sensitivities. This fear of invidiousness, though in some ways admirable, should caution us not to take at face value occasional soothing words on the relative quality of American achievement.

Another version of this theme stresses cyclical variations, shifts from era to era in the emphasis given to certain values. In a seminal essay, Daniel Bell (1972) refers to the "issue-attention cycle" and to the waxing and waning of values over time. He notes that in the 1960s excellence had been at the center of national concern and that it had receded and had been replaced by equality. A decade later, the wheel continues to turn, and we are seeing a renewed interest in excellence—witness the existence of the National Commission on Excellence in Education. If this renewed interest in excellence is not a dethronement of the rampant egalitarianism of a decade ago, there are at least some signs of a dialectic between the two values, which is a topic I will discuss later in this chapter.

Whether one believes that long-range secular trends are at work, or whether we ought to be looking at shorter-range variations, most of us are gradually coming to understand that the variables we want to be looking at are ideological or, if you will, philosophical. One dubious American habit is to see our problems as concrete or "practical" and hence search for technical solutions, which has in fact been a prominent feature of our recent thinking about the schools. It has begun to dawn on us that at least some solutions are to be found in the realm of ideas and ideals; we will be slow to recover past levels of achievement and decorum without giving some thought to some of the transformations in the American sensibility. In the remainder of this chapter I will try to explore how ideological changes have influenced American education during the last twenty-five years by looking at transformations in four areas: authority, educational theory, the idea of merit, and the movement toward modernist values.

AUTHORITY

If you spend any time at all in the schools, you soon realize that a great many of those persons nominally in authority have a sense of having lost it. Some feel that loss so keenly that they feel unable to go on. If they can, they leave the schools, or they simply "go through the motions" until they can retire. About twenty years ago, while I was doing some research in the secondary schools, I met a junior high school principal who was widely admired by his staff, his students, and their parents. He ran his school by a sort of omnipresence: he knew all of the children by name, knew their families, and often knew their family histories. He tended to make decisions—about discipline, for example—quickly, informally, often intuitively, sometimes taking the child aside to talk with him, sometimes (though less often) by talking to the parents.

A few years later I was surprised to learn that he had resigned as principal and had returned to teaching. I learned that he had left the job because he felt he could not adjust to a new administration, which had determined to set things in order and was particularly concerned about the free-wheeling manner in which many principals ran their schools. The principals were told not to "settle so much on the spot" or on their own authority. They were to keep records, to set up fixed procedures, to report things more completely to the central administration, and the like. It did not take this man long to decide that the fun had gone out of the job, and so he returned to teaching; shortly thereafter he retired.

This story does not necessarily bring tears to the eyes of the schoolpeople I tell it to. They are likely to say that an unfettered principal may be a fine thing so long as he is the salt of the earth, but if he were a petty tyrant, I would then feel somewhat differently and would want some controls, or at least some monitoring and accountability. There is, of course, something to be said for that—indeed, the traditional argument for bureaucratic and juridical controls is that these provide evenhandedness and equity to those under the sway of authority. Although this is not the place to argue the issue, it is worth pointing out that in a public school system in a democratic society there exist other means by which wrongs can be redressed. In this case, the decision of the central school administration to tighten things up had little to do with any wish to ensure evenhandedness. It had to do entirely with the need to protect the school system against litigation, to comply with an increasing number of federal regulations, and to meet the demands of activist groups. It is fair to say that the central administration, in wresting authority from the principals, was itself responding to the loss of its own authority as it was forced to meet the actual and projected demands of other institutions and groups, groups that for the most part had only a special or temporary interest in schools and schooling and rarely in the question of educational quality.

That sense of lost authority is felt most strongly at the secondary school level. A high school principal may tell you, as one told me, that he finds himself answerable to the students, their parents, his teachers, his superintendent, the school board, the local press, and the rules and regulations coming from the state legislature, the Congress, and various courts. As it happened, this man is unusually effective and rather enjoyed these challenges, which he took to be a test of his mettle—a test he could pass easily. But a great many of his colleagues do not have his panache, and, faced with a multitude of conflicting pressures, they tend to retreat to bureaucratic authority, avoiding decisions and commitments until the proper rules can be found, cited, and applied. That paralysis of authority—genuine authority—is transmitted to teachers and students and others, and soon enough it becomes the expected ethos to which everyone accommodates.

The effects are seen most clearly in the area of discipline. The extraordinary growth of litigiousness and of litigation have meant that school administrations—and ultimately teachers and principals— have become gun-shy, fearing that a wrong move could land them in the courts or on the front pages of the local press. Much of the time, of course, this fear is exaggerated, but there have been enough instances of gratuitous litigation to reinforce anyone's caution—or paranoia. In my own school district, a judge took it upon himself to overturn a standard disciplinary penalty meted out in a case of serious vandalism by a high school student. That a case of this sort is taken to court, that a judge decides to accept it, and that he rules in favor of the defendant suggest a profound change in the atmosphere of education and in the authority of the schools. Gerald Grant (1982) has provided us with some illuminating—and depressing—reports stemming from his extensive survey of American high schools. Some of his observations are worth quoting in full:

Jurisdiction is so narrowly defined that a student who comes to a school principal after lunch complaining of being beaten up is asked which side of the street he was standing on when the beating occurred. If he was across the street, it would be out of the school's jurisdiction and hence of no concern to the principal. Often when students need help, teachers are afraid to intervene for fear of legal reprisals. One teacher, explaining why she hadn't interfered with a girl who clawed another in her classroom, said, "You'll only be after trouble if you physically handle them." Another teacher was still shaking as she told us about a group of students who had verbally assaulted her and made sexually degrading comments about her in the hall. When we asked why she didn't report the students, she responded, "Well, it wouldn't have done any good." "Why not?" we pressed. "I didn't have any witnesses," she replied. [Pp. 92–93]

These vignettes focus on the helplessness of teachers, but we should also note the thuggishness of the students depicted. As I have written elsewhere (Adelson 1981), the loss of authority in the schools could not have come at a worse time for those deputed to run them. Many youngsters remain in the upper grades of high school who would have left in an earlier era, and among these a small but significant number are resentful and fractious. More important still, we have seen a rise in the number and proportion of antisocial adolescents—there has been an astonishing increase in *all* indices of social pathology among the young during the last quarter of a century, including assaults, suicides, homicides, drug use, and out-of-wedlock pregnancy. The economic demographers—notably Richard Easterlin (1980)—argue that in a crowded youth cohort, that is, when the proportion of the young to the total population is high, we are liable to find a rise in such phenomena, an indirect effect of the demoralization that many youngsters feel when they recognize that their economic prospects are marginal, that they are losing out to more talented competitors in a tight market.[2] There were also larger families, which meant a decrease in the proportion of intellectually able youngsters. Hence, in the postwar era, the schools confronted a horde of youngsters, a large percentage of whom were academically weak or antisocial. It was at that very moment that school officials found themselves stripped of their accustomed powers.

The weakened authority of teachers and principals also led to a weakening of academic demands. Teachers coping with unruly students could not give themselves fully to instruction; those coping unsuccessfully lost the esteem of all students. A demoralization often set in that diminished the will to set and abide by high expectations. Gilbert Sewall (1982) says that his study of a large number of high schools persuaded him that in most of them students rather than teachers decide how much work they will do. Students seem to agree; a large number of high school youngsters, when polled, say they are not given enough homework. It seems evident from these and other reports (see p. 54 of this chapter) that during the late 1960s a sense of impotence overcame many of those managing and teaching in the schools, producing in turn that inanition of purpose necessary for sustained academic effort.

The crisis of authority in the university system did not involve discipline—except during moments of upheaval—so much as it in-

---

2. Among the attractions of this hypothesis is that it tests itself. This is the time we should be seeing a decline in some of these indices. Has it happened? It is too early to know, but on the whole the hypothesis is proving out—there is a distinct decline in drug use, an apparent plateau in the suicide rate, and a slowing down in the growth rate for youth crime. On the other hand, the number of illegitimate births continues to rise.

volved the erosion or collapse of academic standards. One hardly needs to belabor the matter, since the crisis in the universities was the most publicized set of events in education during the years we are considering.[3] The academic faculties lost much of their control over curriculum, grading, intellectual standards, and above all the tacit definition of what the university ought to be. Those losses have not been made up.

One might argue, as Robert Nisbet (1971) and many others did, that the faculties lost their authority because they did not have a strong definition of the university to begin with, that in particular the specifically pedagogical functions of higher education had been treated by many of them with derision or had at most been given lip service. Hence there was an intellectual flaccidity, a confusion of inner purpose, that left the universities unable to defend themselves against the antiintellectualism of the student movement. Be that as it may, the events of the late 1960s had as their primary effect—and perhaps as one of their latent purposes—a serious decline in intellectual quality. The social sciences were the most grievously affected, in my view, especially those disciplines such as psychology and sociology, which proved particularly attractive to the youngsters of the 1970s. One found that credit was given in courses where neither work nor attendance was required; there were a number of embarrassing moments when departments discovered that "A" grades had been given to students who had dropped out of the course at the beginning of the semester. In some cases instructors guaranteed an "A" grade for any student enrolling, as a protest either against the Vietnam War or merely against the competitiveness of academic life. Some courses in psychology became therapy groups or other exercises in self-expression. In other instances the subject matter was entirely politicized; one of my sons, attending an Ivy League university, found that the introductory psychology course (and the only one given that year) consisted exclusively of denunciations of capitalism. To be sure, these cases were in the minority, and the faculty as a whole, even in affected

---

3. Interviewed in 1970, shortly before his death, the great American historian Richard Hofstader said that we were living in an "age of rubbish," and it is easy to see what he had in mind as one re-reads much of the mawkish, vulgar, and self-serving commentary of that period. On the other hand, the crisis also produced some remarkably fine writing, as for example, many of the essays published by *Daedalus* in a vast two-volume survey of American academic thought published in 1974 to 1975.

departments, did not participate nor even approve. There was a great deal of muttering and hand-wringing, but little action was taken. There proved to be little spirit in most departments to impose restraints on the faculty, for fear of diminishing academic freedom. It was all seen as a kind of fever that could be left untreated, since it would ultimately run its course. The uninfected faculty thereupon retreated even further into research or specialized graduate education and withdrew even more decisively from the pedagogical missions of the university.

We now find that a blessed amnesia has begun to settle over us, and with it a tendency to minimize the impact of that period on the grounds that the consequences were limited. In fact they were extensive and enduring, and they have yet to be repaired. Consciously or otherwise, many teachers simply gave up requiring sustained effort from their students. In many instances this was done cynically; in others, out of despair. Some teachers came to believe that the entire academic enterprise had been so compromised by the failure to resist student demands that the game was no longer worth the candle. In other instances a mood of manic zeal persuaded some teachers that they were living in a Golden Age so far as student achievement was concerned. There has never been a more self-celebratory moment in the history of American higher education. College authorities told anyone who would listen that they were privileged to be teaching the most talented group of students the planet has ever seen; many students solemnly agreed.

That self-congratulation produced—or perhaps merely rationalized—the notorious grade inflation that dominated and persists in higher education. Each year grade point averages (GPAs) rose, ultimately to dizzying heights. In some universities the average GPA was at a level that had once been reserved for the highest academic honors, which forced a change in long-standing criteria for the awarding of such honors. One saw the same phenomenon, less concretely but far more vividly, in reading the letters of recommendation written by university teachers about students applying to graduate and professional schools. Where a few years before these letters had on the whole been positive but measured, they were now uniformly euphoric. During this period I served a term as chairman of admissions to our graduate program in clinical psychology and, wishing to test the hypothesis that these letters were no longer credible, decided to read every one of the more than one thousand recommendations submitted that year to see whether I could find anything other than words of extreme praise. As it happens, I did find one from a most unusual source—the abbot of a seminary who said in no uncertain terms that the applicant, one of his seminarians, was mistaken in his view of himself and of his readiness for graduate school. Every other letter was enthusiastic, and a great many were ecstatic, claiming that the applicant was the most brilliant in the last five or ten or fifteen years of the writer's experience. There were of course a great many gifted candidates in our pool of applicants, but about one-third to one-half were mediocre at best, and these students received equally glowing commendation. One might read three such intoxicated letters regarding an applicant who could not compose a coherent complex sentence and whose transcript showed that there had been no college-level instruction in mathematics or science or language or philosophy or history.

And that was, of course, the inevitable and inherent counterpart to the inflation of grades—a devalued curriculum and debased standards of achievement. There was a general retreat from required courses or sequences of courses and from the ideal of a general liberal education. What was most troubling was that the liberalization of the curriculum seemed to have nothing behind it aside from the pious notion that coercion deadens enthusiasm, which in turn inhibits learning. Those in favor of a core curriculum seemed too disheartened or confused to argue their case persuasively. Perhaps the most depressing experience I can remember from that period was listening to a general faculty discussion on whether we ought to institute a new bachelor's degree, the only purpose of which seemed to be to enable some students to escape requirements they found noxious, especially languages. Listening to that listless discussion made it clear that many of the faculty could no longer "remember the answers," that the vision of a liberal education had been eclipsed, and that the only arguments being brought forth were crassly utilitarian—that languages were useful acquisitions and the like. Yet one also knew that most of the faculty sitting there so mutely could achieve a Churchillian eloquence in defense of other and narrower propositions, for example, that their department absolutely had to have two courses instead of one course in nonparametric statistics.

As we all know, the colleges not only offered junk courses of their own but by lowering admissions standards, encouraged the high schools to use junk courses for admission to the university. Or was it the other way around? Do the high schools, through their failure to educate their students adequately, make them unfit for college work?

There is no way we will ever answer those questions, except to agree that each pulled the other down, and despite some grumbling here and there, neither institution objected too vehemently to being pulled. In all likelihood, both secondary and higher education were being responsive to the same obscure but compelling forces in American life, which involved a peculiar mixture of inflated self-esteem on the one hand and an exhaustion of will on the other.

TECHNOLOGICAL AND LIBERATIONIST PROPOSALS FOR REFORM

The American zeal for education provides the energy for programs of innovation and reform of our schools. It is hard to think of another country where we could find so many proposals for the improvement of schooling. The zest for reform was evident throughout the postwar period and, as always, reflected larger social and ideological preoccupations. The Conant Report (Conant 1959) was one of the most influential documents in this century's history of education in helping to establish as normative the idea of a consolidated high school able to offer all students the abundance of opportunities so often not available in smaller and more provincial schools. A second landmark event was the Sputnik "crisis," which led to substantial improvements in the science curricula and an infusion of federal money into mathematics, science, and technological education. These were establishment ventures, in that their intention was to strengthen the existing system rather than to overturn it. In no sense were the aims utopian; they were within reach, given sufficient energy and effort, and in both cases the goals were achieved and became an enduring part of the American pattern of education.

The movements for reform that succeeded those just mentioned took place from about 1960 to about 1975 and are not so briskly characterized because they moved in many different directions. But they can be placed into two general categories, which I will call technological and liberationist. The technological direction encompasses a wide variety of proposals, some narrow, some quite far-reaching, wherein there is some effort to manipulate the materials or specific processes of learning. The simplest examples involve exploiting for the classroom technical devices originally developed for other purposes. The use of cassette tapes for language and other instruction is one obvious example, as is the use of closed-circuit television in the classroom. In most instances these techniques are meant to hasten learning or extend it, but they do not aim at any radical transformation of the teaching process. Although their introduction is often announced by inventors and early enthusiasts as "revolutionary," they generally survive as ancillary methods woven into the quotidian activities of the classroom.

Other modes of technology are—potentially—more ambitious and even radical in intention. The microcomputer is one such device—again, potentially—in that it may have the capacity to transform the very processes of learning, though whether it will do so remains to be seen. Other "technological" approaches are programmed learning, through the systematic use of reinforcers (à la Skinner) and its close cousin, "contract teaching." Though neither of these necessarily involves mechanical or electronic devices, their aim is to rearrange and rationalize the learning process itself. These approaches are based on a technology of response acquisition. The Skinnerian and other behavioral approaches to education were at their inception utopian, in that they promised not merely the transformation of the classroom but a formula for the remaking of human behavior in society itself. These approaches have proved adaptable because parts of them can be borrowed. It is my impression that the Skinnerian emphasis these days is seen in a more deliberate effort on the part of classroom teachers to reward students, both in general and as they acquire specific skills.

The second direction of reform—the liberationist—had a more profound initial impact on education. Liberationists define themselves as radical. For them a major aim of education is to undo the constraints imposed by excessive socialization. They believe that conventional child-rearing chains the "true self," and with it creativity and the capacity to learn easily and joyously. Conventional education then reinforces that enchainment; it merely completes what traditional child-rearing has left undone. Liberationist writing posited—at times merely implied—a "true self" that is essentially virtuous; and it is that optimism about human nature, that tacit denial of original sin, which was part of its attraction in an era marked by political utopianism. The movement was often thought to have stemmed from the philosophy of John Dewey, in that it aimed to be "progressive"; my own view is that much of the time it donned Deweyan colors much as a wolf may dress in sheep's clothing. The immediate sires of most postwar progressive writing were A. S. Neill, Wilhelm Reich, and Paul Goodman. The ultimate progenitor is Rousseau (or some sides of him), and before him the Gnostics and Cathars.

Liberationist writing was a bold attempt to redefine the purpose and practice of education, in part by redefining human psychology. The student was to be seen not as recalcitrant but as avid (under the correct circumstances), and the teacher was to be seen not as a drill master but as a partner or inspirational leader. Subject matter was to take second place to the perfection of the self—the cultivation of sensitivity, creativity, and the like. The writing is by turns polemical, hortatory, and evangelical; it stands in sharp contrast to the modesty and cautiousness of formulation that we find in other presumably "experimental" writers on education, such as William James, John Dewey, and Jean Piaget.

Given these sweeping aims, aims that went far beyond "method" as we ordinarily understand the term, there tended to be little concern with the actualities of the classroom and of instruction—John Holt is an exception. Revolutionary movements tend to be both totalistic and sectarian; that is, on the one hand they aim to produce conversion in the auditor and enlist him totally in the cause, and on the other hand, a sense of exclusivity develops within the movement itself. For these reasons, the new progressivism did not take over American schooling, far from it. It proved to be self-limiting. In those few communities where the new progressivism enjoyed a large constituency, there might have been some efforts to satisfy it by offering special programs or in some cases by setting aside one or two special schools. But the efforts rarely went beyond that, since the more radical the program proposed, the more certain there was to be community resistance. My hometown of Ann Arbor is quite instructive in this regard. The school district hired an ultraprogressive school superintendent who was able to establish an open-classroom school at the elementary level and two small liberationist high schools (one soft-shelled, the other hard-shelled), and do little else. The very fact of a liberationist regime meaning business served to mobilize the conservative elements of an extremely liberal university community to the degree that they were able to elect a school board and in time depose the superintendent and appoint a centrist administrator.

Yet I would not for a moment want to imply that the liberationist movements were without effect; to the contrary, they were to be deeply influential. They were able to give credence and respectability to the idea that the cultivation of "the total personality" was as important a goal as the acquisition of subject matter and of cognitive skills. Hence it became easier to establish courses on such topics as family living and personal adjustment, which could be taken in lieu of conventional offerings in history and the social sciences. By far the major impact of liberationism was the adversary stance it took toward the existing system of public education and toward those who taught and managed in that system. The messages of the movement were these: the schools are extremely dull places for the young; the teachers are rigid and unimaginative and can not engage the enthusiasm of their students; the secondary schools have as their essential but unspoken assumption keeping youngsters out of the labor market; hence they function as prisons, in that they contain an energetic population resentful of their confinement.

Yet even this fairly blunt paraphrase does not quite capture the contempt expressed toward schools and teachers. One has to reread these writings to recall the tonalities (here again I think most of us suffer from some amnesia). The depiction of the ordinary school and the ordinary teacher is supercilious and at times scurrilous: the teachers are considered mean-spirited people serving mean institutions. Often the writer offers himself as exemplary, though of course with the usual moues of humility or self-irony. The contrast is made with some hack or dragon or tyrant. The author's students learn more, are more creative, are suffused with the joy of learning, and love their teacher almost beyond words. These writers were generally young and viewed themselves as maverick. But we saw precisely the same attitudes in establishment figures such as Charles Silberman, who in an extremely influential book, *Crisis in the Classroom* (1970), takes a position that Lerner quite correctly characterizes as extremist in rhetoric and messianic in claims.

Nevertheless the climate of the times was such that these diagnoses of American education proved to be persuasive to elite opinion, soon found their way into the mass media, became conventional wisdom, and ultimately were enshrined in the teaching of the education schools. There was little countervailing argument. If you look through the holdings of a good public library or a good used bookstore, you will find, abundantly, the books by Silberman, Holt, Kohl, Kozol, Friedenberg, Goodman, Herndon, and Lennard. You will find hardly anything from that era by writers representing a contrary position. If you survey the journals of opinion of that time, you find little attention given to problems of primary and secondary education, and what little there is sympathetic to the reform outlook. Most such journals limited their attention to the universities or to the political problems in the primary and secondary schools, especially integration and busing.[4]

This disdainful depiction of the American schoolteacher did grievous damage to the self-esteem of a group, many of whom were already uncertain about themselves and their value—a group that was not seen as "professional" nor as "intellectual" nor as successful in worldly terms. That loss of self-regard made it especially difficult for them to demand a disciplined effort from their students. Having been portrayed as either drones or jailers, many of them yearned to be seen as the very opposite, as charismatic teachers or as laid-back adolescents. Neither role required or inspired self-discipline on the part of the students. Young teachers in particular were tempted to embrace and exemplify the new values and to serve as role models for advanced thinking. Here is a quotation from Fred Bloom (1978), a psychiatrist living in rural Maine:

> A teacher, a woman with twenty years teaching experience, resigned recently from the new community school in our town because she was expected to go on the "team" weekend encounter of the social-studies faculty. On the weekend, she told me, the faculty members play therapy games. Among other games, they lie on the ground and roll back and forth over one another's bodies to develop "closeness" and "trust" among the team. "I went on it last year," she said, "and besides, I can't see why, after twenty years, I have to be shown how to get along. But really, you can't get along at that school unless you go in for that kind of thing." [Pp. 475–476]

The liberationist school has lost influence, at least for the moment. One suspects its success would not be repeated today—not only because of obvious changes in the political climate, but also because we would now insist that some evidence be provided. If such bold claims about schools and teachers were made today, we would surely ask: Is that so? Who said so? Do you have findings? Please show them to me. During the previous decade no serious discussion of educational policy has proceeded very far without some genuflection to the facts—even when we recognize that most of the time the facts are used to justify positions already taken. Nevertheless, the appeal to findings, though it has its limits and corruptions, nevertheless makes it difficult to keep discourse at an entirely sentimental level.

---

4. *Daedalus*, for example, published over a hundred articles on higher education during the quarter-century but until recently only a handful about the schools. The shining exception is *Public Interest*, which has published a steady stream of excellent articles by the most distinguished American writers on education.

What the new empirical literature has shown is in a sense startling, in that it has confirmed many banal, commonsense, and traditional beliefs about the sources of effective teaching—that learning tends to flourish in schools governed by a strong and unified leadership (Rutter et al. 1979), that it requires an orderly environment (Coleman et al. 1982), that mastery of a subject is in large part a function of the time spent in learning it (Walberg 1982), and that homework is therefore important (Keith 1982, and many others).

All of the findings cited are new in that they are quite recent, but curiously enough, they are not at all new, in that similar findings have been in the literature for some time now, ready and awaiting a readership. In an excellent review of many of these, Herbert Walberg (1982) departs from an otherwise straightforward discussion of the data on teaching effectiveness to say with some justifiable exasperation: "The impressive accumulation of these scientific results in the last decade seems to have gone unnoticed by many researchers, educators, and the general public. It might indeed be concluded from widely publicized reports that schools are pathological institutions and that neither educators nor research workers know how to cure their problems and increase their productivity."

As it happens, we did know and do know many of the answers, within limits, although it remains unclear whether we will be able to put into practice what we know. And as it happens, many of the things that we know are embarrassingly obvious—that intellectual achievement requires intellectual seriousness, the willingness to take pains, earnestness, and motivation. But we were led away from these rather trite truths by the dominant intellectual writings of the 1960s. The liberationists did not see the school for what it was or what it might realistically become; they saw it as a simulacrum of a society they despised, which they saw as oppressive and racist. They saw themselves as guerrillas in the service of human freedom. To liberate the student from the teacher symbolized the larger and more splendid liberations that were to take place throughout the world. The other dominant movement of reform was, as we have argued, overly preoccupied with technique. It felt that schooling could be improved by the use of modern devices or of new information on the rationalization of learning.

Both of these approaches elided what we now see as central to sustained academic achievement—the internal morale marked by effort, drive, and persistence supported by purposeful leadership in the schools. The liberationist theorists either ignored those elements altogether or assumed that they would be evoked by the unbinding of a thwarted inner goodness. The technological theorists also ignored them, at least much of the time, or assumed they would be evoked by the right machine or by an up-to-date syllabus or by scientifically devised methods of learning. Neither of these positions is altogether false, yet we can see how illusory they are. Although both positions are now in some decline, they are by no means eclipsed. They draw upon two of the deepest and most enduring themes in American thinking—the idea of perfectability and the love of technique—and one can expect that sooner or later, in one form or another, and for better or worse, these ideas will once again be felt in the American theory of education.

MERIT AND EQUALITY

During the second half of the quarter-century, our conception of equality began to be transformed in ways which were to be extremely important for education. The idea of equality has had a long history in American politics, indeed so long and complex and tortuous as to discourage any effort here to trace its origins, even summarily. The interested reader may want to consult Lakoff's *Equality in Political Philosophy* (1964) for an extensive discussion of the history of the idea, or Eastland and Bennett's *Counting by Race* (1979) for a cogent analysis of equality in relation to racial preference.

"Equality" has been so obsessive a theme during the postwar era that we are liable to think of it as a permanent feature of our political landscape. Yet it has been a central issue—politically and intellectually—only at certain moments of our history. It gained vigor and attention in the 1950s with the explosive growth of the civil rights movement. During that period, equality came to mean racial equality—to end systematic discrimination against blacks, particularly the denial of electoral rights and the sanctioned pattern of segregation in schools and public facilities. These struggles won, indeed with surprising ease, the quest for equality moved ahead toward the achievement of equal opportunity in such areas as schooling, housing, and work, and to the extension of equality to other putatively disadvantaged groups, primarily women.

These extensions of equality enjoyed widespread and enthusiastic assent, certainly among the educated and among political liberals. But in the late 1960s we began to see not so much an extension as a transformation of the earlier idea of equality. Though that transformation drew on some of the most ancient utopian ideals (see Cohn, *Pursuit of the Millennium* [1961] and Manuel and Manuel, *Utopian Thought in the Western World* [1979]), it represented a startling new departure in the American political context and, as we will see, generated a bitter and continuing struggle among intellectuals. The notion of equality of opportunity involved what the late Charles Frankel (1973) termed "corrective egalitarianism"—the idea that a primary aim of social policy is to remove or modify those circumstances that disadvantage some classes of citizens. One might, for example, provide financial subsidies so that poor but able youngsters could attend college. One might even strive to eliminate poverty altogether, by income guarantees for the poorest members of the nation, so as to reduce those economic inequities that hobble the latent talents of those born to impoverished families. That mode gave way to what Frankel termed "redemptive egalitarianism." Whereas in the earlier understanding one sought to give each player a more or less equal chance to succeed, in the newer conception, the fact of inequality itself was seen as unjust, in that it derived from external circumstances that favored one player over another, or from the presence of internal qualities—intelligence and drive—which the player had not earned, or because it was itself capricious—the result of good luck and little more. That being the case, one could not say that a given person was morally more deserving of good fortune than another; and that being the case, the aim of social policy is to minimize differences in fortune or privilege stemming from differences in achievement. The shorthand formula is now familiar: from equality of opportunity to equality of result.

The new position on equality was stated elegantly in one of the few philosophical books in our era to become famous, John Rawls's *A Theory of Justice* (1971), which was—as all commentators have agreed—a book of remarkable originality. As Frankel said, the author's purpose—"which is nothing less than to overturn two centuries of empirical, utilitarian, and positivistic philosophies"—is "breathtaking." Yet the popularity of the book among the educated, the quickness with which it seized the attention of intellectuals, had less to do with its originality than with the way it centered on the ideal of equality. In a long, brilliant, and withering critique of the book, Robert Nisbet (1971) argued that the "passion for equality, first vivid at the time of the Puritan revolution, has been the essential mark of every major revolution in the West" and has in particular been the "mainspring of radicalism." Hence in an era such as the late 1960s, in which a great many intellectuals deemed themselves revolutionary, one would expect to find the wish to celebrate a book of great intellectual power itself celebrating a revolutionary idea of equality.

Rawls's new doctrine did not long escape scrutiny. By drawing such considerable attention, it evoked almost immediately some brilliant displays of contra-egalitarian writing, the most famous being Robert Nozick's prize-winning *Anarchy, State, and Utopia* (1974), which, roughly speaking, did for libertarianism what Rawls had done for egalitarianism. However, the main thrust of the response to Rawls came not from the libertarian movement but from the intellectuals commonly categorized as neoconservative, those associated with *Commentary* and *Public Interest*—Daniel Bell (1972), Irving Kristol (1978), Daniel Patrick Moynihan (1972), Charles Frankel (1973), Robert Nisbet (1974), to mention only a few. The major intellectual debate of the early 1970s pitted these writers against the egalitarians. The issues debated were pivotal in the fission between intellectuals in the postwar era, entirely comparable in gravity and scope to the debate about the cold war in the late 1940s. As we might expect, the debate about equality involved, as a leading issue, a fierce argument about education.

In the traditional understanding of equality, it was posited that economic and other disadvantages acted to constrain the appearance and expression of talent. Jefferson's "natural aristocrats," ordinarily lost to the world by the accidents of privation, were to be uncovered by universal education. Schooling for all was to serve two aims—raising the level of literacy and competence in the general population and bringing into cultivation those talents that would otherwise have lain fallow. The infusion of federal money into higher education after World War II has served both goals: college training was made available to large numbers of young men and women, and an elite education was offered to those who qualified by virtue of intellectual merit.

Soon after the war ended, the prestigious private colleges and universities began to give up the exclusion of students by religion, ethnicity, and social background. Much the same happened at the graduate and professional level and in the recruitment of college faculty. That change took place quickly and for the most part silently—without litigation, protest, or government intervention, as though an agreement had been arrived at tacitly based on a sense of social justice and a reckoning of the nation's needs. The example of Nazi Germany was a sufficient warning of the long-range effects of social bigotry. And beyond that, the country became aware—as did other nations—that its technical progress would depend on the cultivation of intelligence and that the great universities could no longer be enclaves restricted by class and caste.

The effect of that tacit decision was to open the great universities to groups previously excluded or restricted—the Jews most visibly, but also that majority of the American population which had not been so much excluded as discouraged. Access was determined by accomplishment rather than by membership in favored social groups, and accomplishment (or its potential) was determined by objective and universalistic means.

That was the onset of an era of merit. One can find it taking place in almost all industrialized countries. That evolution—from ascription to achievement, and from particularism to universalism—is a fundamental tenet in this sociological theory of modernity. (See Bell 1972, inter alia.) One might even want to argue that in some ways the American system has been more meritocratic than most others, that there are far more openings available in American higher education than in any other country, and that the culling takes place late and is less rigorous. We have had no equivalent of the British 11-plus examinations, nor have we had anything to approach in rigor the Japanese and French examinations for entrance to the university. But the opening of our universities proved to be a major reason for the extraordinary vitality that marked American intellectual, scientific, and artistic life during the postwar period. This country achieved leadership in many of the arts and humanities and in almost all of the natural and social sciences, and did so much of the time through the accomplishments of native talent that easily and rapidly learned from, succeeded, and in many cases surpassed a generation of European émigrés. And if one looks closely at our indigenous "second generation" of extraordinary achievement—Nobel laureates, for example—we find that it is made up in significant degree of the previously excluded and discouraged—the ethnics and provincials.

Nevertheless, the hegemony of merit proved to be surprisingly brief. Not that it was abandoned—it is hard to imagine that happening entirely in any technological society for any length of time. Yet it did lose its primacy, that unspoken assent previously given by all significant strata of the society. The term "meritocracy" soon came into use among the adversary elites, that term used pejoratively, or dismissively, certainly without much loving kindness. The meritocracy, it was implied, was composed not of the meritorious but of those who had the knack of taking tests, or making the right moves in school, or ingratiating themselves with selection committees. Furthermore, the tests themselves were suspect, in that there was said to be no clear relationship between doing well on them and doing well later in life. Nor was there much relationship between doing well in school and later success. Perhaps success was a matter of luck, no more than a roll of the dice. The idea that social mobility was fortuitous was the theme of one of the most influential books of the period, Christopher Jencks's *Inequality* (1973), based on his analysis of the first Coleman study.

These critiques might not have had so powerful an influence had it not been for race, which proved once again to make the American case different from those of comparable countries. What would otherwise have remained an argument about social class and social mobility became an argument about race, and in so doing inherited our country's complex historical legacy of racial division and bitterness. The conflation of race and class produced, among many other things, a fierce attack on intelligence testing, largely because of the false assumption that most psychometricians held blacks to be genetically inferior in intelligence. Hostility to IQ testing—much of it ignorant, or uninformed, or based on the inflation of half-truths—was then generalized to other forms of aptitude and achievement testing. That hostility soon extended to the very idea of intelligence as a measurable attribute. A dogmatic environmentalism came to dominate most discourse on these matters among social scientists and among much of the educated public. Differences among individuals, especially in capacity, were held to be due to socialization alone, unless proved otherwise—and the conditions for proving otherwise were essentially impossible to meet. With the passage of time, the rhetorical ante was raised, in that the arguments for equality became ever more shrill. The elegant moral reasoning of a Rawls and the intricate analyses of a Jencks gave way to the vulgarity of William Ryan's *Equality* (1981), which holds that measured variations in intelligence are a scam devised by the "very rich" to swindle the rest of us.

It was a climate in which the idea of merit could not survive, at least not the belief that native gifts, cultivated by learning and effort, would produce achievement and reward, the fruits of which would ultimately add to the common good. Instead the following propositions became commonplaces: Achievement has little to do with talent, nor with effort, nor with schooling. Differences in ability are a fiction, or are not measurable, or are a kind of confidence trick. The ruling class makes sure that the system is rigged to protect its own kind. The gifted can take care of themselves, or are the products of special privilege, or are in any case not worthy of admiration or special attention. There is no reason to stress cognitive skills over all others, since to do so is a bourgeois prejudice, since it takes as much intelligence to survive on the street as to solve quadratic equations.

These propositions were not often stated quite so crudely, but stated they were, and they helped establish a moral and intellectual ambience in which striving, self-discipline, and the intellectual life itself came to be devalued. That in turn produced a loss of morale that was to diminish the moral energy of the public schools.

VALUES

Beginning in the middle 1960s, a great many parents became aware that something was going awry in the schools. Those with children in the middle or high schools could recognize symptoms of demoralization and loss of purpose: that drugs were sold openly and that school authorities were not doing much about it; that courses in mathematics, science, and languages were disappearing; that students were rarely asked to write and were given little work to bring home. Parents also began to feel that they could not get their concerns acted on. On issues of discipline, the school principal might say that his hands were tied because of new developments in the law or because the schools were wary of litigation. On the issue of a softened curriculum, he might point to changes in college entrance requirements or utter pieties about bringing education up to date and keeping it in tune with the times, leading the parents to feel that they were back numbers. Or the principal might agree, wholeheartedly, then go on to say that things were not what they once were, that students were less manageable and less motivated and that many families had become indifferent to the academic progress of their children.

That parents and the general public were becoming disenchanted with the quality of public education is evident from trend statistics collected by the Roper Organization during the last quarter-century.[5] These show a striking loss of confidence in the local schools during the period we are considering: In 1959, 64 percent of Americans felt that

---

5. The statistics that follow are taken from the invaluable summaries published by *Public Opinion* magazine (August/September 1979, February/March 1980, and October/November 1981).

public education was doing an excellent or good job. That figure declined to 48 percent by 1978. Most of the drop took place between 1967 and 1971, where the proportion giving a favorable rating declined by eleven points, from 61 percent to 50 percent. We can infer what may have been involved in that loss of confidence from the Gallup figures on discipline in the schools. Those believing that the schools are too lax jumped from 39 percent in 1969 to an extraordinary 84 percent in 1978—about as close to unanimity as anyone ever achieves in opinion polling. That conclusion receives distinct support from the potential targets of disciplinary toughness—the high school students themselves, a majority of whom report as "big problems" the following: classroom disturbances (64 percent), marijuana use (60 percent), theft (56 percent), and vandalism (52 percent).

The remedies proposed for the schools also show some startling changes. There is a sharp increase in sentiment for a greater amount of homework for high school students, from 39 percent in 1965 to 63 percent in 1978. Many students themselves agree: 48 percent think the work is not hard enough, contrasted with 23 percent who believe it is too hard. Finally, there is a striking jump in the number favoring competence testing: from 50 percent of the general public in 1965 to 82 percent in 1978. Once again, the students agree: in 1977, 65 percent favored a standard examination to earn the diploma, as against 35 percent who were opposed.

These findings offer some compelling testimony: that the public disaffection with the schools has been felt for well over a decade, that there is nothing whimsical about it, and that it has been responsive to the actual vicissitudes of American schooling, specifically the easing of both academic and disciplinary demands. But what is most striking is the extraordinary cleavage it reveals between public and elite opinion on the schools. During the late 1960s we began to see a sharp decline in public confidence, and that was precisely when the liberationist writing of a few years earlier had come to dominate elite attitudes and then the media and ultimately educational practice. By the early 1970s, the public attitude had become cynical when not altogether hostile—the schools had been turned into playpens, at times dangerous ones, where little serious learning took place. Yet these perceptions were either ignored or rejected by vanguard opinion, which found itself drawn to the views of Silberman or Friedenberg to the effect that the public schools were at best stultifying or at worst the moral equivalent of Orwell's Room 101. Though it was rarely put this way, the schools were felt to be havens of rather dreary lower-middle-class sensibility, lacking the presumed spontaneity and freedom of lower-class life or the sensitivity and sophistication to be found in upper-middle-class milieux.

In one form or another that cleavage continues—it is one of the most striking aspects of American education today that there is so little agreement on what is wrong with the schools, how it came about, and what if anything ought to be done about it. The public's sourness about local schooling—now beginning to change, though rather slowly—is simply not shared by a great many experts in education, who may agree that there has been a decline in quality, but take it in stride, seeing it as the price to be paid for universal education. The effort to raise the level of achievement by a more focused means of instruction will produce complaints about repression. The second Coleman report, which was greeted by many with a shrug of the shoulders as involving little more than a demonstration of the obvious, generated a savage response from many in the education establishment, in part because of the ostensibly hard line it implied about discipline. Nor is it the question of quality alone that divides opinion. Shall we teach morality in the schools, and if so, how? The struggle over "values clarification" between some teachers and some parents has turned on the claim of the latter that, under the pretext of teaching children *how* to think about moral issues, a program of moral relativism has in fact been inserted into the curriculum. The occasional disputes about sex education provide another example: though the opinion polls show that most people—even those calling themselves conservative—approve the idea of teaching youngsters about sexuality, a great many parents become uneasy or oppositional if they come to believe that more than information is being conveyed and that social attitudes they find offensive are being taught as well.

These disputes are by no means new to the schools, which have always been an arena for the playing out of arguments about values and ideologies. Nevertheless, these quarrels now seem more intense than before and seem to involve a larger range of issues. Since the mid-1960s, we may well have seen some loss of consensus on the functions of the schools and on the values they are meant to embody and teach. If so, that loss of consensus would have to do with a widespread shift in values among the population at large, from "materialist" to "postmaterialist" values. Portents of that change have been made by social theorists for many years, and the early appearances were noted by some of our keenest social scientists: in David Riesman's *The Lonely Crowd* (1950), in Daniel Bell's writings on

the postindustrial society (1973), and in the work of the psychologist
Abraham Maslow (1962). These early observations have more recently been supported in a variety of studies, most significantly in
Ronald Inglehart's *The Silent Revolution* (1977), which presents data
from most of the industrialized countries of the West. As these nations
advance into a more affluent postindustrial society, one less dominated by a concern for economic survival and fears of scarcity,
material values lose their hold over large segments of the citizenry—
especially those cohorts composed of the young who have enjoyed
higher education—and are replaced by a greater emphasis upon
aesthetic, intellectual, and communitarian values. It is a trend visible
in all developed societies and most striking in the most prosperous of
them—Belgium, the United States, and Switzerland—and much less
so in poorer countries such as Italy and Ireland. Certain political
movements—environmentalism, for example, both here and abroad—
can be understood fully only if we keep in mind the more general
changes in values they rest on.

Of course it is not at all clear whether this shift in values will
survive the moment or, more precisely, will survive the current
worldwide economic recession. Certainly some of the more flamboy-
ant claims made for a new level of consciousness, as by Herbert
Marcuse and Charles Reich, now seem—to put it generously—
overstated. Nevertheless, it seems quite evident that the emergence of
these new values—transient or not, deeply rooted or not—had some
considerable consequences for American education, not merely because new values always tend to jostle the status quo, but even more
so because in this case they provided the agenda for a new and
assertive constituency in American life.

That constituency is made up of a significant social cadre, often
called the New Class—occupationally centered in government, education, journalism, and higher education, of extremely high educational attainment; and usually from affluent and highly educated
families. It considers itself to be a part of or at the least allied with the
intelligentsia. The growth and evolution of this cadre were sensed,
with an uncanny prescience, by a number of astute observers—Joseph
Schumpeter and George Orwell, for example, but most strikingly in
some early essays by Lionel Trilling (1950), who noted the group's
adversarial tendencies and its sense of affiliation with those elements
in the literary and political culture that were hostile to the given
order, which in American terms meant the business culture.

These intuitions about the New Class, which have often been

dismissed as either speculative or tendentious, have now been con-firmed in some remarkable social research by Robert Lichter and Stanley Rothman (1981), who compared the views of the media elite (journalists working for prestigious newspapers, magazines, and tele-vision networks) with the views of a group of high-level corporate executives. As we might expect, the members of the former group are more liberal on political and economic issues and show more cynical attitudes toward American institutions. But the most substantial differences, by far, are to be found in relation to moral questions—homosexuality, abortion, adultery—where the journalists give liberal responses three to four times as often as do the business executives.

Each group takes an adversarial stance toward the other. Each sees the other as too influential and itself as too little, so each would like to replace the other in influence. That competition involves more than pride of place. Though it is an argument about politics and economics, it is also a struggle as to which values will be ascendant—the ideal of self-restraint on the one hand and of individualism on the other.

These differences, so strongly separating two segments of the upper bourgeoisie, are important to us not merely because these are strong and willful elites, but even more so because they reflect a far more general dispute about values and because that dispute has taken place partially in and about the schools. The mainstream culture fears the schools may be captured by those who, out of a misguided sense of compassion, are unwilling to make those demands necessary for the child's intellectual and moral growth. The modernist culture fears the schools are and will remain academic and thus will sustain the mercenary, authoritarian aims of the heartless elements of American society.

REFERENCES

Adelson, Joseph. "What Happened to the Schools?" *Commentary* 71 (March 1981): 36–41.

Barzun, Jacques, *Teacher in America*. 3d ed. Indianapolis: Liberty Press, 1980.

Bloom, Allan. "Our Listless Universities." *National Review* 34 (December 10, 1982): 1537–1538.

Bloom, Fred. "Escape from Suffering: The Sentimentalization of Psychotherapy." *Social Research* 45 (1978): 467–477.

Bell, Daniel. "On Meritocracy and Equality." *Public Interest* 29 (Fall 1972): 29–68.

Bell, Daniel. *The Coming of Post-Industrial Society*. New York: Basic Books, 1973.

Cohn, Norman. *Pursuit of the Millennium*. 2d ed. New York: Harper, 1961.

Coleman, James S.; Hoffer, Thomas; and Kilgore, Sally. *High School Achievement: Public, Catholic, and Private Schools Compared.* New York: Basic Books, 1982.

Conant, James B. *The American High School Today.* New York: McGraw-Hill, 1959.

Easterlin, Richard. *Birth and Torture.* New York: Basic Books, 1980.

Eastland, Terry, and Bennett, William J. *Counting by Race.* New York: Basic Books, 1979.

Frankel, Charles. "The New Egalitarianism and the Old." *Commentary* 56 (September 1973): 54–61.

Grant, Gerald. "Children's Rights and Adult Confusions." *Public Interest* 69 (Fall 1982): 83–99.

Inglehart, Ronald. *The Silent Revolution.* Princeton, N. J.: Princeton University Press, 1977.

International Association for the Evaluation of Educational Achievement (IEA). *International Studies in Evaluation.* Stockholm: Almqvist and Wiksell; New York: John Wiley and Sons, 1973—.

Jencks, Christopher. *Inequality: A Reassessment of the Effect of Family and Schooling in America.* New York: Harper and Row, 1973.

Keith, Timothy Z. "Time Spent on Homework and High School Grades: A Large-sample Path Analysis." *Journal of Educational Psychology* 74 (April 1982): 248–253.

Kristol, Irving. "About Equality." In Irving Kristol, *Two Cheers for Capitalism.* New York: Basic Books, 1978.

Lakoff, Sanford. *Equality in Political Philosophy.* Cambridge, Mass.: Harvard University Press, 1964.

Lerner, Barbara. "American Education: How Are We Doing?" *Public Interest* 69 (Fall 1982): 59–82.

Lichter, S. Robert, and Rothman, Stanley. "Media and Business Elites." *Public Opinion* 4:5 (1981): 42–46.

Lippman, Walter. *The Phantom Public.* New York: Harcourt, Brace, 1925.

Lippman, Walter. "Education vs. Western Civilization." *American Scholar* 10 (April 1941): 184–193.

Manuel, F. E., and Manuel, F. P. *Utopian Thought in the Western World.* Cambridge, Mass.: Harvard University Press, 1979.

Maslow, Abraham. *Toward a Psychology of Being.* Princeton, N. J.: Van Nostrand, 1962.

Moynihan, Daniel P. "Equalizing Education: In Whose Benefit?" *Public Interest* 29 (Fall 1972): 69–89.

Nisbet, Robert. *The Degradation of the Academic Dogma.* New York: Basic Books, 1971.

Nisbet, Robert. "The Pursuit of Equality." *Public Interest* 35 (Spring 1974): 103–120.

Nozick, Robert. *Anarchy, State, and Utopia.* New York: Basic Books, 1974.

Ravitch, Diane, "Forgetting the Questions: The Problem of Educational Reform." *American Scholar* 50 (Summer 1981): 329–340.

Rawls, John. *A Theory of Justice.* Cambridge, Mass.: Harvard University Press, 1971.

Riesman, David. *The Lonely Crowd.* New Haven, Conn.: Yale University Press, 1950.

Rutter, Michael; Maughan, Barbara; Mortimer, Peter; Ouston, Janet; and Smith, Alan. *Fifteen Thousand Hours: Secondary Schools and Their Effects on Children.* Cambridge, Mass.: Harvard University Press, 1979.

Ryan, William. *Equality*. New York: Pantheon, 1981.

Sewall, Gilbert T. "American Secondary Education." Radio Broadcast. *Soundings*. National Humanities Center, 1982.

Silberman, Charles. *Crisis in the Classroom*. New York: Random Hosue, 1970.

Toby, Jackson. "Crime in American Public Schools." *Public Interest* 58 (Winter 1980): 18–42.

Trilling, Lionel. *The Liberal Imagination*. New York: Viking, 1950.

Walberg, Herbert J. "What Makes Schooling Effective? A Synthesis and Critique of Three National Studies." *Contemporary Education Review* 1 (1982): 23–34.

3

The Changing American Child

Herbert Zimiles

This chapter reports some of the retrospective descriptions of change gathered in an exploratory study of how school-age children of today differ from their counterparts of twenty-five to thirty years ago. Several agendas influenced the framing of the study. There was, to be sure, an interest in the substantive question of how children are changing. At the same time, adopting a historical perspective helped to sharpen our understanding of children today. The study also presented an opportunity to gain access to the "clinical knowledge" of children, that is, knowledge derived from professionals who intervene to support the development of children. One of the main shortcomings of research on child development is that it is based on glimpses of children. Our energy is given over to planning the glimpses and distilling what has been learned from them, but we remain tied to a knowledge base and a conceptual framework based on glimpses. To break out of this constricting and distorting mold and to enlarge and

I wish to acknowledge with gratitude the support to conduct this study provided by a research grant from the William T. Grant Foundation.

enrich our conceptual grasp of child development, the study tapped the knowledge of those professionals whose work calls for sustained contact with large numbers of children; indeed, these people are so immersed in their work with children that they lack time to record what they have learned. Accordingly, the retrospective perceptions of professionals who have worked with children for over twenty years were gathered. The study was based on the observations of educators, child psychiatrists, and clinical child psychologists, but only the findings obtained from educators are reported here.

The study investigated children from five to eighteen years old, in order to examine change from a developmental perspective. The study was confined to children from middle-class backgrounds, and the sampling drew most of its informants from the Northeast, but was extended to include both urban and rural regions in the Midwest and on the West Coast. In all, over two hundred teachers and principals were interviewed, most of whom had been teaching for over twenty years. The semistructured interviews lasted between forty and sixty minutes.

The method of retrospective observation is vulnerable to various well-known forms of distortion. People simply do not remember accurately. There is also a tendency to remember the past in more favorable terms (as Clecak [1983] among others has noted), to collapse the achievements of a decade and treat them as though they had the same probability of occurrence as accomplishments in a single semester. Furthermore, it is probable that informants who have taught for more than twenty years are less likely to find their work challenging and, in turn, might evoke less sparkling and enthusiastic behavior from children. The magnitude of the bias associated with fatigue was estimated by interviewing younger teachers and comparing their descriptions of today's children with the descriptions of those children given by older teachers in the same schools.

At the same time, the retrospective method is also vulnerable to the failure to observe change despite its occurrence. Several informants noted that they adapt to change almost as quickly as it occurs without being aware of it. It is a moot point whether retrospective assessments of change are more prone to errors that exaggerate the magnitude of change or to those that obliterate all signs of change. These problems notwithstanding, the advantage of interviewing people with intensive exposure to children and of gauging change on the basis of integrative assessments represented an important methodological gain.

TRENDS OF CHANGE OBSERVED BY EDUCATORS

The Global View

When educators begin to catalog the changes that are taking place in the psychological development of children, three kinds of change stand out: children today *know more, are freer,* and *grow up more rapidly.* These interrelated trends reinforce each other; increased knowledge begets freedom, and freedom allows for the acquisition of knowledge. More autonomous and armed with greater knowledge, children emerge from childhood more rapidly.

Greater Knowledge. Most teachers, especially those of younger children, are impressed with how much brighter children seem and how much more they know. Children are described as streetwise and more worldly. They are more mobile, travel more widely, and know about faraway places. Children have more money and are active consumers; they know more about handling money, shopping, and acquiring material possessions. From watching television, they have a headline knowledge and a sense of awareness of a wide range of phenomena.

More Freedom. Children are more open and self-assertive, and, correspondingly, they are less timid and shy. They have a more questioning and challenging attitude toward authority and are less intimidated by adults. They require less supervision, and less of their life is centered in the home. Children express feelings more easily and are less inhibited about expressing anger, either physically or verbally. They appear to be more accepting of their sexuality and less burdened by feelings of guilt.

Accelerated Development. Almost all teachers speak of how children are growing up more rapidly. At every age level, children look larger and more fully developed than their agemates of two decades ago. Kindergarten teachers no longer find the wide-eyed innocent child in their classrooms. Whatever the criterion—whether it be social poise, physical appearance, onset of puberty, increased investment in the peer group, or the time when sexual interest and activity increase—children are seen as reaching developmental landmarks sooner. Correspondingly, teachers report teaching particular areas of subject matter at an earlier age. The task of growing up and developing competence is being achieved at a faster rate.

In reviewing these advances in independence and brightness, it is apparent that they are consonant with and have been influenced by the values and principles of the child development and mental health movements. The inner strength that is associated with psychological solidity depends on knowing and understanding the world around us. The greater independence and sense of freedom achieved by most of today's children strengthen their adaptive capacities. It is terrifying and degrading to feel helpless and controlled from without. Children's fear of adult authority tends to stifle their own personal expression and may lead to lifelong patterns of frustrating timidity and inappropriate rage. In addition, anxiety associated with repressed conflicts revolving around sexual and aggressive impulses has been found to be a major cause of mental illness and to impair adjustment patterns within the normal range. The theoretical construct of ego strength, invoked to characterize the inner resources available to the individual to cope effectively with environmental challenges and to achieve a feeling of satisfaction and contentment, has both its antecedents and consequences defined in terms of competence and independence.

Influenced by these same trends of thought, the schools have gradually adopted many of the principles of child-centered education that are derived from the psychodynamic theory of development and the educational philosophy of John Dewey. Educators have come to believe that children learn more effectively when they are allowed to engage in active exploration, have greater opportunity for personal and individual expression, and receive more respectful treatment from adults. In order to deliver children from the dominating and often oppressive yoke of the overseeing adult, school buildings have been designed to appear warmer and more informal and to reflect the mood and perspective of children. Rules and regulations are less arbitrary and rigid, and children are offered choices and are allowed to move about and learn from each other. If children appear to be more competent and independent, it is because the schools have helped them to feel this way. Within these broad categories of apparent progress, however, educators spoke of areas of perceived decline that stem from the reordering of priorities and the inevitable trade-offs associated with change.

A More Differentiated View of Change: Some Unintended Outcomes

Greater Background Knowledge. Children come to school with a vastly larger and more diverse background of information than did children of previous generations. In addition to television, the great variety of new books and publications now available to children, the toys, games, and audiovisual devices ushered in by the new technology, as well as the increased opportunity for travel, converge to form a barrage of information. Those children who are guided in the use of such resources, who are themselves gifted, and who are able to integrate their school learning with their out-of-school experiences show prodigious amounts of knowledge and mastery. They pass through school with a breadth of knowledge and a level of sophistication that tower above those of preceding generations.

Although educators see younger children as brighter, as more quick-witted, and as knowing more, they report that as children grow older their development diverges from traditionally defined expectations, and the accelerated pace of intellectual growth appears not to be sustained. For a great many children, school does not seem to be a suitable vehicle for extending and clarifying what they have already learned. Nor do they show a need for such amplification.

The greater knowledge that the young child brings to school is regarded as a mixed blessing by some educators. It is often dismissed as sketchy and incomplete, as lacking in substance and integration. At the same time, teachers are impressed with the greater range of children's knowledge and with the sense of familiarity they convey with a wide variety of topics. These fragments of information may be seen either as seedlings of knowledge that can be cultivated by the alert teacher or as contributing to a sea of confusion that both reflects and reinforces the shallowness and rootlessness of life today. On the one hand, the teacher works with a more knowledgeable person. On the other, he or she works with a more confused person, one who is perhaps already accustomed to being confused and who has less need to sort out and clarify what is being experienced. Teachers fear that children have become habituated to the fragmentary, untidy quality of learning and knowledge that they acquire from random snatches of watching television.

Orientation to School.   Accustomed to paying attention only to what strikes their fancy, to tuning out or turning the dial, today's children find it difficult to settle into the more rigid and less stimulating regimen of the classroom. They have been exposed to expertly planned communications accompanied by dazzling photographic illustration and elucidation, and they grow impatient with the comparatively modest efforts of the classroom teacher. Most teachers bemoan not only the limited attention span, impaired listening skills, and diminished motivation that they find in today's children but also the insuperable difficulties of competing with the slick productions of television. Above all, teachers must contend with the fact that children no longer regard the school as the major window to the world.

In the not-too-distant past, the child, upon first arriving at school, was thought of as an empty vessel to be gradually filled with prescribed information presented by the teachers. Since teachers constituted a major source of stimulation in a child's life, they were in a much stronger position to regulate what and how children learned. However, today's child finds the tunnelled pathway of the teacher less inviting now that bridges and other alternative routes are available. Educators, too, have begun to reexamine traditional methods of teaching and to adopt a less rigid posture with regard to what and how children should learn. The new flexibility allows for more interesting and varied early learning, but it would appear that the message of the teacher in an informal, noisy classroom loses some of its power when it lacks the ritual and bombast associated with more traditional education.

The old-fashioned curriculum, undergirded by holidays and arbitrarily chosen major historical events, led to a wasteful overlearning of certain facts to the exclusion of others. However, it provided a structure and a universality to the knowledge that was purveyed in school and fostered the belief that the school was leading the child through steps that the child must absolutely take in order to reach the promised land. The old methods were unnecessarily rigid and not especially productive as means for organizing and fostering enduring learning. They would surely not be compatible with the heightened sophistication and independence of today's children, nor could they compete effectively with the new sources of knowledge and modes of learning. They had the virtue, however, of presenting a framework that foreshadowed the larger edifice yet to be built and provided a common set of reference points for assimilating and ordering new knowledge. This overly rigid, not always illuminating or exciting framework is in striking contrast to the prevailing mood of rapid change and fluidity and to the preoccupation with novelty that is reinforced by advertising, recorded music, and the media.

An examination of the current pathway of intellectual development reveals that children are reared today under conditions that foster a greater sense of personal autonomy and in a social climate that rejects authority. They acquire much of their worldly knowledge from watching television—a source over which they have almost total control. They are almost never forced to watch television, are usually able to choose what they watch, and can further regulate their experience by tuning out the auditory input and thereby cease to process the auditory stimulation. Having learned so much so comfortably and voluntarily, and since they retain more or less continuous access to this painless source of information and stimulation, children are less ready to acquire new knowledge that is imposed on them by adults under oppressively didactic or coercive circumstances. Children are less responsive to the prescribed forms of instruction offered by the school. The school's offerings seem less useful, and children, in general, feel less compelled and less willing to exert effort in response to an external demand.

Independence and Goal Achievement. Because of their greater knowledge and independence, young children receive less adult guidance and, therefore, have more opportunity to experience the world from the vantage point of the child, that is, more concretely and hedonistically. The young child behaves in terms of functional, means–ends relationships. More autonomous, vigorous, and single-minded in the pursuit of gratification, the child seldom feels obliged to postpone gratification because of the needs or wishes or warnings of a guiding adult. In the name of fostering greater autonomy in children, and because adults feel less needed and also want relief from their responsibility of being needed, there are fewer instances in which the adult interposes a delay in gratification because of the dictates of reality or morality. Because they receive less adult input and guidance, children hear less about the abstract and spiritual dimensions of the events they experience. As self-regulation for young children becomes more pervasive because of advances in technology and preferred styles of childrearing, the conditioning processes that mediate children's learning and socialization experiences are based on reinforcing agents that are more concretely related to the children's goals. Children are less involved with relational and symbolic reinforcers, with rewards that are shaped and defined by the interven-ing, intermediary role of the caring adult. That is, the reward system that governs how today's children navigate in the environment is more directly concerned with concrete associations and linkages to the gratification that children seek, whereas the responses of children in past years were influenced by their affective ties to adults who provided fear reduction and a feeling of safety. Further, the greater autonomy experienced by children today renders the visual world of here and now so vivid and compelling that abstract and hidden ideas and meanings arouse less interest.

More capable of acting to obtain what they need and want and, conversely, less dependent on other people to provide gratification that may entail greater delay, children encounter fewer delays. Conse-quently, we may speculate that they develop less tolerance for the delay of gratification. In addition, by virtue of being less dependent on adults, children have had less experience in inhibiting the rage and impatience that are inevitably aroused by delays dictated by adults whose affective ties must, at all costs, be preserved.

In the light of these trends, it is difficult for children to think in terms of long-term goals and to accept the value of a particular learning task in terms of its future theoretical or practical usefulness. Children are more insistent on seeing the immediate payoff to any action they are asked to take and are reluctant to expend energy on a given activity if its benefits are not tangible and immediately forth-coming. Thus, the concept of a stepping-stone that is part of a long-term process, so fundamental to academic learning, is more difficult for today's child to understand and accept. Moreover, because today's world changes so rapidly and unexpectedly and so many institutions and relationships that at first seemed permanent are now in a state of transition, it is more difficult for children to entertain seriously the idea of a stable, predictable future toward which current effort will prove a fruitful investment. The instability of modern life does not inspire confidence in the ultimate payoff of delayed gratification.

Not only do children want to be shown the usefulness of the skills or knowledge they are being asked to acquire, they are also seen as generally less willing to exert effort or to face the tedium that is entailed in various aspects of academic learning. As a result, skills that require concentration, attention to detail, and sustained repeti-tion and drill, such as memorization and computation, are less well developed. In addition, the rule-governed aspects of academic learning, including spelling and grammar, are also more difficult for today's children.

Adaptation to Visual and Auditory Sensory Input. The patterns of children's responses to auditory and visual aspects of sensory input appear to have changed. Children today seem less tuned in auditorially. They have much more difficulty in analyzing, differentiating, and remembering sounds, and they attend less well to spoken messages. They are much more accustomed to functioning in a visual world. It is as though auditory messages are less important to them than are visual messages, and thus they pay less attention to auditory input.

On the other hand, the visual appearance of things has become so compelling and so fundamental to definition that it is difficult for children to picture something as possibly being different from the way they have seen it. The task of picturing something not seen, such as an object or an action, is more difficult for most children, perhaps because they are saturated with images and pictures and have grown to depend on them as the basic means of apprehending reality. Words amplify and clarify visual images, but the visual image remains the core of experience, the key to apprehending.

Most imagery and fantasy of today's children, as reflected in their writing and other forms of self-expression, are dominated by their television viewing experience. When called on to make up a story or to engage in some other form of construction, children seem more stymied than in previous years and almost invariably turn to television themes. It is more difficult for children to engage in such imaginative exercises as thinking about and acting out how a person might have lived or functioned at another time or in another place.

Reading and Writing. The written word seems less important; children are less fond of writing than in the past. They are less aware of the rules of grammar and spelling and are less interested in the structural properties of written language. The physical act of writing is itself discomforting to some children because they have had less practice.

Similarly, children find it more difficult to process the written word. They are less motivated to read a dense tract of factual material and are less adept at analyzing and remembering what they read. Reading is less often seen as an intrinsically pleasurable activity.

When children do read, it is more often for the purpose of gaining information; they appear much less interested in reading fiction.

Children tend to find clerical tasks more distasteful than they have in the past. They are, for example, less adept at working with catalog systems in libraries and with other modes of accessing and organizing the written word. They have less patience and less skill in attending to detail. They require more assistance in dealing with written assignments, and they often need guidance at every step. Children have come to view reading and writing as vestiges of ritualistic and arbitrary imposition of adult authority, and thus they learn to avoid them. Their resistance to developing skills in reading comprehension, in writing, in following directions, and in performing clerical tasks becomes increasingly important in the upper-school grades, and forms a serious barrier to academic achievement. As always, children want to get out of school what they find useful, while they avoid getting caught up in its numerous oppressive aspects. However, they hold the school in less awe, feel less obligated to "measure up," more openly express their irritation and disdain for school, and resist school more flat-footedly.

Speaking Ability. Children seem much better able to speak before a group. They are exposed to many more styles of verbal expression and conversation on television as well as to modes of elaborated discourse usually reserved for adults. Television also affords access to an endless stream of models of public speaking. When one considers the impact of television, combined with the influence of changing mores with regard to self-assertion and the early social environment provided by preschools, it is not surprising that children are now more poised in their speech.

Knowledge: Organization and Meaning. It is more difficult for children to order their expanding knowledge. A greater portion of their knowledge derives from out-of-school, less explicitly instructional sources. Television and travel experiences add a new dimension of knowledge and experience that enables the child to clarify what was previously taught and to arrive at a new level of understanding. But, more often, such experiences provide fragments of information, glimpses into a realm that is otherwise unknown. The child finds these diverse and seemingly unrelated fragments of knowledge stimulating and even comforting. They introduce a vague sense of familiarity with a wide range of phenomena. At the same time, the child becomes habituated to this quality of untidy, incompletely understood knowledge. As the tolerance for such incompleteness and confusion builds, such fragmented knowledge is easily assimilated as part of the spray of titillation that television affords. Just as adults may find it difficult to learn the grammar of a language they already know because of the tendency to be less interested in the infrastructure of a knowledge system once they are familiar with its superstructure, so do children tend to be less receptive to the study of the foundations of subject matter about which they already know something.

Teachers tend to take a dim view of the wider range of knowledge that children gain from television. They dismiss it as superficial, claiming that such snatches of information are filled with distortions and misunderstandings that create an illusion of knowledge and false images that can be destroyed by the most elementary probe. Yet, some understanding is deepened by access to television; some phenomena receive more elaborated and graphic elucidation on television than they can receive in the classroom. At the same time, the scope of knowledge to which children are exposed is so vast and far beyond what they can understand that children today, more than before, are exposed to many more facts and concepts that do not make sense to them. Many teachers, especially in the area of social studies, state that one of their main educational activities is directed at following up and elaborating on what their students have seen on television.

However, as teachers spend more energy on clarifying knowledge obtained outside the classroom, it becomes more difficult for children to adapt to a framework that is academically centered and classroom bound. Children are ill-disposed to learn such material, and consequently teachers must struggle to teach it. The idea of childhood as a distinct epoch that requires a prolonged and encapsulated period for growth and learning is being revised as children receive less protection and are moved more rapidly into the world of adulthood. It is not surprising, then, to observe that education is moving toward a pattern established for adult education, an education that is mainly directed toward survival training.

In striking contrast to television broadcasting that is geared to people of all ages and backgrounds and packaged in units of thirty to sixty minutes with no attempt to achieve a sense of continuity between shows or cumulative synthesis, school instruction has been traditionally viewed as presenting a "tree of knowledge." The roots and trunk of this tree are learned first—a sound foundation slowly grows. As the elaboration of basic facts permits comprehension of increasingly complex knowledge, exploration of the limbs begins. But this idyllic image of solid organization and structure gradually unfolding over time seems to apply no longer. The structure of knowledge is changing so rapidly that not only does the tree have many more richly foliated branches, but also the exact shape of the tree, including whether it is in fact really a tree at all, is being called into question. As society becomes less traditional and religion becomes a less potent cultural and spiritual force, there are fewer universal themes and less consensus about which events, places, and personages should form the basic framework for most areas of knowledge. While curriculum experts race to keep pace with the rapid accumulation of information and to revise their mapping of instructional knowledge, there is less clarity about what constitutes a solid curriculum structure.

The functioning of families follows the same pattern. During this era of rejection of tradition and ritual, when flexibility is especially valued and new modes of family functioning and organization are being called forth by divorce or by the mother working, family life is less regular and less predictable. Parents are less available to answer questions, provide clarification and reassurance, and present a sense of continuity. These forces, we may speculate, serve to vitiate the child's own expectation of an external order and sense of inner stability and help to explain why teachers believe children today lack structure through which they can organize the facts they learn.

Among the forces that undermine the development of integrative functioning, television stands out. Teachers report that many children arrive at school with their minds filled with the stimulation and anxiety activated by the previous night's viewing. Children deal with the high level of stimulation by talking about it. They are too filled with the experience, and often too agitated, to confront new tasks and learning opportunities. Their heads are in a whirl. Some are bleary-eyed from late-night watching. In very young children, themes played out on television, usually those of violence, dominate their dramatic play, just as they do the conversations of older children. For some children, it may not be an exaggeration to describe time spent in school as a period of recovery from television.

When motivated, children have the skills and self-confidence to do research with great effectiveness. They are seen as being more alert and resourceful, as having more initiative, and as being more questioning and challenging. At the same time, children demonstrate an impatience, an interest in getting on with things, that leads them to perfunctory execution of their schoolwork. They take less pride in getting things just right and seem less concerned with accuracy or with neatness and completeness. As a result, they are frequently seen as functioning below their capacities. Children's knowledge is so far-ranging and fragmentary that it is difficult for them to adopt an attitude of tidiness. And teachers are less ritualistic and repetitious. There is less of a style of and less of an appetite for dwelling on something—repeating and repeating, and mastering. In effect, there is less compulsion, and so there is less compulsiveness.

In noting the hodgepodge of information that television conveys, one teacher deplored the degree to which children are diverted from the developmental experiences that they need most when growing up. She emphasized the progression of learning that is needed to achieve mastery, the importance of learning and discovering things at the right moment, so that what is learned not only is more clarifying and exciting but also forms the foundation for deductive thinking. The opportunity to mull over, digest, and discover at the right moment is lost because of the pell-mell accumulation of information.

Forces that Interfere with Learning. Children, especially those in urban settings, wrestle with imponderable ideas today more than did children of the previous generation. They are concerned with a multitude of things that they do not understand, which may include the reasons for discord between their parents that signal the imminent or actual threat of family breakup, or matters dealing with sex, social problems, politics, the threat of nuclear war, or violence and crime— all of which children cannot control. Television is the source of much of the vague knowledge about these issues, but these issues are also frequently introduced or elaborated on by parents. One reason why parents are more prone to discuss such matters is that they tend to overestimate the maturity of their sophisticated children. Also, in the new spirit of openness it is expected that all subjects should be dealt with. Some parents are themselves so disturbed by these imponderables, probably because of the vivid reporting of the media, that they have a strong need to share their anxiety with other family members. In some cases, parents see that their children have already been exposed to these disturbing ideas and feel the necessity to help clarify issues that they would otherwise choose not to disclose to their children. This vague knowledge enters the lives of children and interferes with learning because of the anxiety it arouses and the distraction it causes. In addition, these more complicated and compelling issues make other phenomena seem trivial by comparison, an idea that can be used to rationalize the resistance to academic learning.

In attempting to account for the decline in reading skills that she has observed over the years, one teacher emphasized how important it is for children to feel secure in their own place, life, and rhythm before they can put themselves in another place. If children are anxious and vigilant, they are less able to suspend this monitoring and processing of potential danger. Television, with its more compelling pattern of stimulation, allows children to abandon their watchfulness, but reading is less capable of permitting a similar diversion of attentiveness.

The intellectual functioning of children is viewed through a sharper lens these days. Teachers have a more differentiated view of the learning skills of children and, in particular, a greater awareness of the existence of learning disabilities. Whether or not it is because of their heightened awareness, teachers believe that today there are more children with various forms of learning disability.

Also more widespread is the impairment of children's learning and thinking that is associated with anxiety over family upheaval and divorce. The fact that something is amiss at home is signalled by characteristic patterns of loss of concentration, depression, and outbursts of anger and rebellion, as well as by a deterioration of the quality of the child's schoolwork.

Individual Differences.   One of the new realities that complicates the work of teachers and also makes it impossible to provide a univocal description of how children are changing is the expanding range of individual differences in knowledge and understanding. As the mass of available knowledge increases exponentially, variation in access to different forms of knowledge and very large differences in children's ability to integrate and correlate what they hear and see (despite the leveling effect of television) serve to compound the range of variation in background knowledge and intellectual competence. Among those children who are exposed to a wide range of intellectual stimulation and who are capable of assimilating and responding to such opportunities, extraordinary feats of precocity are achieved. Teachers are amazed at their wide-ranging knowledge and intellectual maturity and describe teaching college-level concepts to elementary school children.

At the other end of the widening spectrum of abilities and backgrounds in the public school are large numbers of children from alienated sectors of society—minority groups and the very poor—and children with serious physical or emotional disabilities. Such children were previously sidetracked in the public schools—they were segregated and neglected unless they showed special promise, or they were excluded entirely if judged to fall short of the minimum level of aptitude or commitment to education. Now, legislation aimed at ending discrimination against minority groups and the handicapped has mandated the delivery of quality education to large numbers of children who were previously judged to be uneducable, that is, unable or unwilling to adapt to schools as they were constituted.

The New Freedom Reevaluated. The description of children as more free encompasses many different but interrelated aspects of their development. Children are more independent and they begin to function autonomously at an earlier age. For a variety of reasons, parents have come to view children as requiring less nurturance and to give them more independence. Whether it is because more mothers have returned to work due to mounting economic and social pressures or personal choice, or because mothers have greater opportunity and freedom to engage in scheduled educational or leisure activities of their own, or because of the influence of child development specialists who extol the virtues of independence and point to the damaging consequences of overprotection, children today tend to be less closely supervised by their families and are seen as more capable of fending for themselves.

This altered connection between parent and child begins in early childhood. The young child of previous generations occupied a circumscribed life space that would only gradually be enlarged by grownups who, alone, could open the gates to new territories. The child's growing knowledge evolved out of the stable events of a life experience that was highly predictable and from the guided sojourns provided by people close to him. The child was eased into a more complex world. There was more of a sense of tutelage even if socialization did not proceed by means of formal instruction or according to a deliberate plan of childrearing. The child experienced a continuously expanding view that was mediated by the perceptions and response patterns of an accompanying significant person, and the opportunity to view the world from the vantage point of that person. The child's shepherd might not have made an effort to explain matters, might hardly even have spoken, but the framework of introduction to the world was nevertheless often formed by the speech, mood, movement patterns, affective tone, and worldly concerns of the guiding person.

In marked contrast, children of today, by merely flicking a dial, receive a barrage of stimulation unrelated to what they experience in their families. They view a steady flow of pictures of people, objects, events, and places unknown to them and hear a wide variety of cultivated speech patterns and modes of articulation and discourse. This mystifying yet titillating flood of stimulation is an integral part of their reality. As a result, young children are less shielded from frightening, discordant, highly stimulating, confusing aspects of reality. Television allows children to hear and see news of world conflicts, violence, and danger at the same time and in the same manner as their parents, and not when and how their parents choose to communicate this information to them. This early exposure renders children less protected but also less dependent on parents for receiving schooling in the ways of the world.

Attitude Toward Authority. The change in behavior most frequently cited by teachers is that children show much less respect for authority. Today's children are almost universally portrayed as less automatically deferential, more challenging and questioning, and more mindful of their own rights. At first glance, these changes would seem to represent progress or to constitute a reasonable and long overdue effort to reduce the unfair imbalance of power between teacher and pupil. However, so many shades of thought and feeling are associated with the complex issue of children's attitudes toward authority that any change in the delicate equilibrium of the balance of power may produce many different outcomes ranging from measured alterations in response that seem commensurate with the change in stimulus to explosive reactions that entail a major change in adaptation. Depending on the outlook of the perceiver and on the social dynamics of the school environment, children are variously described as bold and self-assured or as rude and defiant.

In some school communities, the greater informality and the new attitude toward authority have fostered in children their intended outcomes—greater independence and inner strength. Less distracted and disabled by fear and feelings of intimidation, children are freer to attend, to question, to participate actively and fully in learning. As the psychological distance between children and teachers is reduced, adults become more approachable and there ensues an easy, exchanging, trusting, and mutually gratifying relationship between children and their teachers. The greater self-assertiveness and self-esteem that have been achieved have enabled children to bring new energy and depth of feeling to their schoolwork.

However, in those settings where authority was perceived as overbearing, the dominant theme has been that of "getting out from under." In such cases, the adversarial character of the relationship between pupil and teacher has been sharpened by the changed climate. The greater license to express feeling and to challenge authority merely places in relief a tension that both teachers and students previously repressed (at a cost, to be sure) in order to get some work done. Although the more open expression of opposition and defiance may have some cathartic benefit, it produces a decline in politeness and civility that leads to a damaging meanspiritedness. The resulting disrespect deepens the schism between teacher and student.

In those cases where the antagonism toward teachers and schools is open and widespread and has extended to the home, parents have become preoccupied with protecting their children from the power of the school. Indeed, new laws redefine and restrict the sanctions that the schools may impose upon children who misbehave, and they also articulate the rights of redress. There is an increase in litigation brought by parents against the schools, and it is not uncommon for children to flaunt their legal rights during confrontations with teachers.

In general, there is less respect accorded the teachers and schools by both the children and their parents. Younger children seem less attached to their teachers, and they are described as more difficult to reach. That older children are disillusioned with adults is even more strongly felt by teachers and openly expressed by students. In response to this growing overt opposition, some teachers tend to withdraw emotionally in their contacts with children.

The Peer Group. During childhood, an individual's primary emotional investments and allegiances gradually shift from his or her elders to coevals, from inside the family to the outside world. Children today are seen as making this transition earlier and more vigorously, as turning with even greater intensity and at an earlier age to their peer group. Children appear to be more influenced by the norms, values, and standards established by their peers and are more apt to confide in and seek advice and comfort from their friends. In the past, the sphere of peer relationships offered companionship and the opportunity to engage in play; it provided an arena for developing skills and gauging and validating one's competence and growth during the formative years. Deep emotional commitment to peers did not develop until adolescence. It now appears that the peer group becomes a primary reference group earlier in a child's life. Most observers of children do not attribute this pattern to an intensification of the affective bond to peers as much as to the attenuation of the connection between child and adult. Thus, this greater dependence on the peer group probably has occurred by default because of the weakening of the bond between child and adult.

Numerous interrelated factors converge to produce this trend. If children reach various developmental landmarks sooner, the tendency to become invested in the peer group at an earlier age is in part merely another reflection of a more generalized pattern of accelerated development. Similarly, as children develop more rapidly they become less dependent on adults at an earlier age. Furthermore, the greater openness and informality of society, combined with the greater competence and earlier independence achieved by children, give them freer rein to face feelings of rivalry with adults, to express more openly the adversarial side of their relationship. We may speculate that this openly expressed competition, in turn, leads children to detach themselves from adults still more. Moreover, in testing the limits of their developing independence, children probably bring about more alienation from adults than they intend. Not only are they apt to reach for levels of independence that they are unable to handle comfortably, but in their quest for and assertion of independence, children are also likely to disappoint and antagonize adults who are themselves not prepared for so early a separation.

Children are drawn to their peer group not only because their increased competence and independence allow them to separate themselves from adults, but also because they have found that they cannot count on adults. Parents are so busy working, extending and completing their education, engaging in travel and leisure, or striving to preserve or restore their own youth that they are simply not available as much, and children have no choice but to adapt to this fact. The resentment aroused by parental unavailability, together with its harsh reality, serves to thrust the child further into the peer group. In effect, children are finding adults less reliable than they supposed them to be, collectively as well as individually and personally. The lack of resolution in adults' lives becomes ever more apparent as divorce rates rise and people more openly admit defeat and show disarray. Children's greater knowledge of world events is replete with evidence of widespread moral turpitude as well as of the failure of adults to solve problems of overriding importance. In addition, the

pace of social change is so rapid that intergenerational communication may have become more difficult and less useful. As Margaret
Mead (1978) suggested, in a rapidly changing society adults may
have less guidance to offer to the next generation.

Some Ramifications of the Acceleration of Development. Children are
seen as growing up much more rapidly. The kindergartners of today
are thought to resemble first and second graders of years back, and
twelve-year-olds remind teachers of the fourteen-year-olds of yesterday. The school-age child (a term that requires redefinition as increasing numbers of children have begun to attend full-time
preschool, and preschool begins at an earlier age) is viewed as more
self-assured, poised, outspoken, more comfortable in dealing with
adults, and more capable of maneuvering in his environment.

Children become (dimly) aware of worldly matters at an earlier
age and develop means of coping with a much wider, more complicated (though poorly understood) array of forces. Having learned to
adapt to a more complex reality and coveting, always, the power and
the competence and the privilege that are associated with being grown
up, children show an earlier readiness to function within an adult
framework. Armed with more knowledge and coping skills, and
finding it easier to model patterns of adult behavior from the steady
stream of stereotypic portrayals that television provides, children pass
through the developmental cycles more rapidly.

These changes, reported in rural as well as urban and suburban
settings (although the rate of acceleration and degree of sophistication
are greater in cities), do not necessarily make education smoother or
more effective. The period of wide-eyed innocence and thirst for
learning is more fleeting and less clear-cut. The distractions of sexuality intrude earlier, and the flirtations and preoccupations with the
opposite sex are followed by what is described by teachers as a less
secretive and earlier period of sexual activity in which students
participate more widely. By the time many youngsters reach the
middle of high school, they have acquired so many material possessions, experienced so much bought entertainment, achieved so sophisticated a degree of sexual awareness, and have been propelled into
such heights of self-reliance by virtue of alterations in the quality of
family support and their own rapidly growing worldliness that they
have achieved many of the most visible and cherished features of adult
status, and it is difficult for them to think of themselves as needing still
more preparation for life.

Several factors contribute to this pattern of accelerated awareness and development: (1) Because it is no longer possible to shield children from frightening and potentially disturbing events, children are forced to confront and come to terms with disturbing forces in the environment at an earlier age. (2) For a variety of reasons, children function more autonomously at an earlier age, and independence is among the most salient defining features of adulthood. (3) Society has adopted a more open attitude toward sexuality. The ubiquitous lewd magazines in the corner store, the greater sexual explicitness of television programming and motion pictures, the pornography available on home video, and the increasingly sexual character of advertising heighten awareness of sexuality and lead to demystification of a key aspect of the adult world. (4) Educators, too, have come to define progress by demonstrating that the same material can be learned by children at an earlier age, thereby joining the race to have children reach adult competence sooner. (5) Manufacturers of toys and clothing are aware of children's fascination with pretending that they are miniature adults, and manufacturers thus find it profitable to play the game of obliterating child-adult distinctions by magically and whimsically helping the child become an adult—at least in outward appearance. Thus, at school, in the home, on the street, and in the marketplace, children are helped to feel that there are fewer barriers between them and adult status.

At first glance, this acceleration of development would seem an accomplishment that is entirely laudable. Insofar as we associate childhood with helplessness, vulnerability, and incompetence and regard the main task of childhood to be that of growing up, then the earlier emergence from this stage of becoming is to be celebrated. Acceleration of development represents still another way in which modern life represents a triumph over darkness. But questions must be raised regarding the cost of this quickened pace of growth and whether it is solid and integrated. Are children maturing faster, or have we found ways to make them look ready sooner although their internal growth remains essentially unchanged? Is the swiftness of change itself disruptive?

At least part of the acceleration of development has been brought about by the greater accessibility to models of adult appearance and demeanor. While growing up, children have always emulated the outward appearance of adults, as when they secretly lock themselves in a room with a mirror to try on a parent's hat or begin to mimic adult expression and mannerisms. This imitative process is reinforced a hundredfold by television. The parade of visual cues that reveal how adults walk and talk and dress, along with the advertisements that punctuate the programming, is replete with messages about the central importance of external appearance. Clearly, a heightened sensitivity to outward appearance spearheads today's accelerated march toward growing up. Thus once children look older, they are given more freedom and responsibility, and they begin to be treated as older people.

The questions that must be asked are long-standing ones. In the past, they were raised in connection with individual cases in which a child was growing up very fast. Now this state of affairs, in one way or another, applies to most children. Does rapid development lead to the assumption of responsibilities that children cannot carry, and will it thereby bring undue stress? Does it result in unnecessary failures that damage self-esteem, and does it lead to baffling or unrewarding relationships and premature sexuality that predispose the child to disappointment and confusion that have enduring adverse impacts? Will it deprive children of valuable time during which they can learn to know themselves and to develop their inner lives, thereby impairing their ability to make a solid occupational choice and to engage in effective educational planning? Is the acceleration of development today skewed in the direction of more visible and surface aspects of the growth process, and will the focus on the observable and the external foster greater emptiness?

THE CHANGING EDUCATIONAL MILIEU

In attempting to weigh the significance of these reported changes, it should be noted that informants were selective in the changes that they chose to mention. In addition, some of the patterns described by teachers were situationally determined, that is, were elicited by changes in the educational environment. When teachers describe how children are changing, they speak mainly from the perspective of how the task of educating children is changing. Thus, the changes they observe in children are interwoven with changes in the educational environment that have elicited these patterns. Changes in the educational climate and method are both cause and effect; they are a response to changes in children and, at the same time, present a stimulus situation different from that of thirty years ago that evokes correspondingly different behavior. Among the changes in the schools that interact with the changes in children are the following:

1. The school has become less proprietary and elitist. It has less exclusive control over establishing standards, selecting students, and determining what is to be taught. The teacher is viewed as a public servant rather than as a trustee of the school.

2. The greater informality of the schools alters the tone of the educational atmosphere. The decline of tradition and ritual and the elimination of oppressive moral imperatives make for a less somber and serious school life.

3. The teacher's role has become more managerial and less purely instructional, partly because there are more teaching specialists and more programmed forms of instruction to carry out the teaching function and partly because schools are seen less exclusively in an instructional light. The acquisition of information is regarded as but one facet of a continuum of cognitive and social development with which the school is concerned, now that we have grown accustomed to looking at the school through a prism of psychological development rather than academic achievement.

4. The school is seen as more continuous with the home and is asked to take on some of the tasks and responsibilities that were in the past associated with the home—to serve meals, provide after-school care, present information and guidance with regard to sex and substance abuse, and offer counseling. Whereas in the past education was viewed as a privilege, as a supplemental, circumscribed activity in the life of the child that offered cultural enrichment dispensed by enlightened professionals, it is now seen as an integral part of the child-care system.

5. Changes in the size and location of the physical plant of the school and in the distance that children must travel to school place new constraints on the role of the school and alter the character of school life.

CONCLUSION

The question of what is happening to children in light of the whirlwind of change in which they are enveloped seems too important to ignore, despite its forbidding complexity. Perhaps the question cannot be answered fully or with complete accuracy, but we need to begin to provide answers, even if they are incomplete and speculative, in order to stimulate a more probing attitude toward the issue of the changing child. This ethnographic study of teachers' perceptions of how children are changing and of the most salient features of children's development today offers a point of departure for more systematic and rigorous study. Without launching into a detailed methodological analysis, two aspects of teachers' retrospective perceptions that bear on the veridicality of the findings warrant further comment because they raise issues that pertain to how educators perceive children.

The opportunity to talk with so many educators made clear an outlook frequently found among teachers that undermines their effectiveness—a fault-finding and pessimistic stance that becomes crystallized in a sour attitude toward children. Whether it is a disillusionment that stems from the discrepancy between their own childhood view of children (based on their own chain of friendships and associations) and their later exposure to a more varied and less cooperative group of children, or the multifaceted educational goals that inevitably leave the teacher with the nagging feeling of not having done enough, or the fatigue that develops from the need to adapt to a steady stream of change in educational policies and curriculum as well as in the children themselves, teachers tend to develop a grudging attitude toward their work and the children they teach. It is an insidious trend seldom rising above the level of self-awareness, the reality of which ought to be more explicitly recognized so that steps can be taken to combat it.

Perhaps more important, it would seem that when teachers talk about today's children, they are not so much describing children who have changed as they are describing different children. Teachers tend to view children as occupying tiers, gradations that call forth correspondingly different levels of attention, commitment, and expectation in how teachers relate to children. With the passage of time, the searchlights of professionals broaden their beam. As a result, the primary reference group of teachers appears to be expanding. The teachers now include a wider range of children in their first tier. In addition, they feel more obligated to distribute their investment of professional effort to all categories of children more equally. Thus, teachers may be comparing the elite students of yesterday with a broader section of today's student population. While these changes in teachers' attitudes toward children make it difficult for them to render definitive intergenerational comparisons of children, the changes represent significant progress in deepening teachers' commitment to the full spectrum of the child population. These changed perspectives among teachers bring with them changes in academic standards and expectations and in the ways that children relate to school and to each other. The dynamics of this altered perception of school and children sets in motion a chain of events that are both cause and effect of how children are changing.

REFERENCES

Clecak, Peter. *America's Quest for the Ideal Self: Dissent and Fulfillment in the 60s and 70s.* Oxford: Oxford University Press, 1983.

Mead, Margaret. *Culture and Commitment: The New Relations between Generations in the 1970s.* New York: Columbia University Press, 1978.

PART III

Life in Schools

4

What Is Learned in Elementary Schools

Thomas L. Good

Several important aspects of schooling are discussed in this chapter: whether our understanding of schooling is improved by viewing learning as a social as well as an instructional process; how teachers influence what and how students learn; the effects on students of variations among teachers' expectations and instructional styles; the consequences for students and teachers of tracking, ability grouping, and pull-out instruction.

FROM HOME TO SCHOOL

As children leave home and start school, they must adjust to the demands of schooling. To profit from schooling they must learn how to "go to school" and how to "do school work." In this section of the chapter I will discuss home learning, nursery school learning, and learning in first-grade classrooms, and I will contrast the expectations others have of children in these three settings.

I wish to acknowledge the logistical support provided by the Center for Research in Social Behavior, University of Missouri–Columbia. I especially wish to thank Patricia Shanks for her professional typing of the manuscript and Gail Hinkel for her editorial assistance.

We know that children's interest in, and skills relevant to, academic scholarship begin to develop long before they enter school. Many educators and researchers have identified family practices (from symbolic appreciation for learning to actual parental instruction) that contribute to early acquisition of basic academic skills. In particular, many studies have focused on students' interest in reading because of the importance of reading to all school subjects.

Do parents' beliefs and expectations determine children's interests, or do parents' beliefs merely reflect their awareness of interests that their children have developed independently? It is virtually impossible to separate antecedent from cause in determining social influence because so many variables occur simultaneously and one person's behavior always affects that of others in the social grouping. Although parents (and teachers) have more control and resources, parents' behavior is influenced by the behavior of their children. However, a study by Hiebert and Coffey (1982) suggests that parents may have some preconceived notions related to gender and developmental status, regardless of the characteristics of individual children.

McGillicuddy-DeLisi (1982) discusses a number of studies that indicate that children's performance on intelligence and achievement tests varies according to family characteristics such as socioeconomic status. These studies generally show that family constellation factors (number of siblings and birth interval or ordinal position) are inversely related to children's cognitive performance. Interaction effects between socioeconomic status and family constellation are often obtained, with effects of family constellation being more marked for families with lower socioeconomic status. Studies of the influence of family characteristics on children's development have been criticized, however, for failing to specify how the environment affects children (for example, see Bronfenbrenner 1979).

To improve on earlier studies, McGillicuddy-DeLisi used both observations and interviews to explore the relationship between parents' beliefs about children's development and their behavior toward their offspring. One-third of the families had only one child, who was three to four years old, and the remaining families had three children, with the second-born of preschool age. Half of the three-children families had near spacing (fewer than three years) between first- and second-born children, and half had far spacing. Within each family constellation group, half the families were characterized as working-class and half as middle-class, based on education and income of parents.

Children in this study were to learn two tasks taught by their parents in a laboratory situation. The study showed that what mothers believed about how children developed predicted their teaching behavior in two different laboratory contexts, even after demographic characteristics were taken into account. Fathers' beliefs about child development were also related to their behaviors with their children after taking into account family constellation and socioeconomic factors. These data provide evidence that parents' beliefs about child development may guide how they interpret and react to children's behavior.

Differences Between Home and Preschool

How well do parents' beliefs and behaviors match those of preschool educators? Young children in American society are exposed to a wider variety of socializing agents today than at any previous time. Most families now share their childrearing role with at least two other major sources of influence—television and preschools. Each of these socialization influences—family, television, and preschools—has been studied independently, usually as potential influences on the social or intellectual development of children. According to Hess, Holloway, Price, and Dickson (1979), however, little research has been done comparing these influences, so that knowledge of how these three influences differentially affect the cognitive and social development of young children is incomplete.

Calling for more integrative research on socialization, Hess and associates compared the differences between parents' and preschool teachers' behavior and toward children in order to look for discontinuities between children's experiences at home and at preschool. These authors argue that disparities may or may not present problems for children or parents, but that it is important to know about differences in order to make judgments about their effects.

The authors note that it is reasonable to expect parents and teachers to differ in their goals and expectations for children and in their behavior toward children. First, experienced teachers have had more contact with a variety of families and children and have more time for planning instruction. Furthermore, the values and practices of the child-care profession are transmitted to teachers through training programs and literature. Third, materials used in training frequently urge teachers to adopt behaviors that offer children freedom to choose their own activities, follow their own interests, and make their own decisions. One can reasonably question, then, the correspondence between what teachers learn in training programs and the techniques parents use.

The authors point out that the settings in which parents and teachers interact with young children differ in several important ways and argue that these disparities in social context are another potential source of dissimilarities between those two types of caregivers. They note that preschool teachers deal with children in groups, there are a relatively large number of contacts between children and adults, and the relationships between staff and children are transitory. Also, staff behavior is constrained and corrected by the norms of the center and by federal, state, and municipal regulations. The physical environments of the preschool and the home differ considerably. In general, the environment of the school is arranged to benefit the children, while the home is organized to serve a wider range of functions and the needs of a family. Preschools regulate and interact primarily with children in groups. For example, a predictable daily schedule (lunch times, naps, and so forth) serves group needs. Yet another and more obvious difference between mothers and teachers is the personal relationship they have with children in their care.

The sample in the Hess, Dickson, Price, and Leong study (1979) was recruited from preschools and child-care centers in the San Francisco Bay area that used a variety of instructional approaches. Sixty-seven mothers and their first-born children participated in this study. All were Caucasian; fourteen were single parents at the time the study began; mothers ranged in age from twenty to thirty-five years; and the families represented a wide range of socioeconomic backgrounds.

Several general patterns resulted from the comparison of beliefs and behaviors of mothers and teachers who filled out questionnaires, were interviewed, and were observed teaching a standard task to a child: (1) mothers and teachers hold similar goals for children, although mothers tend to emphasize prosocial skills more and independence less than do teachers; (2) mothers press for mastery of developmental tasks at an earlier age than do teachers; (3) mothers teach in a style that is more direct, demanding, and explicit than that of teachers; (4) mothers appeal to their own authority to obtain compliance, while teachers invoke rules more often; and (5) teachers tend to be more flexible in requesting compliance. The following incident provides an example of the general differences in teaching behavior between mothers and teachers.

Mother: I want the one that isn't finished . . . that someone took a bite out of like . . . but a pretty big bite. Can you push that button? (Child incorrectly pushes the button under the half-circle.) *Mother*: No. That's too much. That's not enough of a circle.

Compare this behavior with that of the teacher.

Teacher: Can you find the circle that's open at the top? There is no line at the top. (Child incorrectly pushes button under the half-circle.) *Teacher*: That . . . oh that's good. But it's the one that's got more lines on it.

The mother's response included explicit feedback that the choice was incorrect, while the teacher accepted the response and only implicitly informed the child of the error by using such words as "but" and "more."

Also, note that the teacher provided praise for an incorrect response. Many teachers (unlike most parents) prefer not to tell children that they have made a mistake; these teachers often evaluate students on their *effort* rather than the *quality* of their work.

These differences in teachers' and mothers' styles of interacting with young children are generally congruent with disparities that appear on self-report instruments: teachers and mothers varied in their developmental goals for young children, press for mastery, and use of control strategies. This consistency in differences in teachers' and mothers' beliefs across dissimilar measuring devices and separate testing occasions adds reliability to the findings. The authors conclude that the behaviors they identified are not isolated but are part of a consistent pattern of childrearing and socialization.

In related research, Winetsky (1978) illustrates that, when compared with mothers, teachers prefer preschools that offer unstructured settings where activities are chosen and directed by children rather than organized and directed by adults. Observations of mothers and child-care workers interacting with infants support Winetsky's results (Rubenstein and Howes 1979). Child-care staff touched the infants more in non-caregiving situations, engaged them more often in playful activities, and were less often restrictive than were mothers interacting with their infants at home.

However, there is growing evidence that the home environment is *not* the same for all children in a family. Chall and Snow (1982) studied poor and good readers to learn if there were systematic differences in their home environments, and they often found marked differences in the reading abilities of brothers and sisters in the same home. In a home with a good reader it was not uncommon to find a sibling who was a poor or mediocre reader. Similarly, in a home with a problem reader there were often siblings who were relatively good readers.

Results from the Chall and Snow study provide clear evidence that not all children in a family experience the same home environment. However, it would be misleading to suggest that the home does not have considerable influence on a child's academic-related skills. Although the investigators identified striking within-family differences, they also found that home variables significantly affected children's reading skills. For example, more than 60 percent of the variance on word recognition and vocabulary in their sample of students was explained by home variables.

The causes of these differences are not clear. It may be that children in the same family develop different reading abilities because parents allocate their time and energy differently to their different children. Alternatively, siblings may read at different levels not because their environments are different but because they react differently to similar opportunities. It seems plausible to infer from these data that siblings often enter school with different abilities for, and interests in, reading and probably in other subject areas as well.

The conclusion that students arrive at school with dissimilar interests and abilities may seem relatively commonsense at first glance. However, many educators, sociologists, and psychologists hold that home environment, socioeconomic status, and other status variables lead students to have rather predictable problems to which educators must respond. For example, some teachers commonly base their expectations of students partly on their knowledge of and interactions with students' older siblings (Seaver 1973). This study did not clearly show how teachers' perceptions of students' home conditions influenced their behavior, but it seems likely that some teachers *may inadequately assess students' potential* by emphasizing factors such as home background, performance of older siblings, and the like.

Nursery School: A Case Study

To examine more fully the similarities and differences between home and school, I shall describe one nursery school in detail, the types of demands it places on children, and how closely the teachers' expectations correspond to those of parents. The detailed case study is from Kanter (1972). The general climate of the school is similar to that characterized in the Hess, Dickson, Price, and Leong findings.

Kanter contends that in many ways the nursery school functions as a small bureaucracy by preparing students for similar structures later in life. She notes that there are few risks for individuals associated with the bureaucratic organization; clear rules and procedures eliminate uncertainty and insecurity even in decision making. However, bureaucratic organization concurrently may devalue individualistic enterprise. An emphasis on appropriate bureaucratic behavior is a liability, because stress is placed on fitting in and getting along rather than on achievement. She notes that, compared to other kinds of schools, nursery schools have considerable freedom with which to operate.

In particular, the experiences the nursery school provided can be characterized in the following ways: (1) limiting uncertainty (providing explicit rules and procedures; defining relationships, expectations, and appropriate behavior); (2) limiting strangeness (minimizing change; introducing new routines or songs and games slowly); (3) limiting mystery (presenting the world as rational and mundane as opposed to inexplicable, fantastic, and frightening); (4) limiting coercion (by permitting the child as much freedom of behavior as possible and by disguising use of power in cases when it was necessary to control behavior); (5) limiting accountability (the child was not considered responsible for any deviant or antisocial acts; aggressive behavior was attributed to carelessness or accident); (6) limiting unpleasantness (this nursery school, probably like many others, attempted to make everything fun for the children, even potentially unpleasant events, by making them into games or emphasizing their pleasurable aspects); (7) limiting peer conflict (the school de-emphasized competitions—there were no gold stars, no prizes, and no winners—no child was considered better than any other and no child any worse or less deserving; teachers attempted to maintain strict equality with respect to privileges and possessions; by providing a large number of toys and a variety of activities, the teachers hoped to avoid conflicts over scarce resources).

Different preschool programs no doubt respond differently to the needs of young children and instruct them in diverse ways. Kanter correctly notes that how representative this particular school is of all nursery schools is unknown. Although many nursery schools are more demanding, it still seems plausible that the nursery school described by Kanter is similar to those that many students attend. Indeed, on the basis of my observations of several nursery schools, I believe she has described the typical nursery school. However, the "work of nursery school" in the school Kanter describes differs substantially from many parents' beliefs about how children should be instructed. Thus, nursery school is an abrupt change for many children, who go from direct teaching at home to more indirect teaching (and in some cases, to laissez-faire teaching).

Kindergarten

Apple and King (1977) contend that kindergarten serves as a foundation for the following years of schooling and that elementary school children who have attended kindergarten generally achieve better than children who have not. However, they note that attempts to determine exactly which kindergarten teaching techniques and learning experiences contribute most directly to later achievement have not proved fruitful. They suggest that kindergarten training appears to exert its most powerful, lasting influence on the attitudes and the behavior of the children by *acclimating* students to the more structured environment of first-grade classrooms.

They report observations and interviews of children in one public-school kindergarten class. In this class the teacher emphasized the socialization of children during the opening weeks of school. She expected students to learn to share, listen, put things away, and follow the classroom routine.

Children had *no* part in organizing classroom materials or in making decisions, and the teacher made no special effort to make the children comfortable in the room nor to reduce their uncertainty about the scheduled activities. Rather than moderating or changing intrusive aspects of the environment, the teacher required children to accommodate themselves to the materials as presented. For example, when the noise of another class in the hallway distracted the children, the teacher called for their attention; however, she did *not* close the door. During most of the kindergarten session the children were not permitted to handle objects or materials, and they were organized so that they learned *restraint*. They learned that they could handle things within easy reach only when the teacher permitted them to do so. They were also punished for touching things at the wrong time or not following directions in sequence.

In this classroom whole-class activities were stressed. Not only was *every* work activity required, but every child had to start at the designated time. The entire class worked on all assigned tasks at the same time. Further, all children were required to complete the assigned task during the designated work period. The products or skills that the children exhibited at the completion of a period of work were intended to be identical or at least similar. The teacher demonstrated most art projects to the entire class before the children got the materials. Apple and King point out that activities in this class prevented students from developing any pride in the process of the work per se. *Diligence, perseverance, obedience,* and *participation* were rewarded. These are characteristics of children, not of work. In this way, the notion of excellence was separated from that of successful or acceptable work and replaced by the criterion of adequate participation.

Florio (1978) describes a different type of kindergarten class. Her study is based on a two-year investigation of daily life in a kindergarten/first-grade classroom. In contrast to the class described by Apple and King, Florio identified two different kinds of activities—whole-class, single-focus activities that were directed by the teacher; and more loosely organized, multifocus activities that the children initiated and the teacher did not supervise directly.

In this class academic and social competence entail knowing what behavior is appropriate for a particular context. Since the activities and expectations in the two contexts are varied, students must learn subtle differencs if they are to succeed.

The differences in the two kindergarten settings described above are pronounced. Context differences across settings as well as differences within settings must be considered. In the class described by Apple and King, students generally had to accommodate to only the teacher's interests and needs. In the classroom described by Florio, however, children had to learn to work cooperatively with other students as well. These two classrooms indicate that what one needs to learn to be competent and to do the work in kindergarten varies, depending primarily on the particular teacher and school the student attends. Furthermore, the definition of a successful student in a given kindergarten class may not be consistent with the behaviors required of a successful first-grade student, even in the same school.

Thus, children generally receive direct teaching and explicit socialization in their homes; then they attend relatively unstructured nursery schools; and when they advance to kindergarten, they often perform unimaginative tasks with an entire class. Such a sequence of discontinuities and abrupt changes in behavioral management and instructional expectations would appear to pose problems for some students (What is expected of me? Do I follow directions only or determine my own schedule?). However, I must emphasize that kindergartens vary widely (although many programs I have observed are similar to the "everybody-by-the-number" routine that Apple and King describe). This variation is important and must be considered in any analysis of first-grade students' prior schooling experiences.

First Grade

Although some educators believe that school begins with kindergarten, the majority of parents and some educators believe that formal instruction begins in first grade. What, then, do students learn in schools at this level that is distinctive from what they learn at home?

Dreeben (1968) notes that schools and families differ in notable ways. First, families lack formally defined subdivisions. On the other hand, school systems are divided into various levels and within each level into classroom units. Second, the school provides a unique experience in establishing and severing relationships with adults. That is, each year the child gets a new teacher or teachers. Third, there are fewer adults per child at school than at home. Children thus have fewer opportunities for individualized interaction with an adult at school. Fourth, there is typically a much more rigid pattern of events in schools. School is cyclical in that nearly all instructional events take place during each five-day school week, and one week or one day is pretty much like every other. Dreeben believes that schools are more heterogeneous than are homes. He further notes that it is much more difficult for students to express affect in schools than at home. Also, teachers are expected to avoid establishing enduring relationships with pupils premised on affection.

Another major difference is that the central concern of schools is instruction, and teachers assign pupils specific tasks to perform and then assess the quality of performance. According to Dreeben, in the family the performance of day-to-day activities and the expressions of emotion are equally important. However, the school's explicit purpose and official reason for existence is to offer instruction. The school is an organization concerned with the encouragement of activities in which children demonstrate how well they can achieve. In so doing, pupils distinguish themselves from each other over a period of years on the basis of their achievement. Although teachers are likely to consider the quality of students' performance in the various cognitive activities most seriously, this is not the sole criterion on which pupils are differentiated.

Dreeben notes that what is learned in schools can be summarized in part in four important acts: children learn to (1) act by themselves (unless collaborative effort is called for) and to accept personal responsibility for their conduct and are accountable for the consequences of their conduct; (2) perform tasks actively and master the environment according to certain standards of excellence; (3) acknowledge the rights of others to treat them as members of categories; and (4) realize that others treat them on the basis of a few discreet characteristics rather than on the full constellation of characteristics that represent the whole person.

Like Florio, Dreeben stresses that much classroom behavior is contextual and students must learn how to distinguish one context from another. Although Dreeben's analysis suggests that home and school differ in important ways, the recent development of new types of preschools makes this contrast less sharp than it perhaps was in the early 1960s. Furthermore, the varied and sometimes contradictory demands of family, day care, or nursery school are no doubt confusing to some students. Some schools are permissive, unstructured, and allow students to express affect. Other schools hold minimal academic expectations for students; in such schools there is often *less* public evaluation by teachers than there is by parents in certain homes (especially homes where parents frequently demand that their children play the piano, dance, and so forth when other adults are visiting).

Culturally Different Students

All students experience some discontinuities as they move from home to school. Although the language and expectations of home and school are different, most children can understand these differences (for example, children are accustomed to answering questions posed by adults, although teachers' questions may be of a different type from those of other adults). However, the transition between home and school may present problems for some students (including bright, capable students), particularly if the school environment differs radically from students' home environments.

Au and Mason (1981) examined the social aspects of classroom learning and found that poor school achievement by many minority children is related to the nature of the interaction between teacher and pupils in the classroom, and that the social aspects of lessons are as important as their instructional and academic dimensions. They also found that discussion in conventional classrooms generally follows a two- or three-part sequence (the teacher asks a question, a student answers, and the teacher may evaluate the student's answer). This sequence appears to be very simple; however, it may cause many problems for some children. For example, a child may need to know how to bid for a turn and wait to be called on rather than interrupting the turn of another student. Schultz, Erickson, and Florio (1982) suggest that some children lack this knowledge, because rules for participation in specific home activities differ from rules used at comparable times in classrooms. Au and Mason's data suggest that minority children are likely to have much more difficulty than most children do in observing conventional rules for participating in classroom activities. The culture of the school includes rules for appropriate behavior in face-to-face encounters, and some children are better able than others to follow these rules when they enter school.

However, it should be clear that participation in classroom life requires both academic knowledge and skills as well as social skills and knowledge. To be judged competent, students must learn both types of skills.

VARIATION IN CURRICULA AND QUALITY OF TEACHING

Academic Content

What are pupils to learn during schooling? In the United States, answers to this question vary both within and between states. In some states, the curriculum in certain subjects is reasonably explicit. However, it should be clear that there is not only variance in general curriculum goals across states but that the intended curriculum varies among districts. Variation in curricula is perhaps not surprising, but recent evidence suggests that in many states the curriculum offered may vary significantly between schools in a district, and often even within a school (for example, two first-grade teachers in the same school emphasize different subjects; see Carew and Lightfoot 1979).

Brophy (1982) argues that teachers in some schools are allowed more latitude in determining what to teach than are teachers in many other schools. Hence, what children learn depends partly on the curricula their teachers offer. Also, since many teachers depend on textbooks and the associated teacher's manuals for instruction, the textbook a school or district uses heavily influences what students learn.

Teachers also vary in how much of the intended curriculum they actually teach, that is, how much of the school day they use for instruction. Others have also commented on how widely time allocated for instruction (as well as how allocated time is used) varies from teacher to teacher (see, for example, Caldwell, Huitt, and Graeber 1982). Two children who attend the same school may receive different curricula simply because of the teachers to whom they are assigned.

Part of the difference in the amount of curriculum covered could be due to differences in teachers' managerial ability. However, some variation is also due to teachers' beliefs and preferences: How enjoyable is the subject? How important is it? (for example, see Schmidt and Buchmann 1983). As Brophy (1982) argues, the curriculum also varies because teachers' knowledge of the subject matter and their teaching skills vary.

Although some differences in student achievement can be explained by the content teachers present, there is clear evidence that some teachers obtain more student achievement than other teachers, even when all teachers have comparable groups of students and have used similar lesson formats, time, and materials. Thus, variations in quality of teaching have important effects on student achievement (see, for example, Good, Grouws, and Ebmeier 1983).

Some teachers teach less of the intended curriculum to certain groups of students (most notably students they believe to be slow learners, although gender, race, and other individual characteristics are sometimes associated with differential teaching behavior). Such differences in curriculum taught to students in the same class most often occur in classes in which children are ability-grouped for instruction.

Lanier and others (1981) found that students in general mathematics classes spent much more time working on repetitive drill than did students in algebra classes. Hence, whether or not students are grouped for instruction (within or between classes), teachers often focus less on theory and meaning (and more on drill and practice) when instructing students whom they believe to be lower achievers.

Pull-out Instruction

Ironically, some students may receive less or different instruction because of schools' attempts to provide them with extra assistance; these attempts include taking students out of the class for part of the day for special instruction according to their needs. Hill and Kimbrough (1981) studied pull-out instruction in schools that operated four or more special-need programs. State and district administrators had identified these schools as ones that were experiencing difficulties in administering several of those programs (hence, the sample may not represent all districts). Case-study data were collected in twenty-four elementary schools in eight districts across the nation.

These investigators found that pull-out programs posed problems for students who received special assistance as well as for regular teachers. In some schools, children were out of classes for special programs so frequently that teachers instructed their entire classes only one and a half hours daily and therefore were unable to implement the state-mandated curriculum. Fragmented instruction was especially a problem for Hispanic students because they qualified for so many special programs (six or seven daily!). Indeed, even though many Hispanic students had attended school for five years, they had received *no* formal instruction in science or social studies. Special programs.were *replacing*, not supplementing, the core curriculum for many students. Because of scheduling problems (created by multiple pull-outs), many districts allowed special programs to replace core programs. Many low-achieving, disadvantaged students thus received only special instruction, though they were entitled to regular instruction in mathematics and reading as well as supplementary instruction in those subjects.

When students did receive both regular and supplemental instruction, they were still not well served. Hill and Kimbrough found that in several cases incompatible teaching methods and materials were used in special and regular classrooms. Hence, many children became confused by conflicting approaches taken by special and regular teachers. Learning would be especially difficult for students who received conflicting information (for example, it is hard enough to learn the concept of fractions without being taught conflicting conceptualizations at the same time).

Finally, it should be noted that Hill and Kimbrough's data clearly indicate that, in addition to the problems noted above, disadvantaged students in pull-out programs are segregated from more advantaged pupils for much of the school day and are denied the chance to model and to learn from more successful students.

Ligon and Doss (1982) reached similar conclusions in their examination of Title I programs in grades 1 to 5 in the Austin, Texas, Independent School District. They found that Title I instructional services were not supplementary to regular services but instead supplanted the regular program. Students who attended more than one compensatory program actually received *less* regular instructional time than did students who were enrolled in only one program.

Ironically, then, it seems that children who most need additional instruction often receive less rather than more assistance. However, other possible problems are also created for those students and their teachers by pull-out instruction. Children who perhaps have the fewest time-management skills must know when to leave class and when to return, and they must negotiate with their teachers about work they have missed while they were out of the room. Also, these students have to return to their regular rooms, and no matter how carefully they enter the classroom, their re-entry often disrupts regular classroom activities. Considering teachers' generally negative reactions toward interruptions and pull-out programs, it is likely that teachers will react negatively when students try to find out what work they need to make up. Even though teachers' reactions may be due more to the program and the interruption than to students, pupils may view themselves as causing the teachers' irritation.

Florio (1978) suggests that the biggest potential loss for pull-out students is less exposure to the language and the daily activities of their regular classes. That is, because of these students' frequent absences from the room, they are unable to participate in decisions about classroom rules and norms as well as to learn more about the norms of behavior associated with certain classroom contexts. As a result, it is likely that these students will violate teacher and peer expectations.

Mainstreaming

Mainstreaming is a process resulting from another law designed to improve the educational lives of students. In particular, Public Law 94–142 was intended to return students to classrooms and regular instructional programs from which they had been removed because of alleged handicapping conditions (physical or mental). The intention was to place "handicapped" students in the least restricted environment and to allow them to receive normal instruction with regular students whenever possible.

The effects of mainstreaming appear to be problematic. In some classes with certain teachers it works well; in other classes it has negative effects on most students. However, perhaps a more compelling argument against mainstreaming is that legislation mandating mainstreaming may actually have increased the frequency with which students believed to be less capable receive instruction *segregated* from students believed to be more capable because of an increase in the number of special programs housed outside the regular classroom (Sarason 1982).

Effects of Ability Grouping and Tracking

Students in some classes or schools receive differential instruction because of tracking and ability grouping. Students are often segregated for instruction in American schools. Although many researchers have studied the effects of heterogeneous or homogeneous grouping (on the basis of measured aptitude or students' previous achievement), results are inconclusive. Several authors discuss the difficulties of synthesizing this research (for example, Esposito 1953; Good and Marshall 1984; Persell 1977; Rosenbaum 1976). Despite the difficulty of studying grouping effects, recent studies and literature reviews indicate that ability grouping (teaching students of similar ability together) does not generally positively affect the achievement of students of high and moderate ability. Moreover, it often has quite harmful effects on the achievement of low-ability students.

Good and Marshall (1984) note that the negative effects of teaching low-ability students together are more evident if one examines only studies that include classroom observation. These studies consistently show that students in low-ability groups get less exciting instruction, less emphasis on meaning and conceptualization, and more rote drill and practice. A review of this literature is beyond the scope of this chapter; however, it is instructive to examine one study that illustrates why the segregation of students for regular instruction is seldom effective.

A First-Grade Classroom. One of the most interesting studies of instruction in first-grade reading groups in one classroom was conducted by Eder (1981). This study examines instruction comprehensively and considers both student and teacher variables as explanations for what takes place during reading instruction. Eder found that students who were likely to have difficulty in learning to read were generally assigned to groups whose *social contexts* were not conducive to learning. In part, this was because assignments to first-grade reading groups were based on kindergarten teachers' recommendations, and a major criterion of placement was students' *maturity* as well as their perceived ability.

The academic abilities and the socioeconomic backgrounds (from middle-class homes) of most of the students in Eder's study were similar. Importantly, none of the students could read prior to entering first grade. Their progress in reading could therefore plausibly be related to the reading instruction they received in first grade, although there were no doubt differences in reading potential among students. Despite the similarities among students, the first-grade teacher still grouped them for reading.

Eder studied reading-group behavior throughout the year using qualitative and quantitative observational codes. She made videotapes of many reading-group sessions.

Eder found that the teacher discouraged interruptions of a student's oral reading turn within the high group but not in the low group. Eder thought that the teacher may have been concerned with maintaining the interest of the low group during other students' reading turns (in general, their reading turns tended to be longer and filled with more pauses); the teacher may also have thought that students in the low group were less interested in the material; therefore, she was more willing to encourage most forms of participation or responses from low students but demanded more appropriate behavior and responses from students in the high group.

According to Eder, the most immature, inattentive students were assigned to the low group. It was therefore almost certain that the teacher would have more managerial problems (for example, distractions) with this group than others, especially early in the year. Indeed, because the teacher was often distracted from listening to a student reader (because of the need to manage other students in the group), students in the low group often provided the correct word for the reader. Students in the low group had less time than students in the high group to correct their mistakes before other students or the teacher intervened.

Students in the low group spent 40 percent of their listening time not attending to the lesson (versus 22 percent in the high group). Low-ability students frequently read out of turn, adding to the general confusion. Eder reports twice as many teacher "managerial acts" in the low group as in the high group (157 versus 61), and found that interruption of students' turn to read increased over the course of the year. Due to management problems, frequent interruptions, and less serious teaching, low-achieving students may have been inadvertently encouraged to focus on social and procedural aspects of the reading group rather than on academic tasks.

It is difficult to describe what students learn in school. However, it seems plausible that students in the high-ability and low-ability reading groups in the classroom Eder studied learned different *norms for attention.* The extent to which students applied these norms to other subjects and to other classrooms is unknown; it appears, however, that, having learned a willingness to interrupt other students, the low-ability group will experience difficulties in some instructional settings. I suspect that students in the high-ability group learned other norms as well ("It's okay to think" versus learning to depend on others in difficult or ambiguous situations). I believe that such differences ultimately contribute to students developing either a passive or proactive orientation toward learning.

There is ample and compelling anecdotal evidence that once students are removed from low-ability reading groups they respond in better and more appropriate ways. Eder and Felmlee (1984) found that when a student (in the study described above) was moved from a lower to a higher group, his attention during reading instruction improved. Similarly, Weinstein (1982) found that when a student in a low-ability group was moved up (in this case the teacher was reluctant to make the change), the student's expectations and achievement improved notably. Presumably, as Eder argues, the ecology of a low-ability group sustains an environment in which it is more difficult to learn.

High Achievers and Ability Grouping

Assignment to ability groups affects the educational lives of children from all socioeconomic levels as well as from all racial and ethnic groups. It is important to note that the influence is relative. That is, in the richest school districts the children of bright, talented, and successful professionals are commonly placed in the bottom reading groups, not because they are not capable of reading (in some schools virtually all students come to school reading but are still grouped), but because they are less capable than their classmates. Hence, students placed into low-ability groups are taught with students who are relatively less talented (even though students who are placed in the low-ability group in one school district would be considered model students in another), suffer the effects of low status in the class, and perhaps pick up subtle cues from parents and teachers that they have problems ("Are you perhaps not trying hard enough?"). It seems that such children are prime candidates to become "underachievers," because it may be easier for them to be passive and to feign indifference than to try, which might lead to failure. One wonders how much potential and creativity are wasted by the unnecessary and premature assignment to ability groups in first-grade classes.

Also, students in low-ability groups cannot work with students who have somewhat better social and academic skills (for example, skills for obtaining information from adults). If allowed to work with students who are effective role models, many students in low-ability groups would likely acquire much more useful social information than they do presently (for example, learn how to ask a question in a way that the teacher answers and does not perceive the question as needless or aggressive; learn to "self-motivate" and "self-evaluate").

Teacher Expectations

Even students who receive instruction in the same group do not receive the same or appropriate treatment. In the last fifteen years many studies have examined the relationship between teachers' beliefs about individual students' achievement and teachers' interactions with students. Brophy and Good (1970) developed a model for studying this relationship:

1. The teacher expects specific behavior and achievement from particular students.
2. Because of these varied expectations, the teacher behaves differently toward different students.
3. This treatment communicates to the students what behavior and achievement the teacher expects from them and affects their self-

concepts, achievement motivation, and levels of aspiration.

4. If this treatment is consistent over time, and if the students do not resist or change it in some way, it will shape their achievement and behavior. Students for whom teachers' expectations are high will be led to achieve at high levels, whereas the achievement of students for whom teacher expectations are low will decline.

5. With time, students' achievement and behavior will conform more and more closely to the behavior originally expected of them.

In subsequent work (for example, Brophy 1982; Brophy and Good 1974; Cooper and Good 1983; Good 1981), it has become clear that individual teachers react differently to differences among students. It has been estimated on the basis of many studies that perhaps one-third of teachers behave in ways that sustain the poor performance of low achievers. Some of the ways in which teachers express low expectations toward students whom the teachers *perceived* to be low achievers are listed below:

1. Seating low-achieving students farther from the teacher or in a group (making it harder to monitor low-achieving students or treat them as individuals).

2. Paying less attention to low-achieving students in academic situations (smiling less often and maintaining less eye contact).

3. Calling on low-achieving students less often to answer questions or make public demonstrations.

4. Waiting less time for low-achieving students to answer questions.

5. Not staying with low achievers in failure situations (providing clues, asking follow-up questions).

6. Criticizing low achievers more frequently than high achievers for incorrect public responses.

7. Praising low achievers less frequently than high achievers after successful public responses.

8. Praising low achievers more frequently than high achievers for marginal or inadequate public responses.

9. Providing low-achieving students with less accurate and less detailed feedback than high-achieving students.

10. Failing to provide low achievers with feedback about their responses more frequently than high achievers.

11. Demanding less work and effort from low achievers than from high achievers.

12. Interrupting the performance of low achievers more frequently than that of high achievers.

Unfortunately, the *effects* of differential behavior by teachers on students' behavior, attitudes, perceptions, and achievement have not been studied systematically. However, there is growing evidence that students are aware of differential teacher behavior and that certain practices have negative effects on students' beliefs and achievement (Weinstein 1982).

What students learn over time (for example, what they conclude from specific patterns of teacher behavior) about the meaning of schoolwork and their role as students is uncertain, and we have no research evidence about when and how students become motivated to achieve or to perform well in particular subjects, or about how students learn work habits (for example, how to prepare for an exam, or whether it is better to ask teachers for information or to feign knowledge).

Passivity Model

Teachers also differ in the way they express expectations, and sometimes these differences in style are very dramatic. Some teachers criticize low achievers more frequently per incorrect response than they do high achievers, and they praise low achievers less per correct answer than they do high achievers. In contrast, other teachers praise marginal or incorrect responses given by low achievers. These findings appear to reflect two different types of teachers. Teachers who criticize low achievers for incorrect responses seem to be intolerant of these pupils. Teachers who reward marginal (or even wrong) answers are excessively sympathetic and unnecessarily protective of low achievers. Both types of teacher behavior illustrate to students that effort and classroom performance are not related (Good and Brophy 1977).

Over time, such differences in the way teachers treat low achievers (for example, in the third grade a student is praised or finds teacher acceptance for virtually any verbalization but in the fourth grade the student is seldom praised and is criticized frequently) may reduce the efforts of low-achieving students and contribute to a passive learning style. Other teacher behaviors may compound this problem. Low-achieving students who are called on very frequently one year (the teacher believes that they need to participate if they are to learn), but who find that they are called on infrequently the following year (the teacher does not want to embarrass them), may find it confusing to adjust to different role definitions. Ironically, those students who have the least capacity to adapt may be asked to make the most adjustment as they move from classroom to classroom. The greater variation in how different teachers interact with low achievers (in contrast to the more similar patterns of behavior that high-achieving students receive from different teachers) may be because teachers agree less about how to respond to students who do *not* learn readily.

Even within a given year low achievers are asked to adjust to more varied expectations. This may be true in part because many low achievers have several teachers (in addition to the regular teacher they may have a remedial mathematics, reading, or speech teacher). The chance for different expectations is thus enhanced. During a given year, certain teachers may also be more likely to vary the instructional styles they use to teach low achievers. For example, they may give up on an instructional technique prematurely (for instance, when the phonetics approach initially fails, the teacher tries another instructional method). I believe that many low-achieving students' interactions with different teachers are sufficiently varied so as to pose problems for these students ("What am I expected to do?"). In time, this varied teacher behavior reduces students' initiative (for example, students become reluctant to raise their hands or to approach the teacher; or they make fewer attempts to think about the meaning of an assignment or a particular subject; see Good 1981).

When teachers provide fewer chances for low achievers to participate in public discussion, wait less time for them to respond when they are called on (even though these students may need more time to think and to form an answer), criticize low achievers more per incorrect answer, and praise them less per correct answer, the implications are similar. It seems that a good strategy for students who face such conditions would be not to volunteer or not to respond when called on. Students are discouraged from taking risks and chances under such an instructional system. To the extent that students are motivated to reduce risks and ambiguity—and many argue that students are strongly motivated to do so (Doyle 1980)—students would likely become more passive in order to reduce the risks of critical teacher feedback.

What we need to begin to consider now are the circumstances under which differences in teacher behavior are useful and for which types of students. For some types of students, variations in teachers' instructional behavior and expectations will surely have positive effects in many instances.

CONCLUSION

There are notable differences in what constitutes successful learning in the home, the nursery school, kindergarten, and primary school. Differences among adults' expectations of performance in these settings are not necessarily inappropriate, and indeed under certain conditions may stimulate students' academic and social development. Still, these differences can cause major problems for some children. A more precise definition of student success at various levels may help educators to plan schooling that allows students to develop key skills and attitudes sequentially.

It seems counterproductive for kindergarten teachers to emphasize *cooperation* and *effort*, when most first-grade teachers focus on *competition* and the *quality* of work. Similarly, it is not useful to train students to make their own decisions and then in the following year to place them with a teacher who does not allow them much choice. Yet, an examination of schooling reveals that such discontinuities often occur and that there is little coordinated effort that allows students to develop progressively more self-reliance and independence. My own observations indicate that many nursery school students have more opportunity for self-direction, self-evaluation, and choice than typical sixth-grade students.

In certain contexts, it is beneficial for students to learn to cope with different styles of teaching and to figure out "what the teachers want." However, it seems a poor strategy to have young students wondering whether or not it is appropriate to ask a teacher a question. Yet that is the circumstance for students who may have both a first-grade teacher who emphasizes self-reliance ("Try it first and then ask me") and a pull-out instructor who emphasizes successful practice ("Don't practice silly mistakes; if you don't understand, ask me before you do it").

Some students experience too many unexplained discontinuities in the classroom. For example, what are the effects on students if problem solving in mathematics is taught one year as "take your time and come up with one or two best approaches for stating the problem" and the next year as "come up with as many hypotheses as you can, and then begin to respond to the problem"? What effects do such discontinuities have on students' beliefs about mathematics? For example, do they conclude that mathematics is an arbitrary set of rules—a system they cannot figure out or do not want to?

I am *not* advocating fewer techniques of presenting subject matter or less variation in classroom reward structures, but rather that performance expectations need to be better coordinated across educational levels. In many cases such coordination will reduce or eliminate large discrepancies in definitions of what constitutes acceptable student performance; however, in other cases, the coordination will require an explanation of the differences in performance expectations so that students can concentrate on learning new strategies and work procedures.

Clearly, some discontinuities are appropriate and teachers and administrators need to determine how these new, desirable expectations and performance standards can be taught to students in ways that facilitate achievement. For example, I believe that when mathematics teachers in the same school know their programs differ, the students' learning could be greatly facilitated if teachers give brief recognition of and explanations for such differences to the students at the beginning of the year: "Last year we approached problem solving this way for several good reasons; . . . this year we are going to look at it in a different way . . ." However, this calls for knowledge of what teachers in adjoining grade levels emphasize, and I have observed that all too often this information is not available to teachers. Obviously, it would be useful to gather relevant data and to use them to assure more continuity in instruction from level to level.

Many young students who are believed to be less capable receive less meaningful and less appropriate instruction than do students who are believed to be more capable. Although teachers need to offer special help to students who have deficiencies, teachers need to be especially careful that work they assign to low-achieving students is meaningful and varied. Too often, young students who have problems in school do not understand what they are to do. Students who are asked to do drill work apart from any meaningful context are likely to view such work as arbitrary and boring; under such conditions teaching problems will worsen, not improve.

Low-achieving students are often taught in ways that discourage thinking. For example, the lowest reading group often reads material that two or three other groups in the class have already read. Under these conditions, it is unlikely that the teacher or low-group students will be interested in the story. Hence, students in low-achieving groups may need different but appropriately challenging material and different sets of questions if they are to maintain motivation and interest in reading.

It seems to me that teachers of young children often use ability grouping unwisely (for example, too many groups are formed, which creates supervision problems; the criteria for group assignment are vague or based on relatively minor differences among students). Unfortunately, when low-achieving students are assigned to separate learning conditions (whether they are tracked, pulled-out, or assigned to a low group in the regular classroom), they too often receive instruction that is less serious (often trivial) and more likely to be devoid of substance (drill and facts rather than meaning and conceptualization); in these conditions both students and teachers become trapped in the managerial and procedural aspects of instruction.

When low achievers are taught separately they experience problems other than content fragmentation. Because they often have more teachers, lows must adjust to variations in behavior among different teachers. It is thus not suprising that many slower students view adults and school as arbitrary. Because these students cannot determine their proper role, they often respond passively to school. Most attempts to help students who start with somewhat low academic and social skills will therefore widen, not lessen, the gap between their skills and those of other students. Furthermore, low achievers have little contact with students who have relatively more social and academic knowledge. Such separation denies low achievers an excellent chance to master skills that are critically important to school success (for example, how to ask questions). Failure to learn these skills further increases the likelihood that slow students will develop a reactive or passive stance toward schoolwork.

Although grouping for instruction, even ability grouping, may be appropriate for certain students or particular content goals, my observations in elementary schools and my knowledge of extant literature have convinced me that students perceived to be high or low achievers are unduly segregated for instruction. I believe that excellence of education (productive individual learning of content and concepts as well as enriched respect for individual differences) can often be accomplished through heterogeneous large- or small-group instruction.

It seems unfortunate to deny low-achieving students access to other students during instruction, and teachers need to explore other options for instructing young children. One option is to use whole-class instruction more frequently. This instructional format has been used successfully for certain topics in mathematics (see Good,

Grouws, and Ebmeier 1983), and seems feasible for reading instruction in topics such as phonics, spelling, and study skills, as well as for comprehension instruction. Yet another possibility is to allow students to work in mixed-ability groups. Even in the area of reading (where ability grouping for young children is most pervasive), students can be taught in groups that are formed on some basis other than ability. Thus, although students may need to receive some differential instruction related to their abilities (for example, oral reading for slower readers), there is reason to believe that low-achieving students can benefit from inclusion with more competent students during classroom instruction.

Finally, it seems imperative that all students *learn how to learn*, develop positive but appropriate expectations of their performance, experience success, and master basic skills. To achieve these basic goals, important policy decisions may have to be made at the kindergarten through third-grade level. For example, it may be necessary to provide additional resources so that classes in grades K to 3 are smaller. At a minimum, resources used for instruction at this level need to be coordinated, and increased effort should be made to help all students develop more positive school-related skills.

REFERENCES

Apple, Michael, and King, Nancy. "What Do Schools Teach?" *Curriculum Inquiry* 6:4 (1977): 341–357.

Au, Kathryn H., and Mason, Jana M. "Social Organizational Factors in Learning to Read: The Balance of Rights Hypothesis." *Reading Research Quarterly* 17:1 (1981): 115–152.

Bronfenbrenner, Urie. "Context of Child Rearing: Problems and Prospects." *American Psychologist* 34 (October 1979): 844–850.

Brophy, Jere. "How Teachers Influence What Is Taught and Learned in Classrooms." *Elementary School Journal* 83 (September 1982): 1–13.

Brophy, Jere, and Good, Thomas L. "Teachers' Communication of Differential Expectations for Children's Classroom Performance: Some Behavioral Data." *Journal of Educational Psychology* 61 (October 1970): 365–374.

Brophy, Jere, and Good, Thomas L. *Teacher-Student Relationships: Causes and Consequences*. New York: Holt, Rinehart and Winston, 1974.

Caldwell, Janet H.; Huitt, William G.; and Graeber, Anna O. "Time Spent in Learning: Implications from Research." *Elementary School Journal* 82 (May 1982): 471–480.

Carew, Jean, and Lightfoot, Sara. *Beyond Bias*. Cambridge, Mass.: Harvard University Press, 1979.

Chall, Jeanne, and Snow, Catherine, "A Study of Family Influences on Literacy Acquisition in Low-Income Children in Grades 2–8." Paper presented at the annual meeting of the American Educational Research Association, New York, 1982.

Cooper, Harris, and Good, Thomas L. *Pygmalion Grows Up: Studies in the Expectation Communication Process.* New York: Longman, 1983.

Doyle, Walter. *Student Mediating Responses in Teaching Effectiveness.* Final Report. Denton, Texas: North Texas State University, 1980.

Dreeben, Robert. *On What Is Learned in School.* Reading, Mass.: Addison-Wesley, 1968.

Eder, Donna. "Ability Grouping as a Self-Fulfilling Prophecy: A Micro-Analysis of Teacher-Student Interaction." *Sociology of Education* 54 (July 1981): 151–161.

Eder, Donna, and Felmlee, Diane. "The Development of Attention Norms in Ability Groups." In *The Social Context of Instruction: Group Organization and Group Processes,* edited by Penelope Peterson, Louise Cherry Wilkinson, and Maureen Hallinan. New York: Academic Press, 1984.

Esposito, Dominick. "Homogeneous and Heterogeneous Ability Grouping: Principal Findings and Implications for Evaluating and Designing More Effective Educational Environments." *Review of Educational Research* 43 (Spring 1953): 163–179.

Florio, Susan. "Learning How to Go to School: An Ethnography of Interaction in a Kindergarten-First Grade Classroom." Ph. D. dissertation, Harvard University, 1978.

Good, Thomas. "Teacher Expectations and Student Perceptions: A Decade of Research." *Educational Leadership* 38 (February 1981): 415–421.

Good, Thomas L., and Brophy, Jere. *Educational Psychology: A Realistic Approach.* 1st ed. New York: Holt, Rinehart and Winston, 1977.

Good, Thomas L.; Grouws, Douglas A.; and Ebmeier, Howard. *Active Mathematics Teaching: Empirical Research in Elementary and Secondary Classrooms.* New York: Longman, 1983.

Good, Thomas L., and Marshall, Susan. "Do Students Learn More in Heterogeneous or Homogeneous Groups?" In *The Social Context of Instruction: Group Organization and Group Processes,* edited by Penelope Peterson, Louise Cherry Wilkinson, and Maureen Hallinan. New York: Academic Press, 1984.

Hess, Robert; Dickson, W. Patrick; Price, Gary G.; and Leong, Deborah J. "Some Contrasts between Mothers and Preschool Teachers in Interaction with Four-Year-Old Children." *American Educational Research Journal* 16 (Summer 1979): 307–316.

Hess, Robert; Holloway, S.; Price, Gary G.; and Dickson, W. Patrick. "Family Environments and Acquisition of Reading Skills: Toward a More Precise Analysis." Paper presented at the conference on the Family as a Learning Environment, Educational Testing Service, Princeton, N. J., 1979.

Hiebert, Elfrieda, and Coffey, M. "Parents' Perceptions of Their Young Children's Print-Related Knowledge and Interest." Paper presented at the annual meeting of the American Educational Research Association, New York, 1982.

Hill, Paul T., and Kimbrough, Jackie. *The Aggregate Effects of Federal Education Programs.* Santa Monica, Calif.: Rand Corporation, 1981.

Kanter, Rosabeth M. "The Organization Child: Experience Management in a Nursery School." *Sociology of Education* 45 (Spring 1972): 186–211.

Lanier, Perry E.; Buschman, James; Confrey, Jere; Prawat, Richard S.; Weisbeck, Chrisanne; Coe, Pamela; and Mitchell, Bruce. *The Ecology of Failure in Ninth-grade Mathematics.* Progress Report for July 1, 1980–September 30, 1981. East

Lansing: Institute for Research on Teaching, Michigan State University, 1981.

Ligon, Glynn, and Doss, David. "Lessons We Have Learned from 6,500 Hours of Classroom Observation." Paper presented at the annual meeting of thᶜ American Educational Research Association, New York, 1982.

McGillicuddy-DeLisi, Ann. "The Relation between Family Constellation and Parental Beliefs about Child Development." In *Families as Learning Environments for Children*, edited by Luis M. Laosa and Irving E. Sigel. New York: Plenum Press, 1982.

Persell, Carolyn H. *Education and Inequality: The Roots and Results of Stratification in America's Schools*. New York: Free Press, 1977.

Rosenbaum, James R. *Making Inequality: The Hidden Curriculum of High School Tracking*. New York: John Wiley, 1976.

Rubenstein, Judith, and Howes, Carollee. "Care-Giving and Infant Behavior in Day Care and in Homes." *Developmental Psychology* 15 (January 1979): 1–24.

Sarason, Seymour. *The Culture of the School and the Problem of Change*. 2d ed. Boston: Allyn and Bacon, 1982.

Schmidt, William H., and Buchmann, Margret. "Six Teachers' Beliefs and Attitudes and Their Curricular Time Allocations." *Elementary School Journal* 84 (November 1983): 162–171.

Schultz, Jeffrey; Erickson, Frederick; and Florio, Susan. "Where's the Floor? Aspects of the Cultural Organization of Social Relationships in Communication at Home and in School." In *Children In and Out of School: Ethnography and Education*, edited by Perry Gilmore and Allan A. Glatthorn. Washington, D.C.: Center for Applied Linguistics,1982.

Seaver, W. Burleigh. "Effects of Naturally Induced Teacher Expectancies." *Journal of Personality and Social Psychology* 28 (December 1973): 333–342.

Weinstein, Rhona. "Expectations in the Classroom: The Student Perspective." Paper presented at the annual meeting of the American Educational Research Association, New York, 1982.

Winetsky, Carol S. "Comparison of the Expectations of Parents and Teachers for the Behavior of Preschool Children." *Child Development* 49 (December 1978): 1146–1154..

5

Between Elementary School and High School

Beatrice A. Ward

Lounsbury, Marani, and Compton (1980) estimated that on a given school day in 1977, five million seventh graders attended school in the United States. If we multiply this number by the three or four grades that typically constitute junior high and middle schools, we find that at any one time fifteen to twenty million students attend these "in-between" schools. Because of the unique characteristics of the student age group in these schools, the historical reasons for establishing such schools, and the current trend toward provision of a "middle" as opposed to a "junior high" school education program, the context in which these schools function differs from that of elementary or high schools. The purposes of this chapter are to present key features of this schooling experience and to provide an overview of the students' perceptions of their junior high and middle school life. We categorize these perceptions according to whether students are enrolled in typical or in more effective schools.

STUDENTS OF AGES TEN TO FOURTEEN

An Educational Research Service brief (1977) summarizing research on middle schools described students from ten to fourteen

The author is indebted to John R. Mergendoller and Alexis L. Mitman, Far West Laboratory for Educational Research and Development, for their assistance.

years old as "inbetween-agers," "early adolescents," and "transescents." Eichhorn (1980) used the term *transescence* to refer to "the stage of development that begins prior to the onset of puberty and extends through the early stages of adolescence" (p. 59). He noted that since puberty does not occur for all youth precisely at the same chronological age, "the transescent designation is based on many physical, social, emotional, and intellectual changes that occur throughout these developmental stages" (p. 59).

Lounsbury and others (1980) suggest that seventh graders are representative of the youngsters enrolled in a junior high or middle school. They stated that seventh graders come in "many sizes and shapes, with a variety of ethnic and religious backgrounds, interests, likes and dislikes, and hopes for the future." They noted that youngsters at this age are alike mainly in their unlikeness because of differences in physical and social maturity.

Nonetheless, one can assume most youngsters will undergo an obvious growth spurt and develop secondary sexual characteristics during their junior high and middle school years. Interactions with and acceptance by the peer group into which a student aspires to membership will receive high priority. Reliance on adult opinion and authority will decrease. Ability to deal with abstract as well as concrete concepts may occur, though Epstein and Toepfer (1978) challenged this view based on their studies, which suggested that brain growth slows between ages twelve and fourteen.

Providing appropriate learning programs in junior high and middle schools, given the differences that exist among students, is challenging, to say the least. Eichhorn (1980) suggested that a program that provides the security of structure but with enough elasticity to explore learning and socialization was most effective. He noted that friendliness and encouragement on the part of teachers, administrators, and other staff members were necessary. He stated that students of ages ten to fourteen functioned best in a school in which an "aura of learning" permeated the entire school.

REVIEW OF THE HISTORY OF THE JUNIOR HIGH AND MIDDLE SCHOOLS

Charles W. Eliot (1901), president of Harvard, provided impetus for the creation of junior high schools through his work as chairman of the Committee on Secondary School Studies and in speeches to the National Education Association in 1888 and 1892. The committee proposed that several subjects taught in high school, such as algebra, geometry, and foreign languages, be initiated in the last years of elementary school, or that elementary school be reduced to six years, thus providing a period of six years for secondary education. John Dewey (1903) added to the discussion by stating that elementary school was too long and secondary school needed at least six years to do an adequate job of developing the cultural appreciation needed for competent citizenship.

In his book *Adolescence*, G. Stanley Hall (1904) described the nature of adolescents and emphasized their individual differences. As Gruhn and Douglass (1971) noted, this book "had a significant influence in shaping the philosophy of the six-year program of secondary education and of the junior high school as part of that program."

A study by C. M. Woodward (1901), which concluded that withdrawal of students, particularly boys, from school in St. Louis rose sharply after age twelve, further influenced the move toward creation of junior high schools. He commented that the restraints of the elementary school program at the upper grades were "petty and very irksome" and involved frequent repetitions of things already covered in other grades.

The actual introduction of the junior high school as part of the education system in the United States is placed somewhere around 1910. Various locales are suggested for the first school of this type. Lipsitz (1977) stated that it was a laboratory school in Berkeley, California. Hansen and Hearn (1971) identified an early model in P.S. 62 in New York City, which was converted in 1905 to a school with grades seven and eight. Sweat (1977) alleged that the first junior high school opened in Richmond, Indiana, in 1910.

By 1918 the Commission on the Reorganization of Secondary Education (1918) described a junior high school as follows:

In the junior high school there should be a gradual introduction of departmental instruction, some choice of subjects under guidance, promotion by subjects, prevocational courses, and a social organization that calls forth initiative and develops the sense of personal responsibility for the welfare of the group. [P. 19]

This view of the junior high school prevailed in the education system of the United States until approximately 1960. Beginning in the early 1960s, questions began to be asked about these schools. Some persons noted that junior high schools were "ill-conceived, watered-down high schools, plagued by a lack of fit between the schools' organization and their students" (Lipsitz 1977, p. 94).

The move to create middle schools came in response to these concerns. Ideally, the following characteristics were to differentiate philosophically between junior high schools and middle schools:

— The middle school is child-centered; the junior high school is subject-centered.
— The middle school has a flexible schedule; the junior high school has a six-period day.
— The middle school emphasizes learning how to learn; the junior high school focuses on acquisition of a body of knowledge.
— The middle school uses variable group sizes; the junior high school employs standard classroom groups. (See Educational Research Service 1977; Sweat 1977; Gore 1978.)

These philosophical differences, however, are not as distinct as originally intended. As noted by Lounsbury and others (1980):

The middle school today . . . is still very much a mixed bag. There are hundreds of middle schools operating that are wholly departmentalized, homogeneously grouped, subject matter centered, and featuring interscholastic athletics. These schools display nearly all that typified what became the typical junior high school. On the other hand, there are many middle schools that operate in open spaces, that feature real team teaching, extensive exploratory programs, adviser-advisee arrangements, and nearly all the theoretically acceptable practices. The vast majority, of course, are somewhere in between and cluster around the middle. [P. 65]

In fact, data obtained on junior high and middle schools that were recognized by the U.S. Department of Education in 1983 and 1984 as examples of effective schools for students of ages ten to fourteen suggest that whether a school is labeled a junior high school, middle school, an intermediate school, or some other name is unimportant. What is important is the manner in which the school is organized and the education program that is provided. The following discussion outlines some of these features and describes the experiences students have in schools that are more effective as compared with schools regarded as more typical.

SCHOOL ORGANIZATION

Several patterns of grade-level organization occur in "in-between" schools. Lounsbury and others (1980) found that about 66 percent of the schools they studied included grades six, seven, and eight. Thirteen percent included grades seven and eight, and 12 percent included grades five through eight. Gore (1978) reported that in New England, middle schools with grades six through eight and those with grades five through eight accounted for 93.1 percent of the 315 middle schools surveyed.

Based on these data, it appears that removal of grade nine from the "in-between" school and the addition of grade six, and possibly grade five, are growing practices. Reasons given for various grade-level organizations include noninstructional matters such as keeping a high school open, using a new school building, and aiding desegregation. Instruction-related reasons include provision of more subject-area specialization in grade six, remedying problems caused by the social and developmental differences between ninth-grade students and younger students in a junior high or middle school, and providing an education program especially designed for the transescent students.

Regardless of the reasons for assigning particular grades to a junior high or middle school, within these schools students are assigned to subject areas and teachers in a variety of ways. Most typical is a schedule that includes six academic periods and lunch each day. Some schools require students to move from one teacher to another each period. Others keep fifth-grade and sixth-grade students with the same teacher for several periods. Still other schools assign students to a team of teachers (usually three to five teachers) for a block of time. The teachers allocate the time to several subject areas and determine which teachers will instruct which groups of students and for how long. These decisons may vary from day to day.

Underlying all these arrangements is a desire to make students' transitions from elementary school to junior high or middle school and on to high school as easy and successful as possible. Providing more time with one teacher or with several teachers is seen as a means for easing the move from a self-contained elementary classroom to the junior high or middle school. Moving to a departmentalized program by grade eight prepares the students for the arrangements found in most high schools.

The following examples are taken from the *Catalog of Bay Area Junior High/Middle/Intermediate Schools* to illustrate the various organizational systems found in junior high and middle schools (Far West Laboratory for Educational Research and Development 1982).

School A (Middle School)
Grade Six. Students are assigned to five core teams of two teachers

each. Assignment is based on language ability (beginning English, intermediate English, advanced English, fluent English-speaking, Spanish bilingual, gifted and talented).

The grade six schedule assigns first and second period to two of the four core subjects (language arts, mathematics, social studies, and science). Lunch follows as third period. Fourth period the students take an elective subject. Periods five and six the students return to their core teachers for the remaining two core subjects. Period seven is physical education.

Grade Seven. Students are assigned to four learning-center teams made up of three teachers each. The teams teach language arts, mathematics and social studies. Students are in the learning centers either the first or last three periods of the day. The other periods include science, an elective, and physical education. Students are assigned heterogeneously to the learning centers except for one center which serves the gifted students.

Grade Eight. At this grade level students are assigned to a "cluster" of approximately twenty-eight students. Each cluster moves together through a departmentalized program including English, mathematics, social studies, science, an elective, and physical education. Students are assigned to the clusters heterogeneously except for the gifted cluster.

School B (Middle School)

Grade Six. Students are assigned heterogeneously to the same teacher for a four-period "core" of English, reading, social studies, and mathematics. They also take physical education and an exploratory sequence that includes one quarter each of science, art, music, and practical arts. A pullout remedial reading course is provided for some students during the English part of the core program.

Grade Seven. This program includes a two-period "core" of English and social studies taught consecutively by the same teacher. Students are assigned to the core classes heterogeneously. For mathematics, students are grouped by ability. They take remedial mathematics, regular mathematics, or pre-algebra. Physical education is required. One semester of science and one of reading also are required. Students may take one elective course.

Grade Eight. This program is the same as that offered in grade seven. Algebra is offered to the advanced mathematics students.

School C (Junior High School)
This school utilizes a rotating schedule in which a "red" day has the class periods in consecutive order, one through six. A "blue" day begins with period six and progresses from period five through period one. At all grade levels, students are assigned to mathematics, science and English classes based on ability.

Grade Seven. Students take English and reading from the same teacher in two consecutive periods. Mathematics, physical education, geography/science, and an elective are each taken with different teachers.

Grade Eight. The program is completely departmentalized. Required courses are English, mathematics, physical education, U. S. History, life science/physical science. Students may select one elective.

Grade Nine. Students now may choose two electives. Required courses are English, mathematics, science/social studies (one semester of each) and physical education. The departmentalized organization used in grade eight continues.

From the requirements for transition imposed on students as they move from elementary to junior high or middle school, it is clear that Schools A and B give more attention to providing a bridge between the elementary school with its self-contained classrooms and a departmentalized program. In School C one might expect to find the beginning of grade seven somewhat difficult for students because not only must they work with at least five different teachers, but they must also adapt to a rotating schedule.

All three schools phase students into a departmentalized program of the sort used in most high schools. All the schools also emphasize an academic core that builds students' English and mathematics skills. The area of weakness, if there is one, is that of electives. Since high schools generally offer students a range of courses in all subject areas from which to select the program they will pursue, the limited experience students have in these three schools in selecting among course options may prove to be a detriment in their later schooling careers. One other feature of the programs that warrants note is the extent to which students are grouped by ability for assignment to courses and teachers. The advantages of this arrangement may be that it challenges the more capable students and provides time for other students to master basic concepts and skills. But a disadvantage may be that it restricts peer interactions and therefore limits students' perceptions, particularly those of average and below-average students, of what is expected of a good student in the school.

Based on observations in typical junior high and middle schools (Mergendoller, Mitman, and Ward 1982) and in schools that have been recognized as being more effective than a typical school (Ward 1983)—that is, schools in which students continue to show gains in their basic skills as measured by standardized tests, increase in their ability to use higher cognitive skills, attend school regularly, are seldom suspended, and participate in a variety of cocurricular as well as academic activities—it is apparent that students' schooling experiences differ depending on the effectiveness of the school they attend. In interviews conducted in 1984 as part of the Secondary School Recognition Project of the U. S. Department of Education, students in more effective junior high or middle schools described them as places where "there is discipline." For example, in one effective school, a student who previously had a low level of academic performance indicated that the "discipline in this school has helped; I don't like it, but it helps me learn." Students also pointed out that "teachers help you; they don't let you fail." They described teachers as persons who "explain real good" and "don't just turn the pages in the book." Students noted that when students "do good, [they] get to have special privileges and parties and things." On the other hand, they said that "when you get bad grades, the school won't let you do anything until you start to do better." Students used words such as "helpful," "fun," "understanding," "encouraging," "caring," "a learning place," "challenging," "makes you take responsibility," and "enthusiastically educational" to describe the school they attend. They stressed that "most kids in this school want to do good and you don't get categorized when you do." They indicated that other schools they have attended "don't push you to work; this one does." They underlined that the school requires them "to get organized and get things done."

Students in more typical schools talked about the schools as places where "you have to do work," "you do the things you did in fifth grade," "you have hard homework," "you're around kids," and "teachers are stricter than in elementary school" (Mergendoller and Packer 1981).

Ward (1983) identified eight features of a junior high or middle school, and the configurations of these features differ in more and less effective schools. Three of these are particularly pertinent to a discussion of transescent students' schooling experiences. These are (1) the academic program, (2) the ways in which student discipline is handled, and (3) the instruction that takes place.

Academic Program

In more effective junior high and middle schools, the academic program is designed so that the courses offered within a given subject matter area provide multiple levels of learning opportunities. In English, for example, at each grade level advanced academic courses are offered for students with an advanced level of basic skills in language arts, reading, and writing. An honors class may be offered for students who have average or above-average basic skills and who also work well in independent learning situations. Of course, classes offering the standard curriculum for each grade level are also provided. Remedial reading and writing laboratories are available to assist students who are having difficulty with these basic skills. In mathematics the standard curriculum for the grade level is taught. In addition, basic mathematics skills laboratories are provided, and advanced students may enroll in pre-algebra, algebra, and possibly geometry courses. The skills, knowledge, and concepts to be mastered in each course are made clear to students and parents. Qualitative expectations for high academic performance have also been specified. Students may move from one level of a course to another on a flexible basis, that is, they are not required to remain in a course that is too difficult or too easy for an entire quarter, semester, or year. Students are not required to repeat skills they have already mastered. Evaluation of student performance occurs frequently, and a student and his or her parents receive information regularly and frequently about how well he or she is doing. Homework is required in most courses.

On the other hand, in more typical junior high and middle schools, students are apt to find the format of the classwork and the assignments indistinguishable from those of their elementary schools. For example, Lounsbury and others (1980) reported that middle school students made statements to the effect that they were "still doing things they did in fifth grade." Mergendoller and others (1982) reported that even in typical junior high and middle schools where pre-algebra and algebra courses were provided as a way to expand the mathematics content, the more advanced courses were *not* available to between 60 and 80 percent of the students. Thus, a high proportion of the students in these schools continued in repetitive mathematics programs for much of their junior high or middle school experience. Failure to match courses to students' abilities was also found in a study of students' transitions from an elementary school to a junior high school with grades seven and eight. Rounds and others (1982) reported that all seventh-grade students in this typical junior high school were assigned to a general mathematics course. For the first quarter of grade seven, over 70 percent of the students in these classes were completing computation problems or working with concepts they had already learned in grade five or six. Mooreover, in other subject areas, course content focused on rote memorization—or on what Arnold (1982) called the "Egypt-and-flax" curriculum. In addition, the work in these courses repeated information and skills many students had covered in grades five and six. As one seventh-grade student put it, "Classes are just work, boring work."

Such restriction in the levels of difficulty of the courses available to students in the more typical junior high or middle schools may have advantages and disadvantages relative to a student's academic growth and development. One positive outcome of the repetition of skills and knowledge already taught to and mastered by most students may be reinforcement of necessary skills and knowledge. But a negative result may be that it teaches students that a particular subject area such as mathematics is easy and requires little time and attention in order to "get the answers right." Later, if these students encounter new and challenging learning experiences, they may not be prepared to exert the effort to perform successfully.

From another perspective, depending on the effectiveness of their school, junior high and middle school students appear to differ in the amount of information they receive on how well they are achieving. In more effective schools, a student's performance is monitored frequently, assignments are graded and returned within one or two days, and regular progress reports are given to students and parents at least once midway through a grading period and often every two weeks. In more typical schools such monitoring and reporting appear to be minimal and to be provided haphazardly and infrequently. For example, some seventh-grade students interviewed during the fifth week of a nine-week grading period reported that they had not yet received from their English teachers a marked paper that indicated if their compositions were good, poor, or "just okay" (Rounds and others 1982). Analysis of twenty days of classroom observation for twenty-four target students in this study also indicated that the teachers seldom stated explicitly the criteria by which they would judge the quality of the students' work. An apparent outcome of these two circumstances was that most students thought all they had to do was finish the work and get it in on time. Only the high-ability students realized (on their own) that correctness and quality were important. Other students complained that they did all the work and still received "D's."

While the academic programs in more effective and in typical junior high and middle schools appear to differ on several dimensions, the one dimension they have in common is extensive use of homework. But even here a difference exists. The more effective schools use homework to serve mainly as the drill-and-practice portion of the students' academic program. The more typical schools often include new concepts and skills in the homework. As a result, the students may be required to develop a facility for self-instruction, or they may encounter difficulties and become confused. All in all, in the more typical schools the heavy reliance on worksheets to be completed at home that require the student to apply new skills and knowledge, and the consequent lack of appropriately timed academic feedback and explanation, may hinder the student's performance.

Discipline

Lipsitz (1977) indicated that junior high and middle school students are often noted for their authoritarianism. She suggested that for the first time in their lives they see a need for law and order and that in their zeal to acknowledge societal needs they overlook individual rights and apply a form of justice that is not yet tempered with mercy. At the same time, they also place high value on the fairness of any action that is taken by a person in authority whether it be to compliment, reward, chastise, or punish an individual. Rules are rules and must be applied to and followed by all who are part of a group, for example, a school's student body.

Hence, as one might expect, more effective junior high and middle schools establish both a school-level and a classroom-level discipline program that provides the needed "law and order," assures that rules and sanctions are applied consistently and fairly to all students, and makes expected behavior and consequences for misbehavior known to all students. The rules and procedures are agreed on by the entire school faculty, are made known to parents, are discussed and reviewed with a representative student group such as a student council, and are reviewed with all students at the beginning of the school year and at various times thereafter. Often these standard rules and expectations are given slogans that adults and students use as reminders of the the type of behavior that is expected. For example, one effective middle school, which serves a mixed-income and multiethnic student population, has as its motto: "Walk, Learn, Respect."

The importance of known rules and procedures, consistency in their application, and consistency in imposition of consequences for noncompliance are illustrated by a comment made by a black eighth-grade student in an interview conducted as part of the Secondary School Recognition Program. This student was asked to identify some of the important things that had changed when his junior high school "turned around" from a place of disorder and low achievement to an orderly environment in which student achievement was showing marked progress. The student replied, "The new dude, I mean principal, makes everyone obey the rules. The white kids don't get away with things anymore."

Attention to solution of whatever problems may be contributing to a student's difficulties is also an integral part of discipline programs in more effective junior high and middle schools. When a student fails to follow a rule or procedure, the follow-up process requires the student to describe what caused the misbehavior and to talk with a teacher, administrator, or counselor and outline steps the student will take to solve the problems that appear to exist. These steps often are highly prescriptive. When interviewed in the Secondary School Recognition Program, one student in an effective school said, "I didn't start messing up until seventh grade. Then everybody got on me, my mother, the counselor, the teachers, the assistant principal. I had a contract to be signed every day by everybody to say I behaved and did my work. It's worked. I'm improving a lot academically and now I get along with the other kids."

A survey conducted in a large urban district suggests that several of the program features just described may not exist in all schools (Ward and Tikunoff 1984). For instance, only 33 percent of the sample teachers from junior high and middle schools reported that discipline rules were always made public in their schools so that students knew what was expected of them, 32 percent reported that rules frequently were made public, 21 percent said "sometimes," 11 percent reported "seldom," and 3 percent reported "never." Relative to the ways in which the school handled misunderstandings among students, few schools always handled misunderstandings before they resulted in physical abuse (only 7 percent of the teachers reported that this occurred in their schools, 38 percent said misunderstandings were frequently handled before abuse occurred, 41 percent said "sometimes," 12 percent reported "seldom," and 2 percent said "never").

Discouragement of vandalism is another dimension of school-level discipline in junior high and middle schools. Observations in effective schools suggest that graffiti and other vandalism problems are discouraged and are corrected as soon as they occur (either by the custodian or, on the few occasions when the vandalism is done by students, by the students themselves). The school campuses are clean and free of writing on walls and other forms of defacement (Ward 1983).

The survey mentioned above indicated that vandalism receives considerable but, perhaps, less attention in junior high and middle schools in general. Thirty-one percent of the teachers reported that vandalism was always discouraged in their schools, another 31 percent indicated it was frequently discouraged, 21 percent said "sometimes," 14 percent said it was seldom discouraged, and 4 percent said it never was.

Adult authority and discipline applied in the classroom also are integral parts of the junior high and middle school discipline program. A half century ago, Willard Waller observed:

The teacher-pupil relationship is a form of institutionalized domination and subordination. Teacher and pupil confront each other in the school with an original conflict of desires, and however much that conflict may be reduced in amount, or however much it may be hidden, it still remains. The teacher represents the adult group, ever the enemy of the spontaneous life of groups of children. The teacher represents the formal curriculum and his interest is in imposing that curriculum upon the children in the form of tasks; pupils are much more interested in life in their own world than in the dessicated bits of adult life which teachers have to offer. [1932, pp. 195–196]

Thus for most junior high and middle school students, competent classroom participation involves a balancing of status among peers, acquiescence to teachers' demands, and successful completion of assigned tasks. Successful students learn to balance the expectations of the teacher and of their peers and to court the approval of both parties. Some students challenge the role, demeanor, and prerogative of the teacher in ways that are accepted; others face immediate imposition of disciplinary actions.

Most teachers establish specific classroom behavioral rules and expectations and specific consequences for failure to follow them. In more effective schools, students report that most teachers apply these rules consistently and fairly. One student is not allowed to avoid compliance while another must conform, although circumstances are considered when sanctions are applied. Further, only those students who do not comply with disciplinary standards are sanctioned; students who follow the rules are rewarded or, at a minimum, allowed to proceed with the tasks at hand. Frequent noncompliance with classroom rules generally moves discipline of a student from the classroom level to the school level, and follow-up procedures such as a contract are often used.

Differences between more effective and more typical junior high and middle schools appear to concern the school-level follow-up to students' noncompliance with classroom rules and procedures rather than whether these rules and procedures exist. In response to an open-ended question—What makes it difficult to perform at one's best as a teacher?—junior high and middle school teachers in the urban district survey, which we mentioned earlier, noted that lack of administrator support of teachers' disciplinary actions was a major hindrance to their effectiveness. They said that teachers were left "on their own to handle students who [were] repeatedly disruptive in class" and received "no administrative follow-through with discipline." When a student purposefully challenges the role, demeanor, and prerogative of the teacher and the teacher receives no support in correcting this situation (such as removing the student from the classroom until the problem can be resolved), chaos may result. The student may wrench the authority from the teacher and set the behavior standards in that classroom. In such circumstances, it is apparent that teaching and learning can become ineffective if not nonexistent.

Instruction

Studies of instruction at the junior high and middle school level have looked at whether the general organization of instruction in these schools is appropriate for the students and have examined the specific teaching behaviors that are most effective. Interestingly, when students in effective junior high and middle schools are asked to describe the teacher they most admire and respect, they identify instructional approaches and teacher behaviors and characteristics that are similar to those emerging from research on the most effective teaching behaviors. The discussion that follows presents a sampling of students' views of effective teachers and instruction and summarizes some of the research findings regarding effective teaching in junior high and middle schools. The students' statements are compiled from interviews conducted in 1983 and 1984 in seventeen junior high and middle schools in the Secondary School Recognition Program of the U. S. Department of Education.

Students repeatedly identify seven characteristics as descriptive of the teachers whom they most admire and respect. First, the teachers are accessible to students both during class time and after school. Obtaining help from these teachers is judged an easy task by students at all performance levels. Second, the teachers' actions tell the students the teachers respect them. Students point out that these teachers tell students that they *all* can achieve and meet the expectations specified for high academic performance in their courses. Third, the teachers require students to perform at a satisfactory level. These teachers call students in for a conference as soon as they miss an assignment. Parents are contacted whenever a student fails to correct a problem immediately. These teachers consider it their own responsibility to do everything necessary to help a student do well. Fourth, the teachers are clear about what students are to learn; why students are learning a particular skill, concept, or fact; how students are to go about completing various learning tasks; and what criteria will be applied in judging the accuracy, completeness, and quality of the students' performance. Fifth, the teachers monitor students during class time and require the students to attend to the assigned work. Sixth, the teachers employ multiple approaches to instruction. They use some lecture, some cooperative group assignments, some independent projects, some individual learning sequences or contracts, some discussion, and so forth. Students report that their classes are interesting and help students learn to work in different ways. Seventh, the students indicate that the teachers whom they consider most effective frequently work with other teachers in what educators might describe as a "team-teaching" situation. This team of teachers groups students on a flexible basis to provide special help and to work on special projects.

The students' actual descriptions of the teachers whom they

admired and respected add life to the preceding listing of the behaviors and characteristics of effective teachers. These descriptions included statements such as: "They spend a lot of time with you during enrichment" (an after-school tutorial period). "They give you a lot of encouragement. They say, 'You can do it!' They never put you down." "They re-explain everything to make sure you know how to do it. They explain in detail." "They don't do it for you, but they tell you how to do it." "They discuss with you in plain English." "When you do a good job, they always say something special to you." "They give you a lot of work but you understand it so you do well." "They keep you so busy you don't have time to mess around and do anything wrong." "They tell you how much an assignment is worth on your grade so you always know where you stand." "They give you a lot of homework; almost every night." "They make you work to learn."

However, students in more effective schools also readily point out that not all teachers meet their standards for admiration and respect. They state that "some, but only a few—not very many at all—don't help you, are hard to understand, and always just talk at you or read the pages in the book."

In the real world of junior high and middle schools, teachers will most likely fall from effective to less effective on a scale according to their use of the skills that students list as characteristic of effective teachers and the skills identified through research. Interestingly from the research standpoint, Evertson and her colleagues (1980) reported that a pattern of effective teaching was easier to determine for mathematics classes than for English classes in junior high schools. More effective mathematics teachers were found to be more active, organized, and academically oriented. They spent more time in class lecture and discussion and they had students spend relatively less time doing seatwork. Their discussion periods were marked by asking students many questions. These teachers were also more effective managers and more able to prevent discipline problems. Students rated these teachers as more enthusiastic, nurturant, and affectionate than other teachers. No clear pattern of effective teaching emerged for English classes as a whole.

In another study, Emmer and Evertson (1980) investigated the classroom management techniques of junior high English and mathematics teachers. They found that both more effective and less effective teachers spent approximately the same amount of class time teaching rules and procedures, but more effective teachers were more successful in clearly communicating the rules and procedures to the students and more successful in formulating and enforcing rules and procedures to handle complex situations. Compared with less effective teachers, more effective teachers also referred to their rules and procedures more frequently, ignored disruptive behaviors less, and were more consistent in. applying sanctions to students who did not follow the rules and procedures. Further, the more effective teachers made more of an effort to see that students got a good start carrying out activities, that students continued to progress, and that students completed assignments; to do this, teachers often gave students assignments each day that were collected daily and checked or graded quickly. These teachers also tended to have a system so that students understood how each assignment was related to their grade. In contrast, students in classes of less effective teachers were not given assignments on a regular basis, and their work was not monitored as well or subjected to a regular checking and grading routine.

In addition, Emmer and Evertson found that effective teachers gave clearer directions, stated objectives, and established routines for communicating assignments. They helped students comprehend and complete tasks—for example, by breaking complex tasks into step-by-step procedures. These differences were especially salient between more effective and less effective English teachers.

In an in-depth study of eleven junior high teachers, Rounds and others (1982) found similar differences between more effective and less effective teachers. The more effective teachers were accessible to their students, provided them with help on their assignments, and gave them regular feedback and reinforcement. These teachers usually monitored students' work by moving about the classroom. They gave clear directions and explanations. They established classroom rules and norms and then worked to maintain them, focusing disciplinary actions on the specific students who violated them. Less effective teachers refused to help students and provided feedback that was virtually useless, for example, "Yes, that's wrong." They either did not stress content or stressed content coverage without taking students' learning or interests into account. They often did not have functioning rules, and their disciplinary actions often consisted of empty threats, for example, "I wonder if we are going to have to send someone out?"

Mergendoller and others (1982) found that junior high and middle school students' engagement in learning tasks correlated significantly with several behaviors of teachers, among them the following: the smoothness of the teacher's lesson, the importance teachers attach to academic tasks, teacher's effectiveness in handling discipline problems, the quality of the teacher's academic feedback, the predominant focus of the teacher's feedback, the teacher's efficiency in classroom management, the clarity of the teacher's directions, and the percentage of class time the teacher devoted to academic instruction. Taken as a whole, these correlations suggest that junior high and middle school teachers who show high levels of engagement with their students maintain organized classrooms; are prepared for instruction; conduct smooth, easily understood lessons; keep control of student attention and minimize classroom disruptions and inappropriate student behavior; and communicate to students that they can achieve and learn. Another interesting finding from this study was that when teachers moved beyond total-class, teacher-controlled instruction, it was even more important for them to use well the behaviors listed above. In other words, high "quality of teaching" scores, which were derived from these behaviors, appeared more essential to maintaining students' engagement in small groups, cooperative learning, and other types of non-total-group instruction than in the more traditional total-group situations.

The similarities between the characteristics that junior high and middle school students assign to teachers whom they admire and respect and the research findings regarding effective teaching are apparent. However, researchers seem to have found few teachers who used multiple approaches to instruction, even though this was described as an important characteristic by students. For example, Rounds and others (1982) found that throughout the school day the students "filled in blanks" in mimeographed worksheets prepared by a textbook publisher or by the teacher, watched the teacher give explanations at the board, answered questions directed to them by the teacher, wrote phrases and sentences (only occasionally paragraphs or essays), and took weekly, monthly, or grading-period tests.

Emmer and Evertson (1980) noted that both more effective and less effective teachers rarely gave differentiated assignments or moved beyond discussion, demonstration, and seatwork as approaches to instruction. The differences they reported were in the manner in which the teachers conducted the same instructional activities. More effective teachers wasted less time, interacted more in a whole-class format, and were better able to challenge higher-achieving students by giving extra-credit activities or some other additional work.

In a similar study, Worsham and Evertson (1980) investigated teachers' techniques for maintaining students' accountability for assigned work. More effective teachers were more clear about all aspects of work requirements. This was accomplished by setting specific requirements for a paper's form, neatness, completeness, due date, and make-up procedures. They not only gave clearer directions but also tended to launch into work as soon as the period began and to have students keep their own assignment records in their notebooks. In contrast, less effective teachers often gave insufficient directions or found themselves giving the directions to inattentive students. More effective teachers moved about the classroom as students worked, checking off work as the students completed it. Less effective teachers did not do this. More effective teachers had a consistent routine for turning in and checking work. Less effective teachers tended not to employ routines of any sort. Finally, more effective teachers provided students with regular feedback by assigning grades, making comments on papers, having class discussions of answers, and so forth. Less effective teachers did not use these practices as consistently, and some could not use them at all because students did not turn in papers that could be checked.

In sum, from both a student and a research perspective, it appears that more effective instruction occurs when students know the parameters of expected behavior, know their assignments, know they will be held accountable for completion of the work, know that the teacher expects them to do the work in a highly satisfactory manner, and know that the teacher will provide whatever explanations and assistance are necessary for them to meet these expectations.

CONCLUSIONS

The information presented here suggests that in effective junior high and middle schools and in classrooms in all schools where effective teachers are functioning, transescent students develop a wide range of academic and social skills that prepare them for the move to high school. However, in junior high and middle schools in general, and in some classrooms in even the more effective schools, the cognitive complexity of the tasks assigned to students appears to emphasize a fact-recall, fill-in-the-blank, and rote-learning approach. Further, with the exception of the most able students, who may be placed in advanced classes that cover new subject matter, in more typical junior high and middle schools (but not in more effective schools) the mathematics curriculum completed by most students in grade seven, and perhaps in grade eight as well, includes considerable repetition of skills and concepts the students had already mastered in grades five and six. In addition, many junior high and middle school students enter high school with limited science backgrounds and with minimal experience in using a variety of learning strategies or in selecting appropriate courses from a list of electives.

On the other hand, students' success in junior high and middle schools appears to require them to learn how (1) to get the teacher's attention, (2) to answer questions appropriately, (3) to manage time, (4) to plan projects, and (5) to interact with their peers in acceptable ways. Because the students work with many teachers and students, they must understand and respond to a wide array of requirements for participation. Not until a student leaves high school and enters college or the work force will he or she again face a transition as complex as the social participation requirements faced in the move from elementary to junior high and middle school.

Obviously, junior high and middle school education has strengths and weaknesses. One strength lies in the more effective schools and the model they provide for other less effective schools. A second strength is that these schools provide instructional programs to phase in the use of departmentalized programs; another is the effective teachers who are found in all schools. A fourth strength is the emphasis on a core set of subjects that builds the students' basic reading, writing, and mathematics skills.

The weaknesses in the education program include the repetitiveness of both instructional procedures and content, the limited experience students have in selecting elective courses, the lack of variety in the approaches to teaching and learning used in the more typical schools, and the failure of the more typical schools to provide supporting structures and procedures in areas such as discipline.

Although the typical experience of students at this age level may not be all that we want it to be, this chapter has suggested that some schools, and even more teachers, offer instructional programs that come close to providing the desired learning experiences. In addition, information on the more effective schools and teachers offers avenues for improving the learning experiences provided to all students and can be pursued by educators committed to providing educational excellence for the "in-betweenager."

REFERENCES

Arnold, John. "Rhetoric and Reform in Middle Schools." *Phi Delta Kappan* 63 (March 1982): 453–456.

Commission on the Reorganization of Secondary Education. *Cardinal Principles of Secondary Education*, Bulletin No. 35, Washington, D.C.: Bureau of Education, U.S. Department of the Interior, 1918.

Dewey, John. "Shortening the Years of Elementary Schools." *School Review* 11 (January 1903): 17–20.

Educational Research Service. *Summary of Research on Middle Schools*. Research Brief. Arlington, Va.: Educational Research Service, 1977.

Eichhorn, Donald H. "The School." In *Toward Adolescence: The Middle School Years*, edited by Mauritz Johnson. Seventy-ninth Yearbook of the National Society for the Study of Education, Part 1. Chicago: University of Chicago Press, 1980.

Eliot, Charles W. *Educational Reform: Essays and Addresses*. New York: Century, 1901.

Emmer, Edmund T., and Evertson, Carolyn M. *Effective Management at the Beginning of the School Year in Junior High School Classes*. Austin: Research and Development Center for Teacher Education, University of Texas, 1980.

Epstein, Herman T., and Toepfer, Conrad F., Jr. "A Neuroscience Basis for Reorganizing Middle Grades Education." *Educational Leadership* 35 (May 1978): 656–660.

Evertson, Carolyn M.; Anderson, Charles W.; Anderson, Linda M.; and Brophy, Jere. "Relationships between Classroom Behaviors and Student Outcomes in Junior High Mathematics and English Classes." *American Educational Research Journal* 17 (Spring 1980): 43–60.

Far West Laboratory for Educational Research and Development. *Catalog of Bay Area Junior High/Middle/Intermediate Schools*. San Francisco: Far West Laboratory for Educational Research and Development, 1982.

Gore, E. V. "A Descriptive Study of Organizational, Curriculum, and Staff Utilization Patterns of Selected New England Middle Schools." Paper presented at the Canadian School Trustees' Association Congress on Education, Toronto, 1978.

Gruhn, William T., and Douglass, Harl R. *The Modern Junior High School*. New York: Ronald Press, 1971.

Hall, G. Stanley. *Adolescence*. Vols. 1 and 2. New York: D. Appleton-Century, 1904.

Hansen, J. H. and Hearn, A. C. *The Junior High Program*. Chicago: Rand McNally, 1971.

Lipsitz, Joan. *Growing Up Forgotten: A Review of Research and Programs Concerning Adolescence*. Lexington, Mass.: Lexington Books, 1977.

Lounsbury, John H.; Marani, Jean V.; and Compton, Mary F. *The Middle School in Profile: A Day in the Seventh Grade*. Fairborn, Ohio: Middle School Association, 1980.

Mergendoller, John R.; Mitman, Alexis L.; and Ward, Beatrice A. *Junior High/Middle School Program Variation Study*. San Francisco: Far West Laboratory for Educational Research and Development, 1982.

Mergendoller, John R., and Packer, M. J. *Seventh Graders' Perceptions of Teachers: An Interpretive Analysis*. San Francisco: Far West Laboratory for Educational Research and Development, 1981.

Rounds, Thomas S.; Ward, Beatrice A.; Mergendoller, John R.; and Tikunoff,

William J. *Junior High School Transition Study, Vol. 2: Organization of Instruction, Elementary School – Junior High School Comparison.* San Francisco: Far West Laboratory for Educational Research and Development, 1982.

Sweat, C. H., ed. *Why the Junior High/Middle School: Its Basic Functions.* Danville, Ill.: Interstate Printers and Publishers, 1977.

Waller, Willard. *The Sociology of Teaching.* New York: Russell and Russell, 1932.

Ward, Beatrice A. *Common Features Identified across Majority of Secondary Schools Recognized as Successful Education Settings.* San Francisco: Center for Interactive Research and Development, 1983.

Ward, Beatrice A. and Tikunoff, William J. *Conditions of Schooling in the Los Angeles. Unified School District,* A Survey Conducted for United Teachers Los Angeles. San Francisco: Center for Interactive Research and Development, 1984.

Woodward, C. M. "When and Why Pupils Leave School." In *Education 1899–1900.* Vol. 2. Washington, D.C.: U. S. Government Printing Office, 1901.

Worsham, Murray E., and Evertson, Carolyn M. *Systems of Student Accountability for Written Work in Junior High School English Classes.* Austin: Research and Development Center for Teacher Education, University of Texas, 1980.

6

Public Secondary Schools in the United States

Philip A. Cusick

What are secondary schools like for students? What are the adjustments students must make upon entering them? What may students reasonably expect to learn in them? What is the dominant view of learning held by the staff members, and how do they go about instructing students? Finally, how do the limits and the possibilities of the experience change from the time a student enters high school at the age of thirteen or fourteen to the time the student leaves at seventeen or eighteen? By addressing such questions, this chapter discusses public secondary schools in the United States.

THE STRUCTURE OF SECONDARY SCHOOLS

In the United States, public schools have followed a comprehensive model, which, according to Conant (1959, p. 17), has three main objectives: "First, to provide a general education for all future citizens; second, to provide good elective programs for those who wish to use their acquired skills immediately on graduation; third, to provide satisfactory programs for those whose vocations depend on their subsequent education in a college or university." Whether a comprehensive secondary school that attempts to fulfill all three functions under the same roof or on the same site and also encourages its students to intermingle in a variety of elective courses and activities can be successful is really not an answerable question. There is such great diversity among secondary schools that the question would have to be addressed almost school by school. And there is even the question of whether the unit of analysis should be the school per se or whether individual students or particular groups (for example, minority students) should be used as the referent. But while schools and referent groups differ, the comprehensive model does have a certain basic structure, and all comprehensive schools share some distinct elements. This chapter begins with a discussion of those common structural elements, enters into a further discussion of the curriculum in secondary schools, and finally addresses the specific questions mentioned at the beginning of this chapter.

The structure of an organization confronts both staff members and clients. Regardless of his or her predilections, ambitions, or talents, each person in an organization faces a set of constraints, and while each person may accommodate to these constraints differently, each must accommodate to the same set. The set of constraints defines the possibilities of success and of failure. It defines the rewards one may strive for and the sanctions one may incur. It combines the realities of organization in terms of time, space, and resources with the set of understandings that the participants share about those realities. There is a certain logic within an organization that binds events and behavior into an abstract coherence, and it is that logic that is used to judge certain things as worthwhile and to dismiss others as meaningless. This structure is what insiders must recognize to succeed and what outsiders must comprehend in order to understand the actions of insiders.

Certain elements underlie the structure of secondary schools, and the combination of these elements has some secondary effects that are also part of the structure. The first of these elements is that in general secondary schools pursue the egalitarian ideal: They hold out the promise of social, political, and economic equality for all. Because they are open to all, secondary schools are generally large, diverse, and comprehensive; they are publicly funded from state taxes and local property taxes; and since state taxes are allocated on a per-pupil basis, the schools are accountable to the voting and taxpaying public. From these characteristics flow a number of secondary characteristics. From adherence to an egalitarian ideal, comprehensiveness, public funding, and accountability comes the obligation to take, retain, and educate all students regardless of their ability, ambition, or inclination. Equally important is the belief that this "paying public" has the right to influence curriculum. This is the basis of the endless attempts on the part of one group or another to have more or less attention and resources given to reading, music, athletics, special education, extended bus service, free lunch, the firing of an administrator, the recalling of a board member, creationism, the "basics," accountability, frugality, or equity. Even in the poorer districts where state support far exceeds local funding, there is still the attitude that the local citizenry should exert control over the curriculum.

An additional element underlies all of the above. That is a firm belief that the acquisition of positive knowledge is or can be made interesting and appealing to everyone. By positive knowledge I mean knowledge that is generally accepted as having an empirical or traditional base, that is socially useful, and that lends itself to expression in verbal and abstract forms. It includes computer science, English literature, welding, and physical education. This belief is important because it justifies diversifying the curriculum in order to appeal to diverse students.

From the foregoing flow additional characteristics. Since secondary schools are obligated to serve a large number of diverse students, and since they are funded on the basis of attendance, a tremendous effort is needed to (1) insure attendance even by students who may not be particularly interested in school and (2) maintain order and discipline among this large and diverse group. School administrators see attendance as a more serious problem than order and discipline. They feel that if they can attract students to school and class, then order will follow; hence in all secondary schools a tremendous effort is directed at reducing absenteeism, which in some schools can run as high as 30 percent on a given day. While in many schools that figure may be as low as 3 or 4 percent, low figures are maintained only by the constant effort of administrators. The impetus to retain students is strengthened by the funding processes and by the belief about positive knowledge. If a student leaves, the school failed that student, and the school loses funding. Concerning order and discipline, administrators generally agree that schools are much more orderly than the public perceives. But they also agree that order and discipline are maintained at a very high cost, with most of the available administrative and supervisory efforts allocated to those areas.

The structure as defined has an additional effect on administrators. Because of the schools' publicness, administrators are obligated to spend a considerable amount of their time maintaining good relations with various segments of the community. While attendance and discipline may devour more time and energy in urban than in rural or suburban areas, maintaining good relations with the community is particularly time-consuming in the latter, where the administrators have almost no anonymity. Faced with communities that are both wary and demanding of the school, the high school principals in small communities are under constant surveillance by the community. They lead lives that are almost totally public. They are among the most visible persons in the areas, called on for myriad community functions, asked to help with the students' private lives, and, of course, expected to maintain the highest standards of decency and discretion. Public relations is generally not regarded as a "problem"; rather, it is a fact of life when one is in charge of a publicly funded institution designed to serve the needs of all the citizens and is open to influence by those citizens. But this fact of life does have a serious effect. Just as attendance and discipline take up a great amount of administrative and supervisory time, so does public relations. In fact, attendance, disciplinary, and public relations matters require the greatest proportion of the supervisory and administrative resources in public secondary schools.

In sum, while secondary schools may be quite different from one another, some characteristics are common to all: a commitment to an egalitarian ideal, large size, diversity, public responsiveness, and per-pupil funding. From these come some additional characteristics, such as accountability, public influence on curriculum, and a heavy commitment of resources to maintaining attendance, discipline, and good public relations.

THE CURRICULUM

As we mentioned previously, an organization has a structure, and the events and behaviors that occur within the organization are shaped by that structure. Having described the basic structure of secondary schools, we can address the curriculum. Secondary school curricula consist of a broad range of diverse and discrete courses. As Abramowitz and others (1977) concluded in their study of 2,000 secondary schools: "High schools offer a smorgasbord of programs, practices, options, and services. Students can choose from an array of courses on the basis of their personal needs and career goals. If high schools fit the rigid inflexible patterns suggested by some critics they do so only in scheduling classes and/or evaluating student performance" (p. 59).

To illustrate this diversity we consider two different secondary schools. In one school each student is required to take eight semesters of English, four of history, two each of science and mathematics, two of physical education, and one of government (see Cusick 1981). Within the school's departments is a large number of courses divided into levels of difficulty. Just in English a student can choose from among Shakespeare, mythology, tradition and revolt in literature, music as expression, speech, yearbook, newspaper, drama, mankind's voice today, investigative paper, mystery stories, man to man, philosophy, mass media, learning center (an option for illiterate or marginally literate students), what's happening (a second option for the same students), troubleshooter (yet a third option for these students), developmental English, black literature, grammar, careers, journalism, social problems, mastery learning project, writing, American literature, or, simply, English. In addition to thirty separate courses in English, the school offers sixteen options in social studies, twelve in mathematics, fifteen in business, ten in vocational training, eight in science, eight in art, seven in music, and three in home economics. Physical education, driver education, and co-op education are also available.

In the second school, there is an equally broad array of courses. There, to satisfy the one-year requirement for social studies, a student may take world history, economics, psychology, sociology, anthropology, state history, or World War II. Students from these schools can attend an area career center to study advanced courses in welding, hairdressing, laboratory work, woods, metals, building trades, secretarial work, and data processing. Other students can, and some do, attend the local community college for advanced work in mathematics, science, or arts. Both this school and the first have classes wherein students can earn advanced college credit.

Unlike the first school, where the day is only five periods long and ends at 12:45 P.M., the second school has a day of eight periods. Students can graduate from the second school in three years, while students must attend the first school at least three and one-half years in order to graduate. The second school's more flexible day enables third- and fourth-year students to leave the building as early as the end of the fifth hour (11:15 A.M.) to go to paying jobs for which some of them are receiving high school credit through a co-op program. Two-thirds of the seniors and half of the juniors choose that option. In addition, students over seventeen may take a full-time job during the day and attend evening school. And each of these schools has a full complement of courses to fit the needs of various categories of special students. In both schools one must accumulate from seventeen to twenty-one credits to graduate, but the required courses are few. The board of education requires students to take government, one year of general mathematics, one of science, three of English, one of physical education, and one of social studies. With these minimal requirements and an optimal number of electives, the curriculum of these schools may be described as open, fluid, and diverse.

The reasons for this curriculum diversity are equally varied. Education is generally regarded as a function of the individual states, but the states do not set the curriculum as much as they "suggest" certain elements to be included. In Michigan, the state requires that each school "offer" social studies, consumer education, special education, bilingual education, career education, sex hygiene, health and physical education, the effects of alcohol and drugs, and basic language, but it requires only that each student "take" a semester of government. Most secondary schools in Michigan are also accredited by the North Central Association, which suggests that a school "offer" a basic program of language arts, science, mathematics, social studies, foreign language, fine and practical arts, and physical education, but then leaves each school to plan its own curriculum to serve its own students. In effect, the curriculum of secondary schools in Michigan is somewhat "up for grabs" because (1) the state does not articulate what constitutes an education, (2) the North Cental Association depends on voluntary compliance of its members for support, and (3) the local schools are accountable to their various publics.

Furthermore, the attitude that the "needs" of the students should be served prevails within the schools, and if schoolpeople do not have a view of what those needs might be, then they are in a weak position to determine a curriculum compared to a group that has a clear idea. Schools are always pressured by various groups wanting resources allocated to the basics, music, athletics, bilingual education, affirmative action, or whatever, and such groups have the opportunity to attack the school establishment at a number of points. They may petition a local board; become involved in board elections; or use courts, state legislatures, or local parents' organizations. The fact is that the diversity within secondary school curricula can in part be accounted for by the vulnerability of the school to particular pressure groups; this vulnerability is also in part responsible for the diversity within and across schools. Since the efforts of groups may be locally initiated and directed, a particular school may have elements that are quite unlike those of neighboring schools.

A second element, external to the schools but internal to the educational establishment, serves to diversify the curriculum further. The Elementary and Secondary Education Act (ESEA) of 1965 channeled federal funds for schools through state departments of education. These agencies were allocated funds for administering the ESEA grants and programs and with those funds were able to expand their size and subsequently their scope. The effect was the addition of many educators who do not have contact with students but retain responsibility for educating students. These people have become advocates for a number of ideas and programs such as accountability and testing, bilingual and special education, career education, and vocational and co-op education, the addition of which further fragments and diversifies the curriculum. The explanation of the diversity of the curriculum within secondary schools suggests that two general external forces operate on schools to keep them diverse and fluid. The first of these is the specific advocacy groups. The second is a large and growing group of educators who are distant from students and who can more easily access and affect schools.

An additional source of diversity within the school curriculum has to do with the school's internal structure. For their survival, schools depend on the continuous attendance of large numbers of students who, it is assumed, have very different educational needs. This term *needs* is left purposely vague and undefined, but it is assumed that each student has some idea of his or her own set of needs, and the school is constructed to allow him or her to select experiences appropriate to those needs. To the degree that there is any educational philosophy behind such a structure, it consists of some precepts from progressive education, such as "education should be geared to life; the teacher should try to be empathetic with students; learning should be based on experience; and experiences should be broad" (Swift 1971). Of course, the basic premise about the obligation of the school to serve diverse students with diverse programs is never seriously questioned. Hence, all one has to do to justify an extension of the curriculum is to argue from that premise. And since the definition of *needs* is left undefined, it follows, theoretically at least, that the number of options and electives offered in a high school is potentially unlimited.

Then, too, there is a great deal of wariness within schools about imposing a set curriculum on students. If done overtly, such action would constitute a form of tracking, and tracking has incurred a bad name because in the past it resulted in overt discrimination against black students, poor students, and, particularly, black poor students. Avoiding formal tracking while maintaining the kind of tracking inherent in offering courses that demand prerequisites works out well for several reasons. It means that no one in a position of authority has to decide whether algebra II is more important than woods, or welding more important than French III. If administrators had to make decisions like those within schools, they might conflict with the certification offices of the state, the teachers' unions, and the contract and salary agreement, none of which discriminates among teachers of different subjects. In short, a teacher is a teacher, and a subject is a subject, and a high school education is a high school education.

Because the structure of the high school is such that administrators must spend most of their time on attendance, discipline, and public relations, the day-to-day responsibility for the curriculum falls to the teachers, and administrators generally have two sets of demands for teachers. The first is that they instruct and "get along with" the students; the second is that they not burden the already busy administrators with additional disciplinary problems. Left alone in the classes and charged with maintaining order, instructing, and getting along with the students, teachers are themselves the creators of the vast number of electives offered. The diverse courses are created by teachers to fulfill what they perceive to be the needs of the students. The open-elective course system encourages teachers to find those common interests and then to attract students to their classes on the basis of those interests.

In conducting studies of the curricula of particular schools, we found a large number of interesting courses, and when we asked about their genesis, we found that each was created by an individual teacher to respond to what the teacher perceived as the needs of some students (Cusick 1983). For example, a requirement was for a credit of English. The teacher who liked and studied philosophy created a philosophy class as an English elective; one who liked music created a "music as expression" class as an English elective; one who liked the classics, a classics class as an English elective; one who himself wrote poetry developed a creative writing class as an English elective; one who had a background in forensics, a speech class as an English elective. A business mathematics teacher enjoyed computers; he started a computer club, sent the club members out to sell candy, flowers, and T-shirts, and with the proceeds bought some small computers. He then worked out a curriculum elective through the school's administrators, continued to sell candy and flowers, bought more computers, and now has four classes of computers and one of business mathematics. In the schools we studied, this entrepreneurial approach by teachers is the rule, not the exception. One teacher, hired to teach chemistry, which he admitted he did not like, did like his physical science class, so he created additional electives in physical science, recruited more students, and turned his teaching assignment into four classes of physical science and one of chemistry.

It can be argued that the schools studied were quite loosely run and therefore atypical, but the structure described is the structure of most secondary American schools, and the kind of freedom that teachers have to create classes is what one would expect to find in such a structure. With little supervision from administrators who are busy with matters of discipline, attendance, and public relations, having to appeal to students who are relatively free *not* to elect their classes, and left alone with their students for almost all of the day, teachers work to find ways to create appealing classes based on their personal interests. And, of course, no matter what approach a teacher takes, whether it is to appeal to the gifted, the nonreaders, tougher students, the disadvantaged, or those interested in poetry, music, outdoor education, computers, co-op, or whatever, each teacher is relatively free to find a group of students for whom his approach and subject seem effective and assert that what he is doing is "good for kids." Indeed, it may be, but rarely is a teacher asked to defend or prove the assertion. The mere assertion and the demonstration of a sufficient number of students enrolled in a class are reason enough to continue offering a course.

It may be that the case for diversity is being overstated. After all, in most schools there are a schedule, time periods, fifteen to thirty students to a class, and five or six classes a day. Across schools, one may expect great diversity, but it may be that with some strong community support and a critical mass of homogeneous students, such as the college-bound students, a single school may offer a limited and unified program. The key is the makeup of the critical mass of students in the school. The diversity and disparity are greater in schools with a more diverse populace, less so with a more homogeneous populace. While openness and diversity are less within some schools, across schools they are still great.

Thus, we argue that in order to understand public secondary schools, one has to appreciate the fundamental elements that constitute the structure. These schools are sometimes characterized as monolithic or sterile or are sometimes accused of attempting to impress a uniform education on everyone, but those characterizations and criticisms have most often been uttered by those whose main desire is to fragment and diversify the curriculum further. A more accurate characterization of secondary schools is that schoolpeople themselves long ago adopted an educational perspective that sees a curriculum as reasonable and good when it is fragmented, diverse, open, and fluid and offers as many options to students and as much freedom to teachers as time and space permit. Each student, in the name of satisfying his or her educational needs, is allowed to put together an appropriate set of experiences. The constraints, beliefs, behaviors, structure, and curriculum all combine to support that perspective.

This free market system of education has some advantages and disadvantages. Advantages are that it really does hold out a promise of equality to all, that almost all adolescents take part in it, and that schools really are responsive to their clients. Possible disadvantages, however, are the little emphasis that such a system places on the building and maintaining of a community within the schools and the absence of normativeness that goes with a lack of community. Given the dominant perspective, one would expect to find little community. After all, a strong normative structure is simply inconsistent with the extant system. The choice that the satisfying of individual needs should take precedence over the preservation of a community was made long ago and embedded into the structure. This is what sharply differentiates the public schools from the private schools. Private schools, whether religious, academic/elitist, or special purpose, are characterized by a dual emphasis—the student and the organization. Students know when they enter that they are expected to become a certain kind of person, that there is a normative society toward which they are expected to strive, and that a great deal of organizational energy is devoted to preserving that central ethic.

But the public schools are committed to the education of all, even those who give repeated evidence of not being interested in the acquisition of positive knowledge, and they have adopted a perspective that favors the individual over the community. While the public system has the obvious advantage of being able to demonstrate universalism, the private schools are more able to articulate a coherent relation between their goals and activities. And it may be, as some have suggested, that the community of the private school, serving a pedagogical end of inspiring and motivating students to do better and work harder, is something that public schools were too quick to discard. It may even be that while the public system offers broad advantages to those students sufficiently sophisticated or guided to take advantage of the best available, such a system might further disadvantage those who lack both sophistication and strong guidance. The strongest argument for diversity and fluidity has been that they help extend education to the less advantaged. It would be unfortunate as well as paradoxical if the sum of these efforts further disadvantaged those whom they were intended to assist.

SPECIFIC QUESTIONS

The logic of the argument for diversity in secondary schools is that schools are founded on some basic beliefs such as egalitarianism and universalism are good, that the acquisition of positive knowledge is or can be made interesting and appealing to everyone, that schools should be comprehensive, and, since public schools are publicly funded, they should be geared to the diverse needs of their diverse constituents. The beliefs support the accompanying behaviors, and the beliefs and behaviors combine to form the structure. The logic of the curriculum follows the logic of the structure, and the result is large schools with diverse and fragmented offerings. Given these characteristics, we now address specific questions.

We begin by asking, what are schools like for students, and what adjustments do students have to make to succeed in them? And, specifically, how do answers to these questions differ for different students? Some students enter secondary schools with an interest in learning, some sophistication of their own, or lacking that, some strong parental guidance to help them select an appropriate education and provide them with some motivation to continue and do well. For those students who see themselves competing for good jobs, who know they will attend college, who know they need the more competitive courses, who will enroll in five years of English, four of mathematics, three or four of science, three or four of languages and social studies, public school can be an interesting and rewarding place with a clear relationship between present activities and future goals. On the other hand, many students may not wish to go to college but may have some reasonably clear career plans and may take the advanced vocational classes or a cooperative program that is developed with area employers. For them also, school can be an interesting and rewarding experience. For the latter group perhaps even more than for the former group, the openness, fluidity, and diversity of the system and the openness of the curriculum to alternatives are clear advantages. While the latter group may be less than enthusiastic about some of the academic requirements, the elective system has provided options for them, and in most districts they can if they wish take a reduced academic load in their third and fourth years while making up their credits through working; or, if they wish, they can take adult and evening classes while they work during the day. In the past decade, the articulated desire by various publics for more work-oriented experiences has been taken seriously by schoolpeople, and more and more opportunities in vocational and career education have been made available. Even for students who have neither the desire nor the ambition to attend college nor have any clearly articulated work plans, secondary schools keep open the promise of equality and of increased skills and abilities, and they offer innumerable opportunities for sports, friendships, activities, and affective relations with sympathetic and understanding teachers. Any of these, if entered into with a willing and open spirit, can be sufficiently rewarding to offset some of the inevitable tedium that accompanies life in schools.

On the other hand, there are many students for whom the acquisition of positive knowledge is not interesting, who refuse to enter into any rewarding relationships within the school, who after nine or ten years of school still read and write poorly if at all, for whom simple arithmetic remains a mystery, and who continually end up in the lowest classes with others like them where their ennui and defiance of the system discourage the most sympathetic teachers. For such students school may indeed be a deadening experience, and the sooner they can find their way out the better.

What school is like for students depends on the way they enter or refuse to enter, take part or refuse to take part, engage or refuse to engage in the institution. A student enters the institution as an individual. An education is available, but it is up to each student to wrest it out and to find those good classes, appealing teachers, and rewarding relationships with teachers and peers. A student may make something of the available opportunities but is equally free to drift in and out of the lowest classes, falling to the bottom of whatever he or she enters, and to interact primarily with the administrator in charge of discipline and attendance. Secondary schools can do a great deal for students interested in and attracted to the acquisition of positive knowledge, but they can do little for those students who find the schools neither interesting nor appealing.

But this discussion of differing students is only part of the answer to the quesion of what school is like for students. One may also ask, How do schools differ? A great deal of effort is currently being given to describing a "good school." According to the analysis presented here, a good school is one that is attended by a critical mass of good students, students for whom the acquisition of positive knowledge is interesting and appealing. A "good school" per se does not exist apart from that mass of students who are sufficiently interested to motivate teachers, enter into the spirit of the classes, and keep the school interesting and alive. It has been argued here that students determine what they obtain from school, but it has to be easier to obtain high quality in schools where there is a sufficient number of interested and aggressive students who keep up the level of discourse, who do the work assigned, and who have parents asking about grades and teachers preparing classes carefully and handing work back on time.

While the major assertion is that there is an excellent education to be had by the aggressive and sophisticated student, it is also true that an excellent education is easier to find in the schools with a critical mass of such students. In schools where that mass is lacking, where there is a preponderance of remedial classes, where college-preparatory classes are not really college-preparatory, where there are not enough students for honors or advanced academic or vocational classes, where there are high dropout rates, and where attendance and discipline problems devour all the available supervisory efforts, then it is more difficult to obtain a quality education. The "good schools" are likely to be located in places where the students begin with some advantages, there is a moderate level of income, and there are parents who care about an education. Considerable disparity exists among the public schools, with those located in the middle- to upper-income areas much more likely to offer the fourth year of mathematics, third and fourth years of language, fifth year of English composition, better vocational facilities, and better opportunites for student employment. For the most part, the schools located in financially disadvantaged areas are much less able to provide these elements. For students in those schools, it is more difficult to wrest out an education. The structure holds across schools, but the quality of the education differs according to the clientele.

The public schools have been subjected to serious criticism of their structure. But the structure, according to this analysis, can be quite beneficial to those students who enter the institution with some moderate levels of ability and motivation. The students whom the system may be failing are those who enter with neither ability nor motivation; and in schools with a large number of such students, where they literally compound each other's problems, and where a mass of them can dominate everything else including administrative behaviors and teacher approaches, the criticisms may be justified. But the problems do not stem from the structure per se; rather they develop when the structure combines with that particular clientele.

What may a student reasonably expect to learn in the public schools? In the free-market system of the public high schools, each student is encouraged to and allowed to construct his or her own education. But another kind of analysis is possible. Consider, for example, the type of values students learn when placed in a situation that embodies certain values. Students may learn, for instance, how to behave in a bureaucracy where rules, roles, and regulations are important; they may learn how to behave relative to authority; they may learn to be responsible for their actions; they may learn about the uses of informal peer systems and about the necessity of taking charge of their affairs and creating a coherence across activities; and they may learn about the necessity of putting up with some of the inevitable tedium of organizational life in order to garner its rewards. All of those elements are important to a successful adult life, and all are taught, at least implicitly, in secondary schools.

What is the dominant view of learning held by staff, and how do they go about instructing students? This question necessitates a discussion of a second set of criticisms that have been leveled at the public schools. The instructional mode is such that classes are segmented into forty- or fifty-minute periods, and faculty members are assigned to dole out the material to groups of students five or six times a day. One can well understand the criticisms that such a system might generate—that the system is sterile, wooden, unimaginative, deadening, and monotonous. But the critics do not have a sufficient appreciation of the problems associated with massing a large number of adolescents in the same place for several hours each day and keeping them dry, warm, accounted for, and in reasonable order. The situation necessitates the bureaucracy, and the bureaucracy engenders additional constraints. It is easy to criticize or even ridicule the bureaucratic elements—hall passes, attendance and accounting procedures, absence policies, public address systems, and the plethora of forms for counting this or that—but in almost all schools the students are kept dry, warm, accounted for, and reasonably orderly.

The view of learning and teaching is dominated more by bureaucratic necessity than by pedagogical theory. The fact of thirty students in a room for fifty minutes five times a day dominates the teacher's consideration and severely limits the range of possible approaches. In order to instruct, teachers must maintain order even among the only potentially disorderly, concentrate on developing a normative society in which the students take responsibility for one another as well as for themselves, and work from a written or verbal abstract discussion of reality; and they have only the students' assumed interest to assist them. The emphasis in this system is on teacher activity and student passivity. It is easy to see why public school pedagogy draws criticisms from learning theorists, but it is also easy to see why people who teach and administer in public schools are so defensive about and even hostile to criticisms from those who fail to appreciate the logistics of the situation.

How do the limits and the possibilities of the experience change from the time students enter high school at age thirteen or fourteen to the time they leave at seventeen or eighteen? The structure is such that the system becomes progressively more diverse as students approach graduation. The options and electives increase from the first to the fourth year. By the time a student is a senior, he or she may be in school only a few hours a day, making up other hours in co-op or work-study or career-center programs. Or a student may still be taking five academic classes with one study hall. It all depends on the choices the student made along the way. That of course is in keeping with the beliefs of schoolpeople that as the students grow they should be given more options and with the reality that by the time they have reached sixteen to nineteen years of age, unless they are provided with options in school, they may decide to drop out and find options in other places. Again, the activities follow the structure.

CONCLUSION

According to the argument presented here, various elements characterize secondary schools, the combination of which results in a structure wherein certain patterns of curriculum and of student and staff behavior emerge. Basic to these elements is the schools' obligation to the egalitarian ideal. In a democratic society it is assumed that the problem of identifying and rewarding excellent people will work itself out if the opportunities for learning and personal development are made universal. In modern democratic societies schools are charged with protecting that opportunity, and in American schools that charge is combined with local control, per-pupil funding, and the general assumption that education is a right, not a privilege. The combination of these elements creates a school structure that logically has certain features, such as a proliferation of electives; teacher autonomy; administrative preoccupation with attendance, discipline, and public relations; and the freedom of students to choose what will be their high school education. The system has many positive aspects: it is genuinely inclusive and democratic. But it is open to a number of criticisms: that the system has no set academic standards and gives a very vague definition of a high school education, and, hence, that what a high school graduate actually knows cannot be assumed. And, paradoxically enough, in this free and open system there is the possibility that those who receive the least from the schools and are hence least able to claim that they know anything are just those the school is trying hardest to help, namely those who come from the disadvantaged groups of society, who have the least ascriptive advantages, and who receive the least encouragement and guidance from home.

REFERENCES

Abramowitz, Susan, and Tenenbaum, Ellen, with Terrence Deal and E. Anne Stackhouse. *High School '77*. Washington, D.C.: National Institute of Education. 1977.

Conant, James B. *The American High School Today*. New York: McGraw-Hill, 1959.

Cusick, Philip A. "An Rx for Our High Schools." *Character* 12:7 (1981): 1–5.

Cusick, Philip A. *The Egalitarian Ideal and the American High School*. New York: Longman, 1983.

Swift, David. *Ideology and Change in the Public Schools*. Columbus, Ohio: Charles Merrill, 1971.

7

Making the Grade in College in the 1980s

William F. Neumann

What do colleges require of students today? It depends! It depends on which colleges or universities students attend, what their major fields of study are, who their teachers are, and who the other students are. Finally, what colleges require of students depends on the students themselves and what kind of persons they are. Answering this question specifically, then, is not easy, but answering it generally is not much easier. The safest generalization one can make about the American system of higher education is that it is large and diverse. Of course, everyone knows that, but it is not until one looks closely at this system that one can begin to appreciate its true dimension and variety.

In 1980, 12 million students were enrolled in 3,253 different colleges and universities. Five hundred thousand professors taught 2 million classes preparing students for some 1,500 different degrees.

Institutions of higher education differ in a number of significant ways, all of which may affect what these schools require of students. There are four-year and two-year colleges, church-affiliated and nonsectarian schools, coeducational and single-sex schools. There are residential and commuter schools; there are urban, suburban, and rural colleges. There are liberal arts schools, technical schools, state colleges, graduate schools, teachers' colleges, community colleges, research universities, and multiversities. They all may differ dramatically in cost, selectivity, reputation, prestige, age, history, tradition, wealth, and stability. There are often clear differences in the composition of the student bodies and faculties and profound differences in curriculum and educational philosophies.

Within these sundry institutions the faculties differ in a number of ways that have a direct effect on how they teach and what they consequently require of students. Faculty members may be tenured or untenured, of junior or senior rank, and, depending on their status, are either secure and confident or insecure and anything but confident. College faculty are usually hired for their expertise in their subject area and not for their teaching ability or experience. Some faculty members are notoriously ineffective and boring teachers, while others are great teachers. Others are great researchers. Some are both great teachers and researchers, and others, unfortunately, are neither. All too often promotion is awarded on the basis of research, which places many faculty members under great pressure to publish, and as a result they neglect their teaching. Some senior faculty members resent and avoid teaching introductory and undergraduate courses, preferring to teach graduate courses more closely related to their current research interests. George Wald, the Nobel Prize winning Harvard biologist, claims that he is the first professor in the history of his department to volunteer to teach the freshman introductory biology course. Wald explains that this teaching assignment was customarily foisted on the relatively defenseless junior faculty members. It has been suggested that junior and community college faculty members—often taken from the ranks of high school faculties—are more effective teachers of undergraduates because they have teaching experience, and because they are not under pressure to publish to keep their jobs.

We can also point to obvious differences in subject areas that require very different skills from students. Literature, humanities, and social studies majors will almost certainly be called on to read more than are hard science majors, while the latter will most likely need more highly developed quantitative abilities.

The composition of the student body of an institution—its degree of heterogeneity, qualifications, preparation, maturity, experience, sophistication; its sex and age—and the nature of its interactions with the institution will certainly affect what the school requires of its students. At most colleges the student body is steadily becoming more diverse. Minority student enrollment has increased, and extensive government-supported financial aid programs have allowed greater numbers of working-class students to enroll in college. In 1982, for the first time in our history more women than men were enrolled in institutions of higher education. The popular image of the typical college student as being between the ages of eighteen and twenty-two, attending college full time, and perhaps working part time is also changing. Fully 40 percent of those 12 million students enrolled in 1980 were part-time students, and many of them were working full time. College administrators and faculty realize that they simply cannot expect the same level of involvement from a married student who has children, holds a full-time job, and attends school part time that they expect from the "traditional" eighteen- to twenty-two-year-old student. Inventive college administrators have designed an array of alternative programs to attract and serve these new "nontraditional" students. There are night schools, extension programs, correspondence schools, and weekend colleges. One university, for example, offers an MBA program in which students can take classes taught on the train as they ride to and from their jobs in New York City each day. The Independent Study Degree Program of University College of Syracuse University, a combined correspondence and residential program offering both undergraduate and graduate degrees, includes among its many full-time working students the captain of a trans-oceanic oil tanker.

Given the astonishing variation both between and within our many institutions of higher education, and given that for almost any general statement I might make about these institutions there is certain to be an obvious exception, let me offer some tentative generalizations regarding the collective requirements and expectations (intended and unintended) imposed on students by virtue of the common character and nature of contemporary colleges and universities. But first, we must take note of some important changes in our system of higher education that have taken place since 1960.

CHANGES IN HIGHER EDUCATION SINCE THE 1960s

The launching of Sputnik by the Russians in 1957 sent shock waves across American colleges and universities. At approximately the same time, the young people born during the baby boom of the early 1940s began flocking in unprecedented numbers to our unprepared colleges and universities, where these new college students were packed into classrooms and dormitories. The immediate and obvious response of colleges to both of these challenges was to raise their academic standards for admission, retention, and graduation. Making and maintaining acceptable grades became the dominant feature of academic life, and those students who did not "make the grade" were quickly dropped by the college or university and sent home in what amounted to public disgrace—they had "failed-out."

Becker, Geer, and Hughes (1968) provide a vivid account of the varied academic demands of college life on undergraduates during the early 1960s. Their account, based on two years (1960 and 1961) of participant observation at a large midwestern state university, illustrates how concern about making acceptable grades dominated student life and, more important, how in academic matters students were under the complete control of the faculty and administration:

Faculty and administration set almost all the terms and conditions of student activity in the academic area; their control here is most nearly complete. They decide what students are to do, when they are to do it, something of how it is to be done, and what rewards or punishments will be given to those who do not meet the standards. [P. 8]

They characterize the relationship between the "powerless" students and the faculty members as one of "subjection" and add that they do not think this relationship is necessarily unwarranted or inappropriate:

We must understand, of course, that the term does not express an unfavorable judgment. We use it as a technical term to refer to a hierarchial arrangement in which all the decision-making power is in the hands of the superior group. The faculty, of course, believe with a good deal of reason that this is an appropriate pattern, since they, after all, know a good deal more about their subject matter than students do and so ought not to be expected to give up any power in this area. [P. 8]

Although students enjoyed comparatively more freedom in other aspects of college life (their social activities and interpersonal relationships with other students), even here the university exercised some authority and control. Students living in university-supervised residences, and undergraduate women in general, were expected to conform to a number of regulations. Women, and occasionally men, had curfews or "hours" every night after which they had to be present in their residences. Surprise room checks and bed checks were common practices on many campuses. Students had to receive special permission to be absent from their campus residence overnight and had to leave addresses and phone numbers where they could be reached in the event of an emergency. Undergraduate living quarters were usually strictly segregated by sex, and members of the opposite sex were forbidden to be in one's room except at specially designated, supervised times, and never overnight.

But the complete control by the university over students was not to last. The years shortly after Becker, Geer, and Hughes finished their fieldwork saw the beginning of more than a decade of student activism and rebellion. It began with students' involvement in the Civil Rights Movement and culminated in the often violent protests against American involvement, especially the involvement of American colleges and universities, in the Vietnam War. These protests rocked campuses across the country and traumatized the entire system of higher education.

Surprisingly, the general curriculum of most colleges and universities has survived these shocks and has demonstrated a truly remarkable degree of continuity (Veysey 1973). But it has not survived without some changes that influence what students must do to get through college successfully.

These changes in the undergraduate curriculum have been documented by Grant and Riesman (1978). Based on over seven years of fieldwork at more than four hundred colleges and universities— including intensive visits to thirty campuses—they observed several significant changes in the character of higher education since the upheavals of the 1960s:

While both individual students and institutions have been unevenly affected by these changes, there is no doubt that almost everywhere requirements have been relaxed, the paths toward a degree have been made more multiple and open, and the gold standard of academic currency (in some cases more nominal than real) has been diluted by grade inflation. . . . Requirements evaporated either piecemeal or through large-scale demolition. Open admissions, always a reality in many state universities and colleges, became a political issue when it implied recruiting of, and providing academic enrichment for, minorities who possessed what would hitherto have been deemed inadequate high school preparation. Parietal regulations disappeared with such astonishing speed that it is a surprise to come upon a college that still forbids co-residential living and thus defends what students would regard as hypocrisy. [P. 181]

Of the many changes they discuss, the one they single out as the most important is the disappearance of general education and distribution requirements: "The most important change was the virtual or complete abolition of fixed requirements in many departments and of mandatory distribution requirements, whether of breadth or depth, including class attendance and the time, mode, and kinds of credits needed to secure a baccalaureate degree" (p. 188).

The elimination of these and other requirements has resulted, they conclude, in giving students a truly remarkable amount of freedom of choice and autonomy within their college or university:

> Altogether, the result was a far greater degree of autonomy for the students. They were free to plan their course of study, or not to plan it. They could devise their own majors, delay such a decision, teach courses themselves for credit, and follow their inclinations at their own pace into various forms of "experimental" and off-campus learning. [P. 189]

Other observers of American colleges have noted many of these same changes with dismay and in their writing have painted a very disturbing portrait of contemporary college life. The typical undergraduate has been described as self-centered and narcissistic, compelled by "vocomania" (preoccupation with getting job training), highly competitive, demonstrating little or no social consciousness or consideration for classmates, and totally pessimistic (Levine 1981). They attend colleges (including some of the most respected and expensive institutions) where they are "neglected" and "degraded"; where sex, drugs, cheating, crime, sexism, and racism are rampant (Chase 1980; Lamont 1979). While there is no doubt some truth in all of these charges, it may be well to remember another of Grant and Riesman's findings: "One can still get a classical education in any good college or university if one looks for it, and catalogs show that much of the traditional remains" (p. 179).

Nevertheless, it seems safe to say that today all but a few of the institutions of higher education in our country confront the problems listed above. Furthermore, all but a favored few are in financial trouble, beset by problems of declining enrollment, inflation, and diminishing government assistance. It is tempting to be cynical and say that colleges today require only that students have fat checkbooks. Instead, I will attempt to be objective; I will adopt what I believe is the perspective of the institutions in order that I might lay out some tentative generalizations regarding what colleges require and expect of students.

COLLEGE PRESS AND STUDENT FIT

I will call the functional demands placed on students as actors in the college and university environment *college press*, and the extent to which the students successfully meet these demands I will call *student fit*. The many characteristics of students that provide for student fit are their *attributes*. Student attributes include basic academic skills as well as personality characteristics and other qualities. These attributes may be either inherited or attained. Many of them are learned (most but not all in formal educational settings), while others may be attained through natural developmental growth and maturation. I have made no attempt to rank these attributes in importance or immediacy, nor have I attempted to quantify them.

Basic Academic Skills

In a literal sense all of the attributes discussed in this essay are basic academic skills, but when most people speak of basic academic skills they think of reading, writing, and mathematics. At the college level they would probably also expect students to need analytical thinking skills and an ability to interpret abstract ideas. A recent publication of the College Board (1983), which was the result of the combined efforts of hundreds of college and high school teachers, identified seven "Basic Academic Competencies": reading, writing, speaking, listening, mathematics, reasoning, and studying. There are other educators, however, who would claim that these so-called required competencies reflect an ideal rather than a realistic appraisal. When asked recently what skills colleges required of students, the sociologist David Riesman said he thought "assiduousness in attendance" was all it took. He was serious. Indeed, a major finding of Grant and Riesman (1978) was that the lack of general education and distribution requirements allows all but those students majoring in the hard sciences, mathematics, and languages to avoid these more arduous courses.

There is no overall agreement among educators regarding the level at which college students should be able to read, write, and perform other basic academic tasks. The many participants of the College Board study did not even try: "No attempt has been made to define the level of difficulty or the degree of sophistication that any one school or college should expect of its students. Obviously, different schools and colleges are likely to establish their own definitions in this regard" (p. 4). In general, it seems that colleges require little more than minimal reading, writing, and mathematical skills, and it may be that only reading is absolutely essential in order to get by.

Twenty years ago in an engaging essay titled "College Study:

Expectations and Realities," Louis Benezet (1965) advised prospective college students that they would have to develop a detached academic outlook to make it through college:

For the student to appreciate knowledge and truth as the professor sees it, it becomes necessary for the student also to detach himself from the biases and distractions of everyday existence. He does not realize, for instance, until he proceeds well along in college that almost everything he has read in the daily papers and everything he hears at his family table at home reflect interpretations of truth tortured by self-interest, snap judgment, and wishful thinking. The world of scholarship requires us to get away from the immediate scene. [P. 9]

Now this sounds promising; here are required analytical thinking skills. Unfortunately, Benezet's advice is flawed in two respects. His first mistake is that he assumes that all professors think in this objective, detached manner. The fact is that many college professors present a one-sided or narrow view of the "truth." There are some who feel it is their moral obligation to raise the level of consciousness of their students and intentionally present a slanted perspective, while others simply are not aware of their biases and how they may intrude in their teaching. Second, while it is true that students do have to think like their teachers, they do not have to internalize their teachers' perspectives.

Students have to figure out how their teachers think and what they want, and they must realize that different professors have different values, will think differently, want different things, and, most important, are likely to give greater rewards to those students who can respond in accordance with the professors' values. Such responses may be particularly difficult for idealistic students who come to college sharing Benezet's optimistic perspective and expect objectivity from their professors. Another way of putting this might be to say that colleges require students to be "professor-wise" in the same way that students are described as being "test-wise."

There does not seem to be anything inherent in the makeup of colleges that would require students to enter into the world of abstract ideas. The part of the curriculum that would most likely involve students in or expose them to abstract thinking—the humanities—is generally regarded as being in a state of serious decline (Bennett 1984). Students, we are told, do not consider an exposure to abstract ideas an important part of their schooling; they want training and they want specific courses of study structured to lead directly into jobs after graduation. The vocationalism of higher education is a frequent subject in the literature. A survey conducted by the Carnegie Council on Policy Studies in Higher Education reported that 85 percent of undergraduates were attending college with a specific career in mind (Levine 1981, p. 61). Almost half of all students reported that they would drop out of college if they thought college would not help them get a job. Fifty-eight percent of all undergraduates were majoring in preprofessional studies.

Self-Sufficiency

Surely all of us can remember being warned in high school that when we got to college we would be on our own, that no one would be looking over our shoulders to make sure we got our homework done on time, attended class, studied, or learned anything for that matter. And how we looked forward to that happy day, only to find once it arrived how difficult it was to be on our own.

As discussed earlier in this essay, students in college today possess considerable autonomy. A corollary of autonomy is self-sufficiency, and we can see colleges expecting students to be self-sufficient in a number of very significant areas.

The most elementary expectation colleges have of students is that they will be able to manage their own time. This is more than expecting responsibility; it also includes expecting organization skills. The more free time or unstructured time students have, the harder it seems to be for them to impose some structure and coherence. Scheduling and organizing college study, work, and personal activities is especially difficult for beginning and inexperienced students who do not yet have an accurate perception of how much time certain school-related tasks will take. Also, there is the illusion of having "free time" because the class schedule shows only twelve to fifteen hours a week given to class time. In 1982 a group of 375 Miami University freshmen who had received less than a "C" average for their first semester were asked to rank sixty-eight factors related to academic performance that might explain their low grades. "Failure to schedule time wisely" was ranked by 38 percent of the students as their principal problem—more than any other factor it was responsible for their low grades (Hart and Keller 1980).

Just as a schedule with too much free time may make managing time difficult for some students, too much structure—particularly in non-college-related activities like work—can also create scheduling problems. Having less time for study makes the effective use of "free time" all the more important and no less difficult.

We can also find colleges expecting self-sufficiency from students in areas like self-advisement and independent study. In their description of New College, Grant and Riesman (1978) speculate on the demands of independent study:

> But even now no generally applicable method is available by which to measure the personal qualities required for Independent Study—the stamina of the long distance runner or track star which enables students to endure frustration; the absence of narcissism which makes it possible to plow ahead with work that is not utterly dazzling; the ability to pace oneself when the hated monitoring of school and family is removed. [P. 226]

An even more dramatic manifestation of expectations of self-sufficiency by colleges is found in the concept of self-instruction. Here students not only are studying on their own, but they are also expected to teach themselves, and again, scheduling skills are critical. Often self-instruction involves work with programmed texts, tapes, slide-tape combinations, records, or some type of teaching machine, and much of this work is expected to take place in learning labs or independent study centers that are often staffed by other students— not only is a teacher not directly involved, one is not even present. Further expectations are put on students taking self-instruction courses, since these courses also tend to be self-paced. A Carnegie Council survey of 1976 reported that one-third of all undergraduates had taken self-instruction courses, and it has been estimated that soon the average undergraduate will take one-third of all his courses through self-instruction (Levine 1978, p. 189).

The cumulative impact of all these expectations of self-sufficiency on each student is unknown. But I am reminded of an interview I had in 1980 with a freshman student at a well-known eastern polytechnical institute where I was doing a study of student life. It is the policy of the institute not to refuse admission to interested students; instead, they tell an applicant what the college thinks of his or her qualifications and likelihood of success in what certainly is a demanding curriculum. The freshman, John, chose to be admitted even though the college officials had advised him that he would have difficulty and might not make it. I interviewed John shortly after the end of his first semester. He had failed to complete three of the four courses he had taken his first semester—calculus, physics, and chemistry. All three of these courses were self-paced and involved the use of self-instruction videotapes at the campus learning center; there were no teachers. John had passed biology, the only course he had with a teacher: "I didn't like the subject, but I did like the teacher." He explained that his big problem the first semester was that he had put off taking the several mastery tests for his three self-study courses until the end of the term. There had been a rush on the learning center by all the other students who had done the same thing, so John could not take his tests in time, and he had ended up receiving two incompletes and one failing grade. He readily admitted his responsibility for his poor performance: "It was my own fault!" In his second semester, John told me he was repeating two of the courses, and to my astonishment, he was again scheduled for three courses through the learning center. I asked him what his advisor had said about his schedule, and he told me that he had gone through self-advisement.

Sociability

Whatever else colleges may be, they are essentially social institutions composed of individuals and different groups of people (administrators, support staff, teachers, and students) living and working in learning communities, and as such they have a number of direct and indirect expectations for students' social behavior. Specifically, they expect students to be sociable with other students and with the faculty.

Colleges both expect and require sociable behavior among students in a number of situations, such as in sharing library or computer facilities, but it is in the realm of dormitory and residential life that colleges exact the greatest demands. Students who are often complete strangers at the start of the school year are placed in the most intimate proximity and are expected to share virtually every aspect of daily personal life. While getting along with their roommate or roommates may be difficult for inexperienced freshmen, and especially at first when no one knows anyone else, it can easily become even more difficult as time passes and behavior, attitudes, and opinions that were at first accepted as "different" or eccentric become less tolerable and serve as the basis for the growth of genuine animosity between students. It is just as easy for students to grow less accepting and accommodating of each other as it is for them to grow closer.

Although there have always been difficulties and problems associated with dormitory and residential life, there seems to be a general consensus that two recent developments have tended to make the situation more difficult—the relaxation of parietal restrictions and the establishment of self-governing dormitories.

According to Grant and Riesman, the dropping of these regulations happened very quickly and took place in every type of institution:

> With even greater speed than that with which students were gaining control over the curriculum, they were eliminating the last vestiges of parietal restraints on their conduct in nonacademic arenas. It was really quite extraordinary to watch the wildfire spread of conviction on the part of college authorities, even in the more provincial and religiously dominated schools, that students were now adult enough to, as the phrase goes, "take control of their own lives." [P. 213]

Almost every account of college life today addresses the problems associated with the elimination of rules governing conduct in student housing (Levine 1981; Lamont 1979; Chase 1980). The most commonly mentioned problem, and most troublesome, seems to be "the third roommate":

> The "third roommate" has become a campus institution. This person is, of course, the guest—the roommate's boy or girl friend—who stays for extended periods of time, sharing living quarters with his friend and roommate. Although all colleges officially frown on this, few stop it because, as short stays of lovers are permitted, it is impossible to enforce. Few students want to make enemies of their roommates by complaining, and a few of those who do complain are threatened with physical violence. [Chase 1980, p. 144]

Self-governing dormitories, while fine in theory, simply do not seem to work. In the same way that self-regulation does not work to keep campus libraries quiet and make them workable places of study, it is my impression from talking to freshmen at a variety of colleges that self-regulated dorms are in a constant state of disruption. Of course, there may be and no doubt are exceptions, but it seems that placing students in group living and studying situations without any external form of control and authority to mediate interpersonal relationships serves only to place even greater demands for sociability on students.

A second area in which colleges and universities expect sociability from students is in the realm of student-faculty relationships. While colleges most assuredly do not expect the same degree of sociability in student-faculty relationships that they do in student-to-student interactions, they do expect the student to take the initiative in establishing some level of communication with faculty in less formal settings outside the classroom. At most colleges, faculty members are required to keep office hours, and there are some faculty members who require students to make at least one visit to their office each term, but in most cases it is left to the student to establish this contact. I think this is asking a lot, particularly of the freshman who usually has an exalted opinion of what college professors are and who feels he must have a very good reason to take up their office time. Yet reviews of research on student attrition in higher education report that positive student-faculty interactions outside the classroom, and especially in informal settings, have a definite positive correlation with students' persistence in college (Tinto 1975; Pantages and Creedon 1978; Pascarella 1980). Studies have found that positive, informal interaction between community college students and faculty, including the informal sponsorship of students by concerned faculty, was the critical factor in the persistence and eventual transfer to a four-year institution of these students, who are generally regarded as the most likely to leave college early (Neumann and Riesman 1980).

In addition to students finding satisfactory living arrangements and establishing positive relationships with faculty, their having friendships with other students appears important and may make the difference when they are considering leaving a school before completing their studies. This is most true on large campuses where students may feel lost, alone, insignificant, or forgotten, but it is also important on small campuses with more homogeneous student bodies where being different in even some small way may isolate a student.

The fact that substantial numbers of students with acceptable and often excellent grades choose to leave college clearly shows that it takes more than the so-called basic academic skills to get through college. It is also possible that students who leave college because of poor grades have been socially unsuccessful, which may account for their low academic achievement. Whether it is something about the nature of institutions of higher education or something in human nature, sociability seems to be an important basic skill for success in college.

Motivation

One of my most vivid college recollections is of a slight but very dignified and confident professor of English literature, who, after passing out a forbidding reading list, told the somewhat abashed class of freshmen, "If you want to make it through my class you will have to want it, but just wanting it isn't enough. If you want to do well, you will have to like it!" While some people may argue about whether or not you have to like going to college, both educators and students generally agree that you do have to want to do it.

Two of the more comprehensive reviews of the literature on attrition of college students are those by Iffert (1957) and Summerskill (1962). These studies show that reasons related to their own motivations are regarded by students as having by far the greatest bearing on their decision to leave college. Motivation is a broad concept and can be defined in several different ways; consequently, researchers have investigated the question of the relationship between motivation and college persistence from almost every conceivable angle. They have looked at students' precollege record of motivation and commitment, various sources of motivation, reasons for attending college, reasons for selecting areas of study, goal commitment, institutional commitment, educational goals, occupational goals, career goals, development of goals, and degree of clarity or specificity of goals, and, although there is general agreement among researchers that motivational factors certainly do contribute to college attrition, it has not yet been determined which (if any) motivational factors are predictive of students' persistence or attrition or how those factors can be measured (Pantages and Creedon 1978). But two things seem to be consistently true: First, a great many students who leave college report a lack of interest in either their school or their studies; and second, and even more disturbing, many students who began with the desire to go to college report that the experience of attending college had dampened that interest and motivation.

It seems really quite natural for college administrators and faculty to assume that students are motivated. After all, they may argue, there are no compulsory attendance laws requiring college, and since students have to pay for school, it seems reasonable to expect that they want to be there. Of course, this attitude overlooks the many students who are in college only because of pressure from a parent or because they feel if they do not go to college they will be restricted to a life of hard labor and financial insecurity, but there is some validity in it. Presumably, students are in college of their own volition; they are there because they want to be, and they can leave any time they want to.

Colleges expect and require that students be motivated in a number of ways. These expectations are reflected in the commonality of the structure of courses and teaching practices. While elementary and secondary school teachers expend great amounts of time and energy trying to find ways to interest students, to get them involved with their subjects, or at least to get them to do minimal amounts of work, most college teachers generally do not worry about these things. For the most part, they take student interest for granted, especially in elective courses. College faculty members may feel a responsibility to teach, but they see learning as the students' responsibility, and they expect students to force themselves if necessary to get interested in a subject. This perception of the nature of the relationship between college teachers and students is evident in the general tendency of most faculty members to rely on the same method of instruction, the lecture.

The lecture remains the predominant teaching technique at all levels of college instruction. Lectures may be an efficient means of transmitting a quantity of information to large groups of students, but there is ample reason to question whether it is the most effective means of teaching. Listening to lectures is basically a very passive experience, yet teachers expect students to be motivated enough to pay attention and take notes regardless of how many lectures they have already heard that day. While there may be some variation between the lecturing styles of different professors, each lectures consistently in his or her own way for the entire term or all year in the case of some sequential courses.

In addition to most professors using the same method of instruction, college courses tend to be structured similarly. This is especially true of courses in the same subject area or academic department. There will be lectures, exams (often exams for all courses are scheduled for the same week), and term papers. Students find little structural variety among the courses they take toward receiving a college degree. Freshman courses are structured and run in much the same way as advanced courses. Advanced courses may consider the subject in more detail, but they still are similarly structured. The whole process can and does become repetitious, routine, and monotonous, and no matter how bored the students may become, they are expected to be motivated.

The bureaucratic nature of institutions of higher education also requires a form of motivation from students. Although the bureaucracy may be more pronounced and rigid at larger colleges and universities, there is a general impersonality implicit in administrative policies and a reliance on systematic procedures that are in fact dehumanizing and often very frustrating for a student with a unique problem or even a common one. But colleges expect students to put up with bureaucracy even though most of their procedures are designed not to make life easier for the student, but rather to make things easier for the administrators. It is easy to speculate on how repeated bureaucratic frustrations might affect students' motivation during their college years. In a study I did of undergraduate life at one college, freshmen talked about "learning the system" and juniors and seniors talked about "beating the system." Similarly, Levine (1981) noted that according to a Carnegie Council report in 1976, ". . . almost half (43 percent) of all undergraduates believe that many of the successful students at their college make it by 'beating the system,' rather than by studying" (p. 72).

It all seems to come back to being motivated—whether it is to learn the system or to beat the system, to seek beauty and truth, or to get a job and make money. Students must be motivated to get through college.

Direction, or "Knowing What You Want"

The "over-optioned curriculum" is a term coined by Grant (1979) to describe the expansion of curricula and the unbridled growth in the number of courses offered at most colleges and universities in recent years. One does not have to look far to find evidence of this phenomenon. A recent ad in a Boston newspaper announced that summer students at the University of Massachusetts in Boston would be able to select from five hundred courses representing fifty disciplines, and Grant tells of looking through a catalog of a large state university and finding more than seven thousand courses listed. For undirected students who attend colleges, with no core requirements and no prerequisites for advanced courses, and who have no clear idea of what they want to study, the experience of selecting courses and building a personal program of study can be bewildering. I have known many students who have spent years taking a mishmash of courses scattered across the curricular spectrum, while they made very little progress toward completing a specific degree.

Levine estimates that more than 50 percent of all undergraduates change their major at least once during college, and the number of course changes students make each term is astonishing. For example, according to Chase (1980), at Yale, where there are a mere fifty-nine major programs and five thousand undergraduates, students made over fifty thousand course changes during the 1978–79 academic year. Here are students in search of direction. Sociologist Martin Trow places responsibility squarely on the colleges themselves for this situation: "Since colleges have abandoned responsibility for giving the curriculum any purpose or coherence, students must provide this purpose and coherence themselves" (Chase 1980, p. 147).

To be sure academic advisers still work on college campuses, but complaints by students about improper or inadequate advisement abound. Problems with advisement in large institutions have been described by Gnepp, Keating, and Masters (1980):

In large institutions, however, faculty advisors often find that they are responsible for a sizeable number of undergraduates, and that many of their advising tasks are necessary but quite routine and time-consuming. It is not surprising, therefore, that faculty members with extensive research and/or teaching interests are reluctant to spend time with students who want help filling out forms, need their adviser's signature for registration, and so forth. This disinterest (occasionally bordering on antagonism) on the part of many faculty naturally affects the quality of the advisor/advisee interaction. A survey of advising in 1969 in the institute's collegiate unit revealed serious student dissatisfaction with faculty advisors and the advising system. Among the most frequent criticisms made by students were unavailability of advisors, lack of interest in students, lack of knowledge about the requirements and about referral sources, and advisors "too busy" to spend any time with them.[P. 371]

Similar problems with advising systems can and often do occur in smaller institutions.

Empirical studies on the relationship between specificity of students' educational and career goals and students' attrition have established that having clearly defined goals does improve students' chances of completing college (Pantages and Creedon 1978; Tinto 1975). Elton and Rose (1971) reported a major difference in the persistence rates of vocationally decided and undecided freshmen. They found that only 17 percent of the undecided freshmen persisted to graduation while 43 percent of those who professed a career commitment graduated—even though the specific commitment may have undergone one or more changes. In another study, Abel (1966) found that students were twice as likely to graduate if they were certain of their goals.

Financial Security

A friend of mine attending a large urban university received a bill from the university for twenty-five cents. He could not believe it. The paper, postage, and time and labor spent processing the bill, putting it into an envelope, and sending it to him easily cost more than the original outstanding twenty-five cents. Even if he went to the university office and paid the bill in person, thus saving the twenty-two cent postage, his bank would have charged him a thirty-cent fee for processing the check. He was surprised and angry. I was amused but not surprised; after all, I had had years of experience as a student at three different universities. My friend, however, was a first-term freshman, in college for the first time in his life. He said he thought the whole thing was stupid and he was not going to pay the bill. I advised him to save the bill as a souvenir, but by all means to pay it, warning him that if he did not pay the bill, the university might cancel his registration or charge him a late fee. There simply is no getting around financial requirements at colleges and universities. While my friend's story is humorous, and may be more an example of bureaucratic ineptitude than anything else, many students struggle with serious problems in meeting the financial requirements of obtaining a college degree.

These costs of college are for many students a real burden, and they begin even before a student is admitted to a college. Most colleges require fees to cover the cost of processing applications for admission and financial aid. Once a student is admitted, tuition is only the first of a whole array of fees and required expenses. The cost of books, even paperback editions, can be a real burden for many students.

Financial aid programs have dramatically increased the opportunities of many students to attend college, but most of these programs have been unable to keep pace with rapid inflation and increasing college costs, and in many cases institutional resources to assist students have come close to exhaustion. Furthermore, federal programs providing financial aid to students and to colleges and universities have been cut, which has exacerbated an already difficult situation.

Over the years many students who have dropped out of college have said that financial considerations were the reason they prematurely discontinued their courses of study (Iffert 1957; Tinto 1975; Pantages and Creedon 1978). In 1976 the Carnegie Council survey reported that 54 percent of all college students were holding down jobs while going to school. Although in some instances these jobs are related to a student's studies and become an integral part of his or her education, and one could argue that working helps in the development of other attributes deemed necessary and desirable for success in college, in most cases working while going to school interferes with meeting basic course requirements and makes getting through college more difficult.

In addition to encroaching on the time students would otherwise have to spend on their studies, psychological consequences result from having to work while attending college. Students may find it difficult to concentrate on removed academic issues if they are worrying about whether or not they can pay the rent and meet other basic living expenses. In some cases financial pressure may also effectively isolate and alienate students who have to work their way through college and who may feel resentment toward classmates with greater financial resources. I recall an interview I had with a young man, a senior at a small private college, who told me how he resented, even hated, his classmates who did not have to work outside of school. He hated them because they had more time to study and got A's while he got B's. He hated them most when they complained about assignments that he felt they had all the time in the world to do while he worked six nights a week to get by.

MAKING THE GRADE IN THE 1980s

As we have seen, many of the same attributes the various institutions of higher education required of students to make the grade in the 1960s have remained important for making the grade in the 1980s. However, changes in the nature of the college environment, primarily the relaxation and abandonment of parietal restrictions by colleges in certain areas of the curriculum and particularly in the nonacademic aspects of college life, seem to have shifted the emphasis from the traditional academic activities of class participation, tests, term papers, and the like to the more personal and social components of the college experience. In the 1980s basic academic skills remain important, but preeminent now are personal attributes such as self-sufficiency, motivation, and direction as well as social skills and sociability.

REFERENCES

Abel, Walter H. "Attrition and the Student Who Is Certain." *Personnel and Guidance Journal* 44 (1966): 1042–1045.

Becker, Howard S.; Geer, Blanche; and Hughes, Everett C. *Making the Grade: The Academic Side of College Life.* New York: John Wiley, 1968.

Benezet, Louis T. "College Study: Expectations and Realities." In *The First Years in College: Preparing Students for a Successful College Career*, edited by Harry Rivlin, Dorothy M. Fraser, and Milton R. Stein. Boston: Little, Brown and Co., 1965.

Bennett, W. J. *To Reclaim a Legacy: A Report on the Humanities in Higher Education*. Washington, D. C.: National Endowment for the Humanities, 1984.

Chase, Alston. *Group Memory: A Guide to College and Student Survival in the 1980s*. Boston: Little, Brown and Co., 1980.

College Board. *Academic Preparation for College: What Students Need to Know and Be Able to Do*. New York: College Board, 1983.

Elton, Charles F., and Rose, Harriet A. "A Longitudinal Study of the Vocationally Undecided Male Student." *Journal of Vocational Behavior* 1 (1971): 85–92.

Gnepp, Jackie; Keating, Daniel P.; and Masters, John A. "A Peer System for Academic Advising." *Journal of College Student Personnel* 21 (1980): 370–373.

Grant, Gerald. "The Overoptioned Curriculum." In *Toward the Restoration of the Liberal Arts Curriculum, Working Papers*. New York: Rockefeller Foundation, 1979.

Grant, Gerald, and Riesman, David. *The Perpetual Dream: Reform and Experiment in the American College*. Chicago: University of Chicago Press, 1978.

Hart, Derrell, and Keller, Michael J. "Self-Reported Reasons for Poor Academic Performance of First-Term Freshmen." *Journal of College Student Personnel* 21 (1980): 529–534.

Iffert, Robert E. *Retention and Withdrawal of College Students*. Washington, D. C.: U. S. Government Printing Office, 1957.

Lamont, Lansing. *Campus Shock: A Firsthand Report on College Life Today*. New York: Dutton, 1979.

Levine, Arthur. *Handbook on Undergraduate Curriculum*. San Francisco: Jossey-Bass, 1978.

Levine, Arthur. *When Dreams and Heroes Died: A Portrait of Today's College Student*. San Francisco: Jossey-Bass, 1981.

Neumann, William, and Riesman, David. "The Community College Elite." In *New Directions for Community Colleges: Questioning the Community College Role*, no. 32. San Francisco: Jossey-Bass, 1980.

Pantages, Timothy, and Creedon, Carol F. "Studies of College Attrition: 1950–1975." *Review of Educational Research* 48 (1978): 49–101.

Pascarella, Ernest T. "Student-Faculty Informal Contact and College Outcomes." *Review of Educational Research* 50 (1980): 545–595.

Summerskill, John. "Dropouts from College." In *The American College*, edited by Nevitt Sanford. New York: Wiley, 1962.

Tinto, Vincent. "Dropouts from Higher Education: A Theoretical Synthesis of Recent Research." *Review of Educational Research* 45 (1975): 89–125.

Veysey, Laurence. "Stability and Experiment in the American Undergraduate Curriculum." In *Content and Context: Essays on College Education*, edited by Carl Kaysen. New York: McGraw-Hill, 1973.

PART IV

Academic Work

8

Academic Work

Walter Doyle

The focus of this chapter is on the academic work that the curriculum of elementary and secondary schools requires students to do, how that work is organized and accomplished in classrooms, and what modifications in academic work are likely to increase student achievement. The chapter is divided into two major sections. The first section is devoted to an analysis of the intellectual demands inherent in different forms of academic work. Of special importance to this section is the recent research on the cognitive processes that underlie school tasks. The second section is directed to studies of how academic work is carried out in classroom environments. Particular attention is given in this section to the ways in which the social and the evaluative conditions in classrooms affect students' reactions to

The author acknowledges the resources made available at the R and D Center for Teacher Education, supported by the National Institute of Education, and the assistance of Oliver Bown in arranging time for this paper to be written. Kathy Carter provided valuable comments and suggestions. The opinions expressed herein do not necessarily reflect the position or policy of the National Commission on Excellence in Education or of the National Institute of Education, and no official endorsement by these offices should be inferred.

An earlier version of this chapter appeared in *Review of Educational Research* 53 (Summer 1983): 159–199. Reprinted by permission.

work. Both sections contain an analysis of the implications of this
research for improving the quality of academic work in classrooms
and thus increasing student achievement.

THE INTRINSIC CHARACTER OF ACADEMIC WORK

In broad terms the curriculum of the early elementary grades
reflects an emphasis on fundamental operations in reading and
mathematics, the so-called basic skills. In addition, pupils are exposed to information about social studies, music, nutrition, art, and
physical fitness. The emphasis on basic skills is apparent in the way
time is allocated in these grades. In the Beginning Teacher Evaluation Study, for example, it was found that approximately 55 percent of
the day in second- and fifth-grade classes was spent on language arts
and mathematics, and these figures are generally consistent with
those obtained in earlier studies (see Borg 1980; Rosenshine 1980).

As students progress through the grades, the emphasis gradually
shifts from basic skills to the content and the methods of inquiry
embodied in academic disciplines. Older students are expected to
learn algebra, history, biology, and literature rather than simply to
practice reading and computational skills. Also, in the middle school
or junior high school years, students begin to develop the capacity for
formal operational thought, that is, the ability to think abstractly and
use general strategies to analyze and solve problems. Clearly, schoolwork becomes more technical and more demanding over the years.

The Curriculum and Academic Tasks

This brief topical description of the curriculum provides a useful
overview of students' work at different grade levels, but it gives little
sense of the demands inherent in that work. To explain these demands
it is necessary to view the curriculum as a collection of *academic tasks*
(see Doyle 1980). The term *task* focuses attention on three aspects of
students' work: (a) the products students formulate, such as an
original essay or answers to a set of test questions; (b) the operations
that are used to generate the product, such as memorizing a list of
words or classifying examples of a concept; and (c) the "givens" or
resources available to students while they are generating a product,
such as a model of a finished essay supplied by the teacher or a fellow
student. Academic tasks, in other words, are defined by the answers

students are required to produce and the methods that can be used to obtain these answers.

The central point here is that tasks form the basic treatment unit in classrooms. This task perspective can be summarized in two basic propositions:

1. Students' academic work in school is defined by the academic tasks that are embedded in the content they encounter daily. Tasks regulate the selection of information and the choice of strategies for processing that information.
2. Students will learn what a task leads them to do, that is, they will acquire information and operations that are necessary to accomplish the tasks they encounter.

Types of Academic Tasks

Considerable effort has been recently given to defining the cognitive components of "real life" school tasks (see Anderson, Spiro, and Montague 1977). This work is part of a broader movement in psychology toward the analysis of the cognitive processes that underlie various aspects of human aptitude and performance. In this section some of the general concepts and findings emerging from this research will be reviewed to define more fully the character and range of learnings that are contained in the curriculum of elementary and secondary schooling.

General Categories of Academic Tasks. The academic tasks embedded in the curriculum can be differentiated into at least four general categories (Doyle 1980):

1. *Memory tasks* in which students are expected to recognize or reproduce information previously encountered (for example, memorize a list of spelling words or lines from a poem)
2. *Procedural or routine tasks* in which students are expected to apply a standardized and predictable formula or algorithm to generate answers (for example, solve a set of subtraction problems)
3. *Comprehension or understanding tasks* in which students are expected to (a) recognize transformed or paraphrased versions of information previously encountered, (b) apply procedures to new problems or

decide from among several procedures those that are applicable to a particular problem (for example, solve "word problems" in mathematics), or (c) draw inferences from previously encountered information or procedures (for example, make predictions about a chemical reaction or devise an alternative formula for squaring a number)

4. *Opinion tasks* in which students are expected to state a preference for something (for example, select a favorite short story)

These categories can be specified more fully by contrasting individual types of tasks.

Memory Versus Comprehension. The contrast between memory and comprehension tasks is based on a distinction between surface structure (the exact words printed on a page) and conceptual structure (the underlying network of propositions that define the meaning of a text). Memory tasks direct attention to the surface of a text and to the rote reproduction of words; comprehension tasks direct attention to the ideas embedded in the text and to an understanding of the meaning conveyed by the words and sentences.

Memorizing specific information does not necessarily lead to comprehension of a passage, and reading for comprehension does not necessarily enable the reader to recall words or facts. When a reader focuses primarily on memorizing facts or words, general ideas that are implied but not explicitly stated in the text are often missed. On the other hand, when a reader focuses primarily on the general ideas in a passage, specific facts or words are often forgotten. Thus, preparation for one type of task may not be suitable for the other. It is probably for this reason that students typically adjust study strategies to fit the type of the test they expect to take (McConkie 1977).

Procedural Versus Comprehension Tasks. A distinction between procedural tasks and comprehension tasks is especially clear in the field of mathematics. There is a difference between (a) knowing an algorithm, such as the computational steps for adding a column of numbers or multiplying two-digit numbers, and (b) knowing why the procedure works and when it should be used. Procedural tasks, then, are tasks that are accomplished by using a standard routine to produce answers. The work is typically quite predictable because the routines or algorithms consistently generate correct answers if no computational errors are made. Comprehension tasks, with respect to procedures, are tasks that are accomplished by knowing why a procedure works or when to use it.

Learning to use an algorithm does not necessarily enable one to understand it. Similarly, learning to understand why an algorithm works or when it should be used does not necessarily lead to computational proficiency (see Resnick and Ford 1981). It is often argued that extensive drill and practice with computational procedures is a prerequisite for acquiring an understanding of the material. The present analysis suggests, however, that accomplishing one task does not automatically lead to accomplishment of the other. Indeed, memorization, procedural, and comprehension processes may interfere with each other in accomplishing a given task.

Some Emerging Themes

Analyses in such curriculum areas as reading, mathematics, science, and writing have produced some common insights concerning the character of academic work and students' performance on tasks. A summary of some of this research follows.

Comprehension of Texts.   Work in modern cognitive psychology has had a major impact on our understanding of the processes involved in comprehending texts. A central premise of cognitive science is that comprehension is a *constructive* process (see Bransford and Franks 1976). According to this premise, meaning does not result from reception or rehearsal of information. Rather, understanding involves an active construction of a cognitive representation of events or concepts and their relationships in a specific context.

This constructive process is both interactive and sequential, involving information from the environment and from semantic memory (Rumelhart 1981). In comprehending prose, for example, a reader gradually builds a model of the semantic (meaning) structure of the passage. Information from the environment makes contact with information from semantic memory to suggest a likely interpretation. This interpretation establishes expectations about what subsequent events will likely be. These expectations, in turn, guide processing of new information in working memory, that is, they restrict the options for interpreting incoming data. Thus, the reader's interpretation of the word *saw* depends on whether the passage is about looking or cutting a board. Finally, the reader uses new information to update the initial interpretation as he progresses through a passage.

Cognitive psychologists argue that a person's knowledge of the world is organized into associational networks or schemata (see Rumelhart 1981). A schema is a relatively abstract representation of objects, episodes, actions, or situations that contains slots or variables into which specific instances of experience can be fit in a particular context.

This view of how knowledge is organized emphasizes the multiple associations of information in long-term memory. The word *apple*, for instance, is embedded in a network of associations referring to shape, color, texture, use, and relation to other foods. The word *brick*, however, elicits quite different associations. As words are encountered in a text, they activate associations that establish expectations and enable a reader to construct a propositional representation of the text in memory.

Schemata play an especially important role in accounting for ambiguities in passages or situations and in making inferences (see Trabasso 1981). Passages or episodes are seldom fully specified. In building a cognitive representation, therefore, a person must make inferences about associations and causality among concepts and events to complete the picture. Thus, in reading the sentence, "George entered a restaurant," a reader can use a restaurant schema to fill in what is likely to happen. Similarly, the sentences "Michael took the key from Steven" and "Steven called the police" permit the inference that Michael probably stole the key. This process of making inferences appears to play a central role in what is known as *semantic integration* of information from stories (see Paris 1975).

In addition to knowledge structures in long-term memory, readers use the structures embedded in texts to guide comprehension. For example, Meyer (1975) found that readers recall concepts high in the organizational structure or conceptual hierarchy of a passage better than they recall concepts lower in the hierarchy. These findings suggest that readers use the semantic organization of a text to select and process information. Similar results have been reported for story structures (Stein 1979). In other words, comprehension is not solely a matter of imposing personal knowledge on the world. Passages carry instructions that readers use to construct meaning.

From this perspective, then, the task of learning to read means learning to construct semantic representations of passages. Of course, beginning readers must also learn correspondences between letter and sounds, or "code-breaking" processes (see Beck 1977). That is, a reader must be able to recognize that printed symbols represent meaningful units in the language and then become proficient in interpreting these symbols rapidly in continuous text. These decoding operations are not completely separate from comprehension processes for two reasons. First, if a pupil does not know the code of letter-sound correspondences, then access to the content of a passage is obviously impossible. Second, comprehension of a passage often facilitates decoding by creating expectations about what items of information are likely to be presented next.

The Central Role of Prior Knowledge. Work on general comprehension skills in reading has been extended recently by research within particular subject matter domains such as science and mathematics (see Larkin 1981; Resnick and Ford 1981). Much of this work focuses on differences between the performance of experts and novices as well as on the effects of the preconceptions that novices bring to content. The purpose of this work is to identify the competencies and knowledge structures required for gaining mastery in these domains. These studies suggest strongly that performance in academic work, especially in technical subject matter areas, depends on domain-specific knowledge rather than on general problem-solving strategies alone. Thus, attention needs to focus on the schemata that students bring to their academic work. In the absence of appropriate knowledge structures, students are likely to (a) use memorizing strategies to accomplish tasks or (b) exhibit a discontinuity between what they are able to state about a field and what they actually do in solving problems (see Resnick and Ford 1981). In either case, they are not likely to understand what they are being taught.

Implications for Instructional Policy

Although considerably more basic and applied research in instructional psychology is needed, the way instructional designers conceptualize the task of improving instruction provides some promising directions that warrant consideration.

Direct Instruction in Cognitive Processes. One of the most common reactions to results of research in cognitive science is to recommend direct instruction in the processes used by expert readers, writers, mathematicians, or scientists (see Anderson 1977). For example, several investigators have been working to devise and test methods for teaching children to monitor their own comprehension and make inferences while reading (Collins and Smith 1980; Pearson and Camperell 1981). In essence, direct instruction means that academic tasks are carefully structured for students, and students are explicitly told how to accomplish these tasks and are systematically guided through a series of exercises that will enable them to master the tasks. Opportunities for directed practice are frequent, as are assessments to determine how well students are progressing and whether corrective feedback is needed. From this perspective, the role of cognitive science is to define the processes underlying subject-matter competency so that programs of direct instruction can be designed to foster these processes in students and thus improve the quality of academic work.

While the research cited above has certainly indicated that direct instruction can be effective for some outcomes, at least three important considerations are relevant to defining the substance of direct instruction and understanding its uses and potential limitations:

1. Direct instruction may not be possible for some areas because the processes that have been identified as necessary for learning tasks in those areas cannot be communicated in terms that are understandable to learners at a particular level of development or ability. We know, for instance, that riding a bicycle requires skill in balancing the equipment, but telling or showing someone how to balance a bicycle is virtually impossible.
2. Many processes that experts use, especially in academic disciplines at the secondary level, have not been identified. Indeed, there are probably certain inherent limits to our ability to specify the components of expertise and thus a limit to the application of direct instruction to foster competence in advanced academic work.
3. Research on performance differences has indicated that without strong guidance novices, young children, and low-ability students often fail to develop the strategies and higher-order executive routines that enable them to understand tasks or construct the goal structures necessary to accomplish tasks. Direct instruction that concentrates on specific operations for accomplishing a task will produce immediate effects, but it is not likely to engender the higher-level knowledge structures or strategies required for the flexible use of these operations. Successful instruction in decoding or vocabulary, for example, does not necessarily lead to proficiency in reading comprehension (see Becker and Gersten 1982).

A series of training studies by Brown and Campione (1977, 1980) has provided especially important insights into the effects of direct instruction. The studies began with a remedial program focusing on teaching young, low-ability children to use memorization strategies. The evidence from several sources had suggested that such learners have a production rather than a capacity deficiency. They are able to use mnemonic strategies, but in contrast to high-ability children, they do not use them spontaneously. With prompting, low-ability children will use mnemonic strategies, but this improvement is temporary and lasts only while the instructional prompts are available. Moreover, they do not use the memorization strategies flexibly to transfer to other memory tasks for which prompts are not supplied. There is, in other words, a "heart-pacer" effect in which performance is maintained only because the instructional program does most of the work for the students. The investigators found that the durability of strategies could be increased through training children in specific memorization strategies, although the amount of training required was much greater than originally expected. In addition, training to achieve durability *reduced* flexibility. The skills became welded to the items used in training and did not transfer to new items. Consistent with the general work in cognitive psychology, these findings suggested that low-ability children have special problems accessing what they know and flexibly using that knowledge. In addition, training that is focused on specific memorization skills does not produce flexibility.

In a redirection of their research, Brown and Campione (1977) produced some promising results for training in higher-level cognitive operations. Little durability was achieved for young children, but some flexibility was evident among older learners. Direct instruction in making inferences in reading (Hansen 1981) and estimating answers in arithmetic (Reys and Bestgen 1981) has had some success. An approach known as "attack strategy training," based on cognitive behavior modification, has been effective in helping low-ability students learn general strategies for solving arithmetic problems of a particular type (see Carnine and Stein 1981). It is important to realize, however, that direct instruction in higher-level processes and knowledge structures will probably take longer and have fewer immediate effects than will direct instruction aimed at lower-order skills.

Indirect Instruction in Cognitive Processes.   The push toward higher-level processes and toward meaning or understanding places direct instruction in a territory that is usually occupied by what might be called indirect instruction. Such instruction emphasizes the central role of self-discovery in fostering a sense of meaning and a purpose for learning academic content. From this perspective, students must be given ample opportunities for direct experience with content in order to derive generalizations and invent algorithms on their own. Such opportunities are clearly structured on the basis of what is known about an academic discipline and about human information processing. However, these opportunities are only partially formed in advance; gaps are left that students themselves must fill. In other words, the instructional program does only part of the work for students by opening up opportunities for making choices, decision making, discovery, and invention (for good analyses of the contrast between direct and indirect methods, see Resnick and Ford 1981; Shulman 1970).

An emphasis on invention in learning is certainly consistent with the basic premise in cognitive psychology that knowledge and understanding are constructed by individuals. But, as Resnick and Ford point out, there is less evidence that indirect instruction is the most suitable or efficient way to obtain this outcome deliberately. Two factors seem to limit the applicability to indirect methods. First, the ability level and background of the students are likely to be important influences on the effectiveness of indirect instruction. In a comprehensive review of research on the way the aptitudes of students interact with instructional methods, Cronbach and Snow (1977) found that high-ability students profited from unstructured teaching conditions that gave them choices in organizing and interpreting information. Low-achieving students, on the other hand, did not do well under these unstructured conditions or with indirect methods. One possible explanation for these findings is that low-ability students lack the general understandings and processes that enable them to formulate their own generalizations or procedures necessary to accomplish academic tasks under conditions of indirect instruction. As a result, the "treatment" does not actually occur, that is, they do not have the opportunity to practice higher-level operations.

Second, invention does not automatically lead to usable procedures or an understanding of concepts and principles. Students also invent mistakes as they encounter obstacles in learning. Thus, while increasing the opportunity for invention, indirect teaching also increases the chance for students to develop erroneous strategies for finding solutions and misconceptions of content. Special attention in indirect teaching must therefore be given to monitoring and correcting the inferences students actually make.

Summary

The existing research in cognitive psychology leads to the following general recommendations for improving the quality of academic work:

1. Direct instruction in identified cognitive processes and knowledge structures is probably more appropriate than indirect methods for teaching novices, low-achieving students, and pupils in the early elementary grades.
2. Direct instruction that is focused on specific skills is likely to have few long-term consequences unless combined with instruction, either direct or indirect, in higher-level executive processes and knowledge structures for representing tasks and selecting solution strategies. Thus, instruction in decoding needs to be combined with instruction in comprehension monitoring to foster an ability to read independently. If specific skills are taught in isolation, students can develop either magical thinking or an excessive concern for details, both of which interfere with accomplishment of tasks and learning.
3. Indirect instruction is one way of providing practice in higher-order executive routines and the use of knowledge structures to represent problems. Indeed, even in direct instruction some degree of "unstructuredness" is essential to ascertain whether students really understand how and when to use their knowledge and skills. In other words, overly explicit signals or programs for solution strategies obviate the need for students to employ executive routines, and thus students are not able to practice these higher-level processes or demonstrate mastery of them. In addition, many operations that are necessary to achieve expertise in academic areas either have not yet been identified or are difficult to formulate into clearly teachable propositions. In such cases, the only alternative is to allow students to experience content so that they can invent procedures and construct knowledge structures on their own. Such experiences obviously need to be structured in ways that seem at least logically related to intended outcomes so that invention will be productive.
4. Resnick and Ford (1981) have observed that "transitions in com-

petence that emerge without direct instruction may be more common in children's educational development than we have thought up to now" (p. 82). That is, students do not simply learn what is taught but invent their own algorithms and conceptions of content whether instruction is direct or indirect. This propensity to invent can have both advantages and disadvantages. As indicated, invention enables students to learn routines and concepts that are difficult to teach directly. At the same time, invention can lead to "buggy" algorithms and misconceptions of content. This possibility underscores the central role of corrective feedback in learning and the need to base that feedback on an understanding of the processes that lead students to make mistakes.

5. Finally, accomplishing academic tasks is not solely a matter of general strategies. Especially in the upper grades, students need domain-specific knowledge in a discipline to do academic work.

ACADEMIC WORK IN CLASSROOMS

In this chapter, academic work has thus far been discussed in isolation from the classroom context within which it is normally carried out. This isolation is clearly artificial, and this artificiality is especially serious if one is interested in understanding and improving classroom practices. To remedy this situation, a brief summary of recent classroom studies is provided (for more information, see Doyle 1983, 1986).

Classroom Complexity and Academic Work

Research on classroom events and processes suggests that academic work is transformed fundamentally when it is placed in the complex social system of a classroom. The character of these transformations can be summarized as follows:

1. Academic tasks organize students' information processing in classrooms. Whether students pay attention to the teacher's questions or participate in a classroom discussion would seem to depend on the relationship of these events to the accomplishment of tasks. Similarly, if the presentation of a procedure in class focuses on understanding how the procedure was derived and why it works, but the assignment is to solve twenty-five computational problems, then attention is likely to be directed to learning the computational

steps necessary to produce answers efficiently. In other words, the answers a teacher actually accepts define the real tasks in classrooms.

2. In classrooms, teachers are required to think about more than academic tasks in planning and conducting instruction (see Yinger 1980). Because classrooms are crowded, teachers are faced with the task of organizing students into working units and maintaining this organization across changing conditions for several months. In addition, they must establish and enforce rules, arrange for the orderly distribution of supplies and materials, collect and evaluate students' papers, pace events to fit bell schedules as well as the interests of students, and respond rapidly to a large number of immediate contingencies. And all of these functions must be performed in an environment of considerable complexity and unpredictability. In addition to structuring and monitoring academic work, therefore, a teacher must be able to gain and maintain the cooperation of students in activities that fill the available time (Doyle 1985).

3. Academic work in classrooms is connected to a reward structure. Students' answers, therefore, are not just evidence of having accomplished academic tasks. They also count as points earned in an accountability system. Accountability, in turn, drives the task system in classrooms. As a result, students are especially sensitive to cues that signal accountability (for example, announcements about tests) or define how tasks are to be accomplished (see Doyle and Carter 1984; King 1980). In addition, students tend to take seriously that work for which they are held accountable. If no answers are required or if any answer is acceptable, then few students will actually attend to the content. In some instances, answering becomes the task in classrooms. That is, student attention is directed to the answering event itself rather than to the content. And it appears that students sometimes invent strategies for producing answers in ways that circumvent the information-processing demands of academic work; students might, for example, copy, offer provisional answers, request that the teacher make instructions more explicit or provide models to follow closely, and so forth.

4. Tasks that involve understanding and higher-level cognitive processes are difficult for teachers and students to accomplish in classrooms (see Doyle and Carter 1984). Such tasks pose high levels of ambiguity and risk for students, who often respond by

delaying the start of work or by negotiating to increase either the explicitness of a teacher's instructions or the teacher's generosity in grading final products. Teachers, in turn, face complex management problems resulting from slowdowns in the flow of activity and from the fact that a significant portion of the students may not be able to accomplish the assigned work. As tasks move toward memory or routine algorithms, these problems are reduced substantially. The central point is that the tasks that cognitive psychology suggests have the greatest long-term consequences for improving the quality of academic work are precisely those that are the most difficult to manage in classrooms.

5. Because tasks are administered to groups and performance on these tasks is often evaluated publicly, teachers are often under pressure to adjust standards and pace to levels suitable for a majority of students (see Arlin and Westbury 1976). To make this adjustment, teachers often avoid comprehension tasks that typically require considerable skill to accomplish. Moreover, prompts given to low-ability students are also available to other students who may not need such help. As a result, some students end up working on tasks that are considerably below their abilities. Finally, it would seem difficult to maintain individual accountability in a group setting. It is always possible that a student can copy answers from peers or slip through the accountability system in other ways.

6. The need to manage group contingencies and evaluate answers often appears to focus the attention of teachers and students on getting work done rather than on the quality or meaning of work (see Anderson 1981). In their analysis of case studies in science education, Stake and Easley (1978), for example, observed that content goals often appeared to have little salience for either students or teachers. Students seemed primarily interested in grades as intrinsically valuable: "They did not think of themselves as mastering a certain body of knowledge, but more as mastering (and of course not mastering) those things being required by the teacher or the test. The knowledge domain was not a reality—it was a great arbitrary abstraction" (chap. 15, p. 29). In addition, several investigators have recently noted that many teachers spend very little time explicitly telling students how to accomplish academic work. Rather, they assign exercises and then monitor students as they work (see Duffy and McIntyre 1982; Durkin 1979).

7. Finally, the classroom makes academic work especially complex for novices, young children, and low-achieving students, that is, those who are likely to find academic tasks difficult to accomplish anyway. Classroom studies also indicate that low-achieving and immature students are often grouped together for instruction, particularly in reading in the early elementary grades. Such groups are typically difficult for teachers to manage, and the quality of teaching in such groups is frequently low (see a review by Cazden 1981). Any effort to improve the quality of academic work in schools must necessarily address the problem of effectively teaching these students.

Implications for Instructional Policy

Descriptions of classroom realities often evoke the proposal that the classroom system needs to be replaced or fundamentally altered. Such proposals, however, do not seem to have much merit. Replacing classrooms is not likely to happen because there will always be fewer adults than students in schools. Once students are grouped and assigned to teachers for specific periods of time, classrooms are necessary regardless of the format used for activities or the size and shape of rooms. Whatever alternatives are proposed for classrooms, it will still be necessary to manage groups of students through time and space and cope with the ambiguity and risk associated with academic tasks. The central problem is to find ways to make classrooms more productive in the face of the realities of such environments. In this concluding section some possible ways to achieve this goal are reviewed.

Instructional Materials. Studies of classrooms indicate that teachers often rely on instructional materials to carry out the academic tasks system. Students spend a good deal of their time working on exercises and reading passages from textbooks and workbooks. Thus, academic work is defined in large measure by commercially prepared materials. Research also suggests that these materials are often poorly designed and written (Anderson, Armbruster, and Kantor 1980; Beck and McCaslin 1978). As a result, students are sometimes prevented from learning the content because of difficulties inherent in the text rather than in the complexity of the academic discipline or the basic skill being mastered. It is reasonable to propose, therefore, that careful attention be given to academic tasks in the preparation of instructional materials and that more research be conducted to find ways to design such materials and test their efficacy. Some preliminary attempts are being made to design materials in such areas as comprehension monitoring. Efforts are also being made to improve the design of workbooks used in elementary reading (Osborn 1981) and to help students learn to understand the textbooks they read (Adams, Carnine, and Gersten 1982). As more is discovered about the cognitive dimensions of academic work and the processes of learning from texts, the possibility of improving instructional materials should increase substantially.

Training in Managing Tasks. Additional knowledge about academic tasks and how they are carried out in classrooms will increase the possibilities for training teachers to manage academic work more efficiently and effectively. On the basis of present knowledge, at least two areas warrant special attention in teacher preparation. First, accountability appears to be a central component in the academic task system. If answers are not required or any answer is acceptable in a particular area, then students are not likely to take the work seriously, especially in upper elementary and secondary grades. It would seem essential, then, that teachers learn the importance of accountability and explore a variety of ways in which accountability can be handled creatively in classrooms. Second, teachers need to think about curriculum content in cognitive terms and become aware of the various paths students invent to get around task demands in accomplishing academic work, such as delaying, eliciting overly explicit prompts, and so forth. With this awareness, teachers can plan instruction and tests that emphasize understanding rather than the memorization of isolated facts. In addition, they can begin to devise ways to sustain task demands and thus have students use the cognitive processes that are intended for task accomplishment.

It is important to reiterate that the tasks that cognitive science indicates are likely to have long-term consequences, such as those involving higher-level executive routines, are probably the most difficult to manage in classrooms. Tasks that leave room for student judgment are often hard to evaluate and are more likely to evoke attempts by students to circumvent task demands. Special attention needs to be given to managing such tasks if the quality of academic work is to be improved.

In addition to managing academic tasks, teachers also face the larger problem of establishing and maintaining cooperation in classroom activities. Unless skills in this area are well developed, a teacher will have little time to think about academic tasks or little freedom to arrange classroom events to sustain a variety of types of tasks. Indeed, without highly developed management skills, a teacher is likely to rely on memory and routine tasks that typically elicit cooperation from more students, especially those who are inclined to disrupt activities. Major progress has been made in recent years in understanding how classroom management is accomplished (Doyle 1985) and in testing procedures for helping teachers learn these processes (Emmer, Sanford, Evertson, Clements, and Martin 1981; Emmer, Evertson, Sanford, Clements, and Worsham 1982). Additional research is needed, however, to extend this work to the management of academic work (see Doyle, Sanford, Clements, French, and Emmer 1983).

Direct and Indirect Instruction. Research on effective teaching has generally indicated that, at least in basic skill areas in elementary and junior high schools, high levels of student engagement are associated with high achievement and that direct instruction in which the teacher actively manages academic work is likely to sustain engagement (Rosenshine 1983). From the perspective of classroom management, direct instruction is efficient. If academic activities are carefully and clearly organized and the teacher has a central role in the classroom, then he or she will usually be in a position to monitor classroom events and intervene early to stop disruptions. In addition, engagement is generally high in teacher-led instruction so that the task of management will be relatively easy. Indirect instruction, on the other hand, is typically more difficult to manage because of resistance from students and because the pace and rhythm of events are inherently slower.

The quality of the time students spend engaged in academic work depends on the tasks they accomplish and the extent to which they understand what they are doing. It is essential, therefore, that direct instruction include explicit attention to meaning and not simply focus on engagement in academic work as an end in itself (see Good 1982). Moreover, some curricular areas, especially in the upper grades, may not lend themselves to direct instruction. It is in these areas that special attention needs to be given to task management.

Finally, emphasis must be placed on the quality of academic work for low-ability and immature students. These students are likely to find academic work difficult, and their problems increase as such work is embedded in a complex classroom environment. Grouping these students together for instruction often increases the complexity of the task environment for the students and creates formidable management problems for teachers. In the end, the quality of teaching suffers. The practices that lead to such grouping need to be examined carefully, and alternatives for working with low-ability students in classrooms need to be explored.

CONCLUSION

The analysis in this chapter suggests that properties of the classroom environment shape academic work in fundamental ways. Classrooms provide a continuity of experience as well as particular resources that can be used to accomplish academic tasks. In addition, accountability by students for their work drives the academic task system in classrooms. If answers are not required or if any answer is acceptable, then the task system is suspended, and little academic work will be accomplished. In turn, the nature of the answers a teacher accepts and the routes a teacher allows for getting answers define the tasks students are required to accomplish. Finally, students invent and use strategies for managing the ambiguity and risk associated wtih academic tasks when they are embedded in an accountability system, and these strategies also affect the nature and quality of academic work.

Any changes in the classroom system will continue to face these inherent pressures. Major improvements in academic work clearly depend on further inquiry into the event structures of classrooms and how work is accomplished in these environments.

REFERENCES

Adams, Abby; Carnine, Douglas W.; and Gersten, Russell. "Instructional Strategies for Studying Content Area Texts in the Intermediate Grades." *Reading Research Quarterly* 18 (Fall 1982): 27–55.

Anderson, L. M. "Student Responses to Seatwork: Implications for the Study of Students' Cognitive Processing." Paper presented at the annual meeting of the American Educational Research Association, Los Angeles, 1981.

Anderson, Richard C. "The Notion of the Schemata and the Educational Enterprise: General Discussion of the Conference." In *Schooling and the Acquisition of Knowledge*, edited by Richard C. Anderson, Rand J. Spiro, and William E. Montague. Hillsdale, N. J.: Lawrence Erlbaum Associates, 1977.

Anderson, Richard C.; Spiro, Rand J.; and Montague, William E., eds. *Schooling and the Acquisition of Knowledge*. Hillsdale, N. J.: Lawrence Erlbaum Associates, 1977.

Anderson, Thomas H.; Armbruster, Bonnie B.; and Kantor, Robert N. *How Clearly*

Written Are Children's Textbooks? Or, of Bladderworts and Alpha. Reading Education Report 16. Urbana: Center for the Study of Reading, University of Illinois, 1980.

Arlin, Marshall N., and Westbury, Ian. "The Leveling Effect of Teacher Pacing of Science Content Mastery." *Journal of Research in Science Teaching* 13 (May 1976): 213–219.

Beck, Isabel L. "Comprehension during the Acquisition of Decoding Skills." In *Cognition, Curriculum, and Comprehension,* edited by John T. Guthrie. Newark, Del.: International Reading Association, 1977.

Beck, Isabel L., and McCaslin, Ellen S. *An Analysis of Dimensions that Affect the Development of Code-breaking Ability in Eight Beginning Reading Programs.* Pittsburgh, Penn.: Learning Research and Development Center, University of Pittsburgh, 1978.

Becker, Wesley C., and Gersten, Russell. "A Follow-up of Follow Through: The Later Effects of the Direct Instruction Model on Children in Fifth and Sixth Grades." *American Educational Research Journal* 19:1 (1982): 75–92.

Borg, W. R. "Time and School Learning." In *Time to Learn,* edited by Carolyn Denham and Ann Lieberman. Washington, D. C.: National Institute of Education, 1980.

Bransford, J. D., and Franks, J. J. "Toward a Framework for Understanding Learning." In *The Psychology of Learning and Motivation: Advances in Research and Theory.* Vol. 10. New York: Academic Press, 1976.

Brown, Ann L., and Campione, Joseph C. *Memory Strategies in Learning: Training Children to Study Strategically.* Tech. Report 22. Urbana: Center for the Study of Reading, University of Illinois, 1977.

Brown, Ann L., and Campione, Joseph C. *Inducing Flexible Thinking: Problem of Access.* Tech. Report 156. Urbana: Center for the Study of Reading, University of Illinois, 1980.

Carnine, Douglas W., and Stein, Marcy. "Organizational Strategies and Practice Procedures for Teaching Basic Facts." *Journal for Research in Mathematics Education* 12 (January 1981): 65–69.

Cazden, Courtney B. "Social Context of Learning To Read." In *Comprehension and Teaching: Research Reviews,* edited by John T. Guthrie. Newark, Del.: International Reading Association, 1981.

Collins, Allan, and Smith, Edward E. *Teaching the Process of Reading Comprehension.* Tech. Report 182. Urbana: Center for the Study of Reading, University of Illinois, 1980.

Cronbach, Lee J., and Snow, Richard E. *Aptitudes and Instructional Methods: Handbook for Research on Interactions.* New York: Irvington, 1977.

Doyle, Walter. *Student Mediating Responses in Teaching Effectiveness.* Final Report, NIE-G-76-0099. Denton: North Texas State University, 1980.

Doyle, Walter. "Academic Work." *Review of Educational Research* 53 (Summer 1983): 159–199.

Doyle, Walter. "Classroom Organization and Management." In *Handbook of Research on Teaching.* 3d ed. Edited by Merle C. Wittrock. New York: Macmillan, 1986.

Doyle, Walter, and Carter, Kathy. "Academic Tasks in Classrooms." *Curriculum Inquiry* 14 (Summer 1984): 129–149.

Doyle, Walter; Sanford, Julie P.; Clements, Barbara S.; French, B. S.; and Emmer,

Edmund T. *Managing Academic Tasks: Interim Report of the Junior High School Study.* R&D Report 6189. Austin: Research and Development Center for Teacher Education, University of Texas, 1983.

Duffy, Gerald G., and McIntyre, Lonnie D. "Naturalistic Study of Instructional Assistance in Primary Grade Reading." *Elementary School Journal* 83 (September 1982): 14–23.

Durkin, Dolores. "What Classroom Observations Reveal about Reading Comprehension Instruction." *Reading Research Quarterly* 14:4 (1979): 481–533.

Emmer, Edmund T.; Evertson, Carolyn; Sanford, Julie; Clements, Barbara S.; and Worsham, Murray. *Organizing and Managing the Junior High School Classroom.* R&D Report 6151. Austin: Research and Development Center for Teacher Education, University of Texas, 1982.

Emmer, Edmund; Sanford, Julie; Evertson, Carolyn; Clements, Barbara; and Martin, Jeanne. *The Classroom Management Improvement Study: An Experiment in Elementary School Classrooms.* R&D Report 6050. Austin: Research and Development Center for Teacher Education, University of Texas, 1981.

Good, Thomas. *Classroom Research: What We Know and Need to Know.* R&D Report 9018. Austin: Research and Development Center for Teacher Education, University of Texas, 1982.

Hansen, Jane. "The Effects of Inference Framing and Practice on Young Children's Reading Comprehension." *Reading Research Quarterly* 16 (1981): 391–417.

King, L. H. *Student Thought Processes and the Expectancy Effect.* Research Report 80-1-8. Edmonton, Canada: Center for Research in Teaching, University of Alberta, 1980.

Larkin, Jill H. "Enriching Formal Knowledge: A Model for Learning to Solve Textbook Physics Problems." In *Cognitive Skills and Their Acquisition*, edited by John R. Anderson. Hillsdale, N. J.: Lawrence Erlbaum Associates, 1981.

McConkie, George W. "Learning from Text." In *Review of Research in Education.* Vol 5. Edited by Lee Shulman. Itasca, Ill.: F. E. Peacock, 1977.

Meyer, Bonnie J. F. "The Organization of Prose and Its Effects on Memory." In *North Holland Studies in Theoretical Politics.* Vol. 1. New York: American Elsevier, 1975.

Osborn, Jean. *The Purposes, Uses, and Contents of Workbooks and Some Guidelines for Teachers and Publishers.* Reading Education Report 27. Urbana: Center for Study of Reading, University of Illinois, 1981.

Paris, S. G. "Integration and Inference in Children's Comprehension and Memory. In *Cognitive Theory.* Vol. 1. Edited by Frank Restle, Richard M. Shiffrin, N. John Castellan, Harold R. Lindman, and D. B. Pisoni. Hillsdale, N. J.: Lawrence Erlbaum Associates, 1975.

Pearson, P. David, and Camperell, Kaybeth. "Comprehension of Text Structures." In *Comprehension and Teaching: Research Reviews*, edited by John T. Guthrie. Newark, Del.: International Reading Association, 1981.

Resnick, Lauren, and Ford, Wendy W. *The Psychology of Mathematics for Instruction.* Hillsdale, N. J.: Lawrence Erlbaum Associates, 1981.

Reys, Robert E., and Bestgen, Barbara J. "Teaching and Assessing Computational Estimation Skills." *Elementary School Journal* 82 (November 1981): 117–127.

Rosenshine, Barak. "How Time Is Spent in Elementary Classrooms." In *Time to*

Learn, edited by Carolyn Denham and Ann Lieberman. Washington, D. C.: National Institute of Education, 1980.

Rosenshine, Barak. "Teaching Functions in Instructional Programs." *Elementary School Journal* 83 (March 1983): 335–351.

Rumelhart, David E. "Schemata: The Building Blocks of Cognition." In *Comprehension in Teaching: Research Reviews*, edited by John T. Guthrie. Newark, Del.: International Reading Association, 1981.

Shulman, Lee S. "Psychology and Mathematics Education." In *Mathematics Education*, edited by Edward G. Begle. Sixty-ninth Yearbook of the National Society for the Study of Education, Part 1. Chicago: University of Chicago Press, 1970.

Stake, Robert E., and Easley, Jack A. *Case Studies in Science Education*, vols. 1 and 2. Urbana: Center for Instructional Research and Curriculum Evaluation and Committee on Culture and Cognition, University of Illinois, 1978.

Stein, Nancy L. "How Children Understand Stories: A Development Analysis." In *Current Topics in Early Childhood Education*. Vol. 2. Edited by Lilian G. Katz. Norwood, N. J.: Ablex, 1979.

Trabasso, Thomas. "On the Making of Inferences during Reading and Their Assessment." In *Comprehension in Teaching: Research Reviews*, edited by John T. Guthrie. Newark, Del.: International Reading Association, 1981.

Yinger, Robert J. "A Study of Teacher Planning." *Elementary School Journal* 80 (January 1980): 107–127.

9

Children's Motivation to Learn

Deborah J. Stipek

Learning is an active process that requires conscious and deliberate effort from the student. If students are to obtain maximum benefit from the curriculum, educators must provide a learning context that maintains students' motivation to engage in learning activities. This chapter addresses two questions: (1) What are the motivational characteristics of a child who is most likely to achieve at his or her optimal level? and (2) What kind of educational environment fosters these motivational characteristics?

FROM REINFORCEMENT TO COGNITION

Until about the early 1970s, a reinforcement model of motivation dominated the literature in educational psychology. This model assumes that the frequency of a desired behavior increases if an individual is rewarded for the behavior, and the frequency of undesired behavior decreases if the individual is not rewarded or is punished for it. At the practical level a rather extensive educational "technology" has developed out of reinforcement theory. In many educational settings, elaborate token economies are employed to motivate children; this practice prevails especially in programs for learning-handicapped or behaviorally disordered children. Verbal praise or criticism, giving or withdrawing privileges, and grades are common rewards and punishments found in all types of educational settings.

The impact of reinforcement theory on American education is understandable for the simple reason that reinforcers are often effective in controlling achievement behavior. With or without special training, most teachers find that the promise of a reward or the threat of punishment can powerfully affect children's behavior in the classroom, at least temporarily. When certain principles based on recent refinements in the application of reinforcement theory are followed, rewards can be effectively used to elicit from children behaviors that lead to achievement without long-term negative effects (Brophy 1981). Behavioral methods have been particularly successful with children who behave extremely maladaptively in school settings (Haring and Phillips 1972).

Problems with Reward and Punishment

There are, however, potential hazards in overreliance on rewards. The traditional rewards used in most American classrooms are not universally effective. Grades, for example, are ineffective with children in early elementary school because young children have not yet learned that our culture values high grades. Furthermore, unless the value that teachers place on grades is reinforced by parents and peers, children of any age are unlikely to work for such a symbolic reward. A particularly difficult problem is finding an effective means to reinforce the achievement behaviors of adolescents, who are often more concerned with popularity, athletics, or other nonacademic activities than they are with their grades. Indeed, among some rebellious or alienated adolescents, for whom success in school is explicitly devalued, high grades may be perceived as an embarrassment rather than as a reward.

A second problem with external reinforcement is that its effectiveness is often short-lived. Rewards may be effective in eliciting behaviors, but behaviors will occur only under conditions in which rewards are given. When a reward is withdrawn, the desired behavior occurs less frequently or ceases altogether.

These limitations of rewards become increasingly important as children advance in grade in school. The curriculum in the early elementary school grades is generally broken down into small units with frequent opportunities for reinforcement. In the upper grades, assignments are generally larger and less frequent, and they span over a longer time period. Compare, for example, typical language arts assignments for elementary and high school students. The younger students may be given in one day as many as three short assignments for which they can receive reinforcement. High school students are more likely to be asked to write a theme based on assigned reading once every week or two. Consequently, while young children can be reinforced for every sub-component of the academic task, older students must go through many steps without any reinforcement.

For college students, many rewards (for example, obtaining a degree, getting into graduate school, getting a good job) are far removed from the immediate situation in which achievement is required. Even within a given course, a midterm and a final examination are often the only "products" of a semester of academic labor that the professor sees, and consequently, these products are the only "behaviors" of the students that can be reinforced. For many students who are accustomed to being reinforced for every successful academic effort, the promise of such distant rewards will not induce day-to-day activities directed toward achievement.

Rewarding achievement in the classroom may also negatively affect children's desire to pursue achievement-related activities, such as reading outside school. If these activities are done to obtain praise from the teacher or a good grade, the child may overlook the intrinsic value or pleasure that derives from learning activities outside the classroom.

Punishment can also have negative consequences for achievement behavior. Fear of punishment, such as public humiliation or low grades, can cause anxiety, which if extreme can seriously hinder learning (Hill 1984). Such fear can cause attentional problems or, if severe, can block thinking altogether.

Many children spend considerably more energy trying to avoid punishment than they do trying to understand material or learn new skills for which they might receive rewards. Thus, for example, they avoid asking questions or volunteering answers for fear of revealing their ignorance. Or they turn in completed assignments with answers that they know are incorrect rather than taking time to try to figure out the correct answers; they have learned that punishment for not turning in an assignment on time is more severe than is punishment for poor performance. Most of these failure-avoiding behaviors accomplish the student's immediate goal of minimizing punishment, but they are self-defeating in the long run.

These are some of the practical problems related to overreliance on rewards and punishments in educational settings. Revisions in reinforcement theory itself suggest further reasons for reconsidering current educational practice based primarily on traditional reinforcement theory. These theoretical revisions, which are discussed in the next section, have important implications for the use of reinforcements in the classroom.

The Discovery of Cognitions

Traditionally, reinforcement theory was rooted in a mechanistic view of behavior. Individuals' perceptions, beliefs, or other cognitions were not considered relevant. Behavior was explained entirely by the individual's history of rewards and punishments for achievement efforts.

In recent years, theorists have introduced various cognitions into traditional reinforcement models. For example, Rotter (1966) explains that it is not the reward itself that increases the frequency of behavior, but an individual's *beliefs* about what brought about the reward. If individuals do not perceive rewards as contingent on their own behavior, they will not expect the behavior to be followed by a reward in the future, and consequently, the reward will not influence their future behavior. For example, if a child knows that everyone in the class received an A on a particular assignment, he or she may believe that the teacher gives A's indiscriminantly, regardless of the quality of the product or the amount of effort exerted. The child may not try very hard on a similar assignment in the future because the child does not believe the derived reward (the A) is contingent on his or her behavior.

Rotter refers to the individual's beliefs regarding the contingency of reinforcement as "locus of control." Briefly, internal control refers to an individual's belief that an event or outcome is contingent on his or her own behavior or on relatively stable personal characteristics such as ability. The belief that an outcome is caused by factors beyond the individual's control (for example, luck, task difficulty, biased teacher) has been labeled external control.

Rotter claims that a generalized belief system, developed out of past experience in similar situations, influences an individual's achievement behavior, and he has spawned a large body of research that supports his claim (for reviews, see Lefcourt 1976; Stipek and Weisz 1981). Thus, children who have repeatedly experienced failure regardless of the amount of effort they have exerted may believe that success is not contingent on effort, even in situations in which effort would actually lead to success. A child's generalized belief that success is not contingent on effort may override information to the contrary in any specific situation. Early school experiences can therefore have long-term effects on motivation by influencing young children's developing belief systems.

Recently, attribution theorists have refined and elaborated on Rotter's concept of locus of control. Weiner (1979) claims that effort and ability attributions, which are internal and are treated equivalently by Rotter, have different behavioral implications because individuals can control their effort but not their ability. Ability is also generally perceived as a relatively stable cause of behavior, whereas effort can vary from situation to situation. Children who believe that their low grades result from their own lack of effort can expect to be rewarded if they increase their efforts in the future. Children who attribute their low grades to lack of ability and believe that low ability is permanent and out of their control will assume that success is unattainable regardless of the amount of effort they expend. Thus, Weiner distinguishes between two kinds of internal causes of achievement outcomes—controllable, unstable causes such as effort, and uncontrollable, stable causes such as ability. The control and stability dimensions that Weiner added to Rotter's original internal-external dimension allow for much more refined predictions of children's behavior based on their beliefs about the cause of reinforcements they might receive.

The other major difference between Rotter's and Weiner's analyses of achievement-related cognitions is that Rotter emphasizes generalized beliefs that develop from an individual's experience in achievement settings; he assumes these beliefs will hold regardless of the situation. Weiner admits that relatively stable differences in individual's perceptions of the cause of their achievement outcomes may occur, but he emphasizes how the situation may affect individuals' attributional judgments. He claims that individuals make judgments about the causes of their achievement outcomes primarily on the basis of information from the current achievement situation. The information includes the difficulty of the task, others' performances, and the individual's analysis of his or her own competence at that particular task; all of this information affects the individual's judgment. Past experience in similar achievement contexts is relevant, but it is only one of many factors. Weiner's view is somewhat more optimistic than Rotter's since it suggests that we should be able to change children's causal attributions, whatever their previous experiences in achievement contexts, by manipulating current environmental variables.

Dweck and her colleagues have studied how beliefs about the causes of success and failure affect achievement behavior . For example, Dweck and Reppucci (1973) observed that some children with a history of poor performance in school persist and actively pursue alternative solutions to a task when they encounter failure, while the performance of others undergoes marked deterioration in persistence or quality—what they refer to as "learned helplessness." Why do children respond differently to the same experiences of failure? Consistent with Weiner's attributional analysis of achievement behavior, Dweck claims that learned helplessness in achievement situations occurs when students perceive failure to be independent of their behavior. This perception of failure as insurmountable is associated with attributions of failure to stable, uncontrollable factors, such as lack of ability. This attribution results in seriously impaired performance. In contrast, positive achievement behavior tends to be associated with attributions of failure to factors that are in the child's control, particularly to lack of effort.

Dweck and others have developed educational programs designed specifically to alter children's attributions of the causes of their failure from ability to effort (see, for example, Dweck 1975, Schunk 1982). These programs attempt to shift children's analysis of task situations from, "I can't do this no matter how hard I try, I'm just not smart enough to learn it," to "I can do it if I try because I know I'm smart enough."

The most important determinant of children's interpretation of the cause of their sucesses and failures is their perception of their own competence, that is, whether they believe that they possess the necessary ability to obtain some form of desired reinforcement. A child who believes that he or she lacks the basic ability will also believe that no amount of effort will bring about a positive outcome. Bandura (1982) uses the term *self-efficacy* to refer to an individual's perception that he or she possesses the prerequisite ability for effective effort. He and his colleagues have demonstrated the importance of self-efficacy for adaptive behavior for clinical populations (especially phobics) as well as for individuals in learning situations. Schunk has further shown that low-achieving children's self-efficacy, and consequently their learning, can be enhanced by offering rewards specifically contingent on mastery (Schunk 1983a), or by explicitly attributing children's successful performance to their ability (Schunk 1983b).

Confidence in their ability to complete tasks, in addition to the amount of effort they exert, bears on children's strategies and attention while performing tasks. Self-confidence is, for example, related to a distinction Nicholls and Miller (1984) make between "task-involvement" and "ego-involvement." When task-involved, the individual's attention is focused on the process of completing a task; when ego-involved, attention is focused on the self and especially on external evaluations of the self.

The practical implications of this distinction are illustrated in a study by Peterson and Swing (1982). They observed children participating in a lesson on probability and later interviewed them individually. One of the students, Melissa, looked as if she were paying good attention throughout the lesson. However, when subsequently asked what she was thinking about during the lesson, she responded: "Well, I was mostly thinking. . . I was making a fool of myself" (p. 486). Melissa's attention was on herself and not on learning about probability. In contrast, task-oriented Jani responded to the same question by describing in some detail the strategies she used to solve the problems. In a later study these researchers suggest that negative self-evaluations while working on tasks are seriously debilitating to student achievement (Peterson, Swing, and Waas 1984).

In summary, two major changes in traditional assumptions about how to motivate children to obtain the optimum benefits from schooling have occurred in recent years. First, evidence has mounted suggesting that continuous use of rewards and punishment can actually have the opposite of the intended effect of increasing certain achievement-related behaviors—at least in the long run. Long-term negative effects of reliance on external reinforcements can occur because children become dependent on the reinforcements and are consequently not motivated to engage in appropriate achievement-related activities when external reinforcement is absent. Second, it is not the reinforcement per se that influences children's behavior in achievement settings. Rather, children's cognitions, beliefs, and values determine their behavior. It is the child's *interpretation* of the situation, not the objective facts, that determines his or her behavior.

These modifications in traditional reinforcement theory suggest that rewards and punishments should be used sparingly in the classroom, although they should not (indeed, could not) be eliminated altogether. This is troublesome for most educators who have relied almost exclusively on external reinforcement to control children's achievement behavior. Fortunately, alternative strategies are available for maintaining children's enthusiasm for academic tasks. We examine next an intrinsic motivational system (as opposed to one that is based on external rewards and punishments) that many motivational theorists currently believe is relevant to achievement behavior in the classroom. Later, we will consider principles for the effective use of external reinforcement, when it is necessary.

INTRINSIC MOTIVATION

In 1959 White published a now classic paper challenging the notion that external reinforcement is necessary for learning to occur. He presents evidence suggesting that a phylogenetic characteristic of the human species is an intrinsic need to feel competent and that such behaviors as exploration, curiosity, and mastery attempts are best explained by this innate motivational force. Successful mastery of learning activities is naturally reinforcing because this results in feelings of competence. This motive is activated in any situation that provides opportunities for developing new competencies and is therefore particularly relevant to formal educational settings.

White's defense of an intrinsic competence motive rests partly on its evolutionary adaptive value, since it impels the organism to deal more effectively with the environment. Piaget (1952) also makes an evolutionary argument for his similar claim that humans are naturally inclined to practice newly developing competencies ("schemes" in his own terminology). Other theorists have extended in various directions White's and Piaget's basic notions regarding intrinsic competence motivation (Deci 1975; Harter 1981; Hunt 1971).

All of these theorists stress that external rewards are often unnecessary for mastery or for learning behavior to occur. Indeed, as we mentioned in the previous section of this chapter, some motivation theorists argue that external reinforcement can have a negative effect on behavior in achievement situations (see Bates 1979; Deci 1975). An external reward offered to a child for engaging in a task that he or she might have been intrinsically motivated to do is believed to shift the child's attention from the original intrinsic motive to the extrinsic reward. When the reward is removed, the child will no longer engage in the activity. Recent research indicates, for example, that if a child who likes to draw is offered a reward for drawing, he or she is less likely to seek opportunities to draw after the reward is withdrawn than if no reward had been offered (Lepper, Greene, and Nisbett 1973). Note, however, that extrinsic rewards negatively affect task behavior only if the individual views the reward as the reason for engaging in the task. The undermining effects described above have generally not been found in situations in which the reward was used as a symbol of task mastery (Morgan 1984). If a grade is given only to indicate level of mastery—as is necessary for many school tasks because students have no other means to assess whether mastery has been achieved—it will not undermine intrinsic motivation.

The degree to which a task will appeal to an individual's intrinsic motivational drive partly depends on the context in which the task is encountered. In addition to the possible negative effects of providing extrinsic rewards, eliminating personal choice (deCharms 1984; Deci 1975) and stressing external evaluation (Maehr and Stallings 1972) can render undesirable a task that, without these constraints, might have been considered fun. Most tasks in school can be presented in a way that would, to some degree, appeal to students' intrinsic motivational systems.

Intrinsically motivated achievement behavior is considered more desirable than is externally motivated achievement behavior primarily because external reinforcements are not always available. A child who becomes dependent on rewards for engaging in achievement behaviors will fare poorly in educational environments that do not provide constant external reinforcements. Thus we turn now to a discussion of the kind of school environment that will maintain children's intrinsic motivation and contribute to the other positive motivational characteristics.

THE EDUCATIONAL CONTEXT

The preceding theoretical discussion suggests three sets of motivational characteristics that contribute to optimal achievement and therefore should be fostered in schools. First, the educational environment must facilitate positive achievement-related cognitions that result in adaptive learning behaviors and maximum effort and persistence. Children should maintain a positive view of their competencies—a belief that they possess the necessary ability to master school-related material. As a consequence, they should maintain high expectations to succeed at academic tasks. When they fail, they should attribute the failure to lack of effort, not to lack of ability.

Second, educational environments need to maintain children's intrinsic motivation to learn for the sake of learning so that they will continue to learn outside the school or in higher education institutions where extrinsic reinforcements are either unavailable or delayed. If tasks cannot be presented in a way that appeals to students' intrinsic competence motivation, students should learn to view them as instrumental to achieving meaningful personal goals. Third, the educational environment should encourage independent, self-directed learning strategies that will benefit children in and out of structured educational contexts.

We will consider first the effect of current educational practice on these dimensions as related to children's motivation to learn. Then, we will make suggestions for creating educational environments that should help to better achieve these goals.

The Status Quo

It is ironic that before children enter school, they possess the kind of motivational characteristics that we desire to create in formal educational environments. They have positive perceptions of their competence and high expectations for success (see Stipek 1984b). Because success and failure are generally attributed to effort, young children are less susceptible to learned helplessness than are older children (Rholes, Blackwell, Jordan, and Walters 1980). Moreover, their behavior while performing tasks is rarely debilitated by anxiety about the quality of their products or about receiving external approval. The learning activities that preschool-age children spontaneously engage in are also primarily intrinsically motivating. Most young children are pleased when adults praise their learning efforts, but this praise is superfluous in motivating children to engage in the activity. Finally, young children's learning is, for the most part, self-directed; adults tend to serve more as resources than as instructors.

Schooling often depresses these positive motivational characteristics. In school, children's achievement efforts are evaluated and compared to the efforts of their classmates. Because success is usually based on a comparative standard, some children necessarily experience failure. Partly as a consequence of the evaluative aspects of the formal educational setting, children's perceptions of their competence and their expectations for success decline on the average over the elementary school grades (see Stipek 1984a, 1984b). From about the third or fourth grade on, an increasing number of children begin to believe that no amount of effort will lead to success, and they begin to show evidence of learned helplessness. Anxiety about external evaluation also increases over the early school years as self-confidence declines and as children become socialized to seek high grades and other symbols of achievement.

Intrinsic motivation also wanes over the early elementary grades. Rewards (happy faces, stars, and so forth) are made contingent on many activities that children previously found intrinsically satisfying. Consequently, children's attention turns away from the intrinsic motive (that is, to master a skill and to feel competent) toward the more salient extrinsic motive (for example, to get a star on a paper). Most formal educational environments shift children as quickly as possible from an intrinsic motivational system to an extrinsic system that is more under the control of the teacher. Thus, traditional schooling often inhibits rather than capitalizes on children's intrinsic motivational systems, and in other ways diminishes rather than enhances children's enthusiasm to learn. The apparent inability of the American educational system to maintain the interest in exploration and learning that seems to be intrinsic to most children when they enter school has been lamented by many educational philosophers (for example, Bruner 1966; Dewey 1900).

Finally, in elementary school, children are given much less opportunity to choose which learning activities they will engage in than they were given in preschool and in kindergarten. Choice increases somewhat in secondary schools, but the level of independence children enjoy before they enter school is never equaled in formal educational settings.

In many respects, these changes are necessary. Comparisons with other children are to some degree unavoidable when children are educated in groups, and these comparisons will inevitably result in lowered self-confidence for some children. Intrinsic motivation cannot be relied on for many school tasks. Some learning goals will surely seem irrelevant to children who do not understand the competencies required in a modern technological society. Children are very unlikely to "choose" to engage in many of the academic tasks critical to the educational curriculum. Notwithstanding these limitations, however, most educational environments could be improved in ways that would positively affect children's motivation to learn. We turn now to recommendations for such improvements.

Maintaining Positive Achievement-Related Cognitions

Evaluation based on class norms contributes significantly to many children's negative achievement-related cognitions. In the individual competitive model that characterizes most classrooms, rewards are allocated among individuals according to their relative performance. Students' attention tends to be focused on demonstrating ability (or avoiding demonstrating lack of ability) rather than on strategies to master the task (Ames and Ames 1984). Among individuals of equal ability, competition can be effective in optimizing effort because success is in this case largely a function of effort. However, in more typical classrooms composed of competing individuals of unequal abilities, the outcome is determined only in part by effort; increments of effort by any competitor do not necessarily increase his or her probability of success. A competitive model can inhibit high effort in high-ability students because they can succeed without great effort when they are competing against students of lower ability. Competition can have devastating effects on the achievement behavior of lower-ability students because in educational contexts in which success and failure are defined normatively, these children find that no amount of effort will ever lead to success. Inevitably these children lose their sense of efficacy and begin to expect to perform poorly; when they do fail, they naturally attribute that failure to their poor ability. Since effort does not lead to success, they begin to feel helpless and often give up trying altogether.

The inevitable failure of some students and the accompanying negative achievement-related cognitions could be minimized if success is viewed in terms of exceeding one's own standard or mastering a skill rather than in terms of surpassing the performance of others. Both high- and low-ability students can benefit from a mastery as opposed to a competitive evaluation system. Low-ability students benefit from a mastery orientation because success is attainable and effort should always have some payoff. High-ability students always have a higher standard of excellence to aspire to, since the objective is to surpass one's own previous level of performance.

A mastery-based evaluation system is often associated with individualized instructional techniques, but it does not preclude either direct instruction or instruction in small groups. Teachers can provide direct instruction to a small group of students who have reached the same level of mastery and are ready to be exposed to new concepts.

However, the groups should be loosely formed with the potential for frequent changes in composition.

Educational programs based on a mastery rather than a normative model have been tried, and in many cases these programs have resulted in a relatively high level of effort and achievement (see Block 1984; Bloom 1984). Yet mastery-based programs have not been implemented on a broad scale in the United States. Perhaps this is because a competitive classroom model is consistent with the large economic and political context of American schools and a noncompetitive model runs counter to other socializing influences. Children themselves have been known to sabotage teachers' efforts to emphasize personal rather than normative standards. In individualized programs in which students are supposed to be working at their own pace and focusing on developing competencies rather than outperforming classmates, children who are accustomed to a competitive learning environment sometimes introduce normative evaluation by informally creating a "race to the end of the curriculum" (Levine 1983). These tendencies, however, are not inevitable or irreversible.

When a teacher does introduce competition into the classroom, an effort should be made to avoid the serious negative achievement-related cognitions that could occur. Covington and Beery (1976) provide an excellent example of a competitive academic game that protects against these possible negative effects. In a spelling bee involving two teams, each child is given the choice of a difficult, medium, or easy word. The number of points the child's team receives depends on the level of difficulty of the word the child chooses. The words in the three categories of difficulty are determined by each child's *own* spelling ability. Consequently, all children have an equal chance of contributing points to their team. Educational researchers have developed many similar strategies for team competition in which teams are comprised of children with differing ability levels so that all teams have an equal chance of winning (see Slavin 1983). Incentives for high effort can also be created by comparing children on how much progress each child makes rather than on the skill level of each child.

There are other ways of maintaining positive achievement-related cognitions compatible with a de-emphasis on normative standards. The structure of classroom instruction, for example, has been found to affect children's beliefs about their competence (see, for example, Bossert 1979; Rosenholtz and Simpson, 1984). Classroom structures that maximize opportunities for comparing the performance of students have been associated with negative achievement-related cognitions. Teachers must cautiously use whole-class recitations or question-and-answer periods because wrong answers automatically become public and comparable. Giving the same assignments to all children at the same time also facilitates comparisons. Ability grouping, if it is stable and salient, can have negative effects on some children's achievement-related cognitions. In contrast, a highly individualized classroom structure in which children's tasks vary and their interactions with the teacher are either private or in small, flexible groups minimizes the publicness of performance and evaluative feedback.

Note, however, that while some classroom structures facilitate comparisons more than others, the teacher is probably a more important factor than is the structure of the classroom. Whole-class question-and-answer periods, for example, can be done in a way that is potentially humiliating for children who give wrong answers. In this situation, children who lack self-confidence rarely participate because the risk is too high. It is not unusual for a small group of high-ability students to dominate such question-and-answer instructional periods. However, sensitive teachers who integrate wrong answers into their instruction (which gives each child a feeling of having made a constructive contribution to the discussion) can engage the participation of all children; thus teachers can avoid subjecting children to possible humiliation or embarrassment if they give wrong answers.

Given that in almost any educational context children will to some degree be aware of how their performance compares to the performance of other children, the teacher has the additional task of minimizing the negative implications of this self-assessment for the relatively low-achieving child. Within the academic domain of classroom activities, interpreting errors as failure is one avoidable practice that unquestionably contributes to many children's lack of self-confidence. To be sure, it is important for teachers to point out errors and poor performance; students require this feedback to learn and to assess their own mastery. But errors need not be treated as something to be avoided or embarrassed by. It is ironic that errors are considered a natural part of learning skills outside the school. No one would expect to serve perfectly when learning how to play tennis, nor should bad serves cause embarrassment or a belief that no amount of practice will ever bring success. Yet in school, children learn to devalue errors, even on assignments based on new material or concepts. Papers with no errors receive gold stars, smiling faces, and A's, or they are displayed on the bulletin board. Indeed, some high-achieving students will be disappointed by anything less than 100 percent.

Errors should be thought of as a natural part of learning. There is good reason why assignments done without errors should be cause for concern. If no errors are made, the task obviously required no learning. Children who continually turn in papers with no mistakes are clearly not being given challenging assignments that push them to the levels of excellence they could achieve. Thus, if teachers treat errors as something to be avoided, the relatively low-achieving students might be continually humiliated by their errors and high-achieving students might become more motivated to complete assignments with no errors than to engage in activities that challenge their current level of competence. Of course, this principle applies only to performance that reflects the student's true ability level, that is, his or her best effort. Errors resulting from low effort or sloppiness are not to be regarded favorably. It is often difficult to distinguish errors that are the result of low effort from those that result from lack of mastery. Teachers must therefore be good diagnosticians to enable them to make this distinction as accurately as possible.

Thoughtful teachers have developed many clever methods to avoid the negative effects of incorrect responses. One teacher I interviewed developed the simple but ingenious method of marking incorrect responses on written assignments with a dot. Students continued to work on assignments until all answers were correct. Dots could easily be changed into check marks indicating correctness, without leaving any evidence of the original error. Thus, when a student had completed a workbook, for example, only checks, indicating total mastery, were evident. By using a symbol for incorrectness that could be easily changed into the symbol for correctness, the teacher treated errors as a natural step in mastering new material.

Emphasis on a narrow band of academic tasks will also inevitably cause some children to believe that attempts to try for a valued positive outcome will never be rewarded. Giving children who fare poorly in traditional academic tasks opportunities to excel publicly in other activities might sustain a sense of personal efficacy and self-worth and the belief that effort does pay off. In most classrooms the teacher creates an environment in which academic excellence, narrowly defined, is clearly more highly valued than are other kinds of achievements. Musical, artistic, and athletic talent could be responded to just as enthusiastically, even if instruction in these areas is given less time. It is the teacher's task to find the strengths and talents of each child and to provide opportunities for every child to express those talents.

In summary, I have proposed the following strategies for maintaining a sense of self-worth in children: (1) evaluating on a mastery rather than a normative standard; (2) minimizing salient public evidence of individual children's performance; (3) considering errors as a normal aspect of mastering new skills; and (4) providing opportunities for all children to demonstrate competence in an activity that is publicly valued by the teacher. All of these teaching strategies should help maintain positive achievement-related cognitions, including self-efficacy ("I can do it or learn it if I try"), high expectations for success, and, if "failure" occurs (which it should naturally), an assumption that continued effort will correct the failure. These cognitions are certainly more likely to result in high effort and continued interest in learning than will feelings of incompetence or a perception that no amount of effort will ever lead to success.

Maintaining Intrinsic Motivation

Many of the tasks required in school are less intrinsically reinforcing than the tasks children engage in spontaneously in early childhood. It is not realistic to expect to rely solely on an intrinsic motivational system in school. Well-informed teachers can nevertheless capitalize more on children's intrinsic motivational systems and minimize the negative long-term effects of extrinsic reinforcement.

There are, for example, more and less attractive ways to present tasks, and creative teachers who design learning tasks that appeal to children will need extrinsic reinforcers less than will teachers who present tasks in their dullest, least attractive form.

A less obvious principle of task selection concerns challenge. In his writings on cognitive development, Piaget emphasized that children are naturally inclined to practice newly developing skills and that they experience the greatest amount of pleasure in accomplishing challenging tasks. Harter (1974) has empirically demonstrated that optimal pleasure is derived from challenging tasks. Once a skill has been fully mastered, it is no longer intrinsically motivating. Consider as an example the toddler who repeatedly (and sometimes irritatingly) engages in some new activity that seems to serve no useful purpose (for example, tying and untying shoes; opening and closing doors). The skill is eventually mastered, and suddenly the activity that seemed so enjoyable is no longer intrinsically motivating.

This same principle applies to learning activities in the classroom. Tasks that are far beyond the child's current skill level and tasks that exercise fully mastered skills are not likely to evoke intrinsic motivation. My own observations of classrooms indicate that high-achieving children's intrinsic motivation sytems often are not activated because the academic program is not sufficiently individualized to provide them with challenging tasks. These high-achieving students often become so accustomed to errorless papers and high grades that they develop an overly cautious approach to learning situations. Any grade lower than an A is cause for serious disappointment. Consequently, when they are given some choice in academic tasks, they often select the assignment or the course that assures them of the best grade rather than the most learning; they avoid situations in which failure (a low grade) is perceived as a risk. This is unfortunate for the student who could benefit from greater academic challenge, and it is undoubtedly one explanation for many highly competent individuals' avoidance of science and mathematics (see Parsons, Kaczala, and Meece 1982).

In addition to being challenging, tasks need to be presented with an emphasis on developing competencies rather than on external evaluation. Maehr and his colleagues have found in their research that children are most inclined to pursue academic activities outside school that are presented to them in a classroom in which external evaluation is de-emphasized (Maehr 1976). Maehr argues that the emphasis on external evaluation undermines children's sense of autonomy and control in learning situations and consequently their intrinsic motivation.

Maehr's analysis may explain why so few junior high school students approach their algebra homework with the same intensity and zeal that they approach such cognitively demanding activities as "dungeons and dragons" or computer games. Dungeons and dragons and computer games may be more interesting than algebra because of their fantasy characteristics. But fantasy is not the only reason for their greater appeal. Another important difference between these intellectually demanding activities is the context in which they are encountered. An exhilarating feeling of satisfaction can accompany solving a difficult mathematics problem. But such accomplishments usually occur in a context in which external evaluation is highly salient, and anxiety about potential failure detracts from the enjoyment that mastery itself can produce. Algebra may never be done as enthusiastically as dungeons and dragons or computer games, but it could be much less burdensome if external evaluation and the potential for failure were less salient.

But what about tasks that are not intrinsically appealing under any circumstances? Many academic tasks will seem useless and irrelevant to children, and consequently such tasks will not provide children with the feeling of competence that is necessary to activate intrinsic motivation. Alternative strategies for motivating children to engage in such tasks must be sought.

In some cases, intrinsic motivation can be activated by linking the immediate task to the student's long-range goals or to another activity that is more appealing. For children of elementary school age these goals must be in close view. Not until high school are students likely to be motivated to engage in activities that are linked to longer-range goals such as occupational aspirations. Teachers should also avoid making reinforcers (for examples, going outside to play) arbitrarily contingent on completing an academic task. Reinforcement used this way is likely to undermine whatever intrinsic interest the child has in the task. However, beginning work on an appealing project might be made contingent on mastering a particular skill that is necessary for successfully completing the project. Thus, for example, building a model city to scale might be made contingent on mastering certain mathematical principles. This kind of contingent reinforcement should enhance the value of the immediate skill to be mastered.

There are certainly many situations in which some external reinforcement is necessary. If external reinforcement is used sparingly, and if certain principles are followed, the long-term negative effects can be minimized. For example, if the value of the information to be learned is emphasized, the reward is less likely to undermine a child's intrinsic motivation than if the reward itself is emphasized (Morgan 1984). Thus an A can be given to provide the student with feedback about his or her skill attainment, but it should not be viewed as something that is valuable in itself. The teacher is better advised to say to a child, "You have had A's on your last three arithmetic papers; I guess you have mastered these concepts and are ready to go on to some new concepts," rather than "Congratulations, you received the only A in the class."

Gratuitous, noncontingent rewards are not advisable. If reinforcement is not made contingent on some performance standard, it provides no information. Indeed, achievement motivation theorists have recently argued that gratuitous praise can actually cause students to lower their self-perceptions of ability. Praise for poor performance can be interpreted by the student as evidence of the teacher's low expectations for his or her performance. Global, positive reactions should also be avoided. Rather, rewards should be contingent on specific, clearly defined accomplishments. If external reinforcement is used according to these recommendations, it should not undermine children's intrinsic motivation to learn for the sake of learning. (See Brophy [1981] for further recommendations on the effective use of rewards.)

Maintaining Independent Self-Directed Learning

Autonomous learners must trust their own evaluation and ability to diagnose problems when learning new skills. Covington and Beery (1976) suggest many methods for helping children develop skills in self-evaluation. Providing models to which children can compare their own work is one such simple technique. Encouraging children to be self-critical and to trust their own judgment is another strategy that can be used effectively.

Realistic personal goal setting is also necessary for autonomous learning. The ability to set realistic goals is critical for the college student who typically receives little day-to-day guidance in organizing the workload. Clearly an educational program in which the teacher tells students what to do, when to do it, and how long it should take will not enhance students' ability to set realistic goals, although a considerable amount of teacher direction may be required in the first few years of elementary school. Alternative models to this more common situation have been developed. Some models encourage children, under the gentle guidance of the teacher, to set their own learning goals for a specified amount of time. In a few cases there are formal contractual agreements.

Wang and Stiles (1976), for example, found in an intervention study that assignments were more likely to be completed when students were allowed to determine the order in which assignments were done. A study by Rainey (1965) found that high school science students showed more care and involvement in laboratory work when they were encouraged to organize their own experiments than when they were given detailed instructions and directions. Comparisons of classrooms in which the autonomy of students varied have yielded similar results. Deci, Schwartz, Sheinman, and Ryan (1981) observed that elementary school teachers who encouraged student autonomy, as compared to teachers who emphasized direct teacher control, had students with higher levels of task-involvement and a higher sense of competence. Pascarella, Walberg, Junker, and Haertel (1981) report that high school students evidenced more interest in science if they were in classrooms where students had relatively greater control over learning.

DeCharms (1984) has implemented educational programs that are specifically aimed at helping children and teachers to develop personal responsibility for learning. He trains teachers to take more responsibility themselves, to feel greater control over their classrooms, and to encourage students to do the same. Emphasis is placed on participation, choice, and freedom in the classroom. His program has resulted in students' taking greater responsibility for their learning, in higher achievement scores, and even in higher rates of high school graduation among low-income youth.

Thus, many educational models encouraging greater student autonomy and independence have been developed. All of these programs offer an alternative to the more typical classroom in which students are essentially, in the term coined by deCharms, "pawns" of the teacher, in which the teacher serves as the sole evaluator and dispenser of rewards and punishments. Researchers have shown that these alternative models of education often result in a higher level of intrinsic motivation, more independent, self-directed learning strategies, and usually a higher level of achievement.

Teacher Variables

There are certainly other factors that affect the level of students' motivation. The teacher's own enthusiasm for teaching, for example, affects students' enthusiasm. To be sure, a teacher who communicates pleasure in his or her work and who presents tasks as interesting and valuable is more likely to maintain student enthusiasm than is the teacher who communicates boredom and presents tasks as though they have no intrinsic interest or value.

Teachers' expectations are also known to influence students' performance (see Cooper and Tom 1984; Good 1981 for reviews). Students who have teachers who expect them to put forth their best effort and who communicate that expectation are more likely to pay attention and work hard than are students whose teachers expect less.

Whether students respect the teacher also affects the amount of effort they exert in the classroom. This may be especially important in the upper grades when youths are highly evaluative and sometimes distrustful of adults. Without the basic respect of the students, a high school teacher may find useless all of the other principles and strategies discussed in this chapter for optimizing motivation.

Teachers' respect for the children may be as important as children's respect for the teacher. The teacher's communication of positive regard for each child, regardless of the child's academic performance, may be one of the most important factors in children's willingness to take academic risks. "Noncontingent positive regard" (Rogers 1951) may be particularly important in the early elementary grades when children are especially concerned about the teacher's acceptance. The teacher's respect for students' ideas is also important. Clearly, the teacher who ridicules students' ideas is unlikely to obtain maximum participation and effort.

These and other teacher variables all have a bearing on the amount of effort children exert on academic tasks. Optimizing motivation therefore requires consideration of teacher characteristics in addition to teaching and evaluative strategies and other variables associated with learning in the classroom.

CONCLUSION

The recommendations presented may seem reminiscent of the open-classroom movement of the 1960s and out of touch with the current back-to-basics emphasis. In many respects, the educational model recommended here dates back to John Dewey. But these ideas are not antithetical to an emphasis on basic skills or highly demanding academic subjects. To the contrary, the more demanding the task, the more important are the motivational factors discussed in this paper. Academic subjects like science and mathematics probably suffer the most from traditional instructional techniques. These are the subjects that even highly capable students are reluctant to pursue.

Children's disinterest in the most basic of skills—reading—has often been lamented by parents. While children's motivation to read has probably been most affected by the availability of television, the association of reading with a highly evaluative, anxiety-provoking school context may also affect children's motivation. Reading is something that children have learned to do in order to avoid punishment or to gain a reward such as a good grade. The intrinsic pleasure in reading may therefore not be apparent. Thus, the typical response to a parent's admonishment—"Why don't you read a book instead of watching television all the time"—may be something like, "I already read the two books I had to make book reports on this year." Perhaps if teachers required television viewing as homework and tested students on the content, they would watch less television and read more books.

Traditional educational programs may foster more fear than joy of learning. If our goal is for students to exert maximum effort on academic tasks in the classroom and also to be prepared to benefit from higher education programs, and if we want individuals to value learning and to be motivated to seek learning opportunities throughout their adult lives, radical changes in educational environments are going to be necessary.

But what about children who have been in our schools for many years—those who have lost their self-confidence and are convinced that they will never achieve academic success, or those who engage in academic activities only to obtain external rewards, or those who are unable to work independently? What about students who have become alienated from the school environment and have begun to invest their energy in alternative areas in which they have some chance for success, such as sports or less socially sanctioned activities such as gangs? What about students who have become so concerned with external evaluation that they avoid the most challenging intellectual subjects? Is high school too late a time to affect the motivation of these students?

The answer to all of these questions is a definite no. Perhaps the most remarkable thing about youth is their ability to respond to the demands and expectations of a new environment. That is not to say that it is easy to convince a student who has fared poorly in school for many years that he or she can succeed with some effort. Nor is it easy to convince the high achiever that the academic challenge of physics is worth risking the lower grade. But highly skilled teachers and an environment in which self-directed learning is encouraged and external evaluation and competition is de-emphasized can be very effective in reacquainting students with the pleasure of learning.

To be sure, it is preferable to provide from the very beginning a learning environment that is conducive to self-confidence, intrinsic motivation, and independent, self-directed learning. It is easier to maintain than to recreate these desirable motivational characteristics with which young children come to school. But a teacher in any grade can create an educational context that supports these motivational characteristics. Students may resist at first, but many are likely to respond with great enthusiasm, and the benefit from such an education will continue throughout their adulthood.

REFERENCES

Ames, Carole, and Ames, Russell. "Systems of Student and Teacher Motivation: Toward a Qualitative Definition." *Journal of Education Psychology* 76 (August 1984): 535–556.

Bandura, Albert. "Self-efficacy Mechanism in Human Agency." *American Psychologist* 37 (February 1982): 122–147.

Bates, John A. "Extrinsic Reward and Intrinsic Motivation: A Review with Implications for the Classroom." *Review of Educational Research* 49 (Fall 1979): 557–576.

Block, James H. "Making School Learning Activities More Play-like: Flow and Mastery Learning." *Elementary School Journal* 85 (September 1984): 65–76.

Bloom, Benjamin S. "The 2 Sigma Problem: The Search for Methods of Group Instruction as Effective as One-to-One Tutoring." *Educational Researcher* 13: 6 (1984): 4–16.

Bossert, Steven. *Tasks and Social Relationships in Classrooms.* Arnold and Caroline Rose Monograph Series of the American Sociological Association. Cambridge, England: Cambridge University Press, 1979.

Brophy, Jere. "Teacher Praise: A Functional Analysis." *Review of Educational Research* 51 (Spring 1981): 5–32.

Bruner, Jerome. *Toward a Theory of Instruction.* New York: W. W. Norton, 1966.

Cooper, Harris, and Tom, David Y. H. "Teacher Expectation Research: A Review with Implications for Classroom Instruction." *Elementary School Journal* 85 (September 1984): 77–90.

Covington, Martin V., and Beery, Richard G. *Self-worth and School Learning.* New York: Holt, Rinehart, and Winston, 1976.

deCharms, Richard. "Motivation Enhancement in Educational Settings." In *Research on Motivation in Education, Vol. 1: Student Motivation,* edited by Russell Ames and Carole Ames, pp. 275–310 New York: Academic Press, 1984.

Deci, Edward L. *Intrinsic Motivation.* New York: Plenum, 1975.

Deci, Edward; Schwartz, Allan J.; Sheinman, Louise; and Ryan, Richard M. "An Instrument to Assess Adults' Orientations toward Control versus Autonomy with Children: Reflections on Intrinsic Motivation and Perceived Competence." *Journal of Educational Psychology* 73 (October 1981): 642–650.

Dewey, John. *School and Society.* Chicago: University of Chicago Press, 1900.

Dweck, Carol S. "Role of Expectations and Attributions in the Alleviation of Learned Helplessness." *Journal of Personality and Social Psychology* 31 (April 1975): 674–685.

Dweck, Carol S., and Reppucci, N. Dickon. "Learned Helplessness and Reinforcement Responsibility in Children." *Journal of Personality and Social Psychology* 25 (January 1973): 109–116.

Good, Thomas. "Teacher Expectations and Student Perceptions: A Decade of Research." *Educational Leadership* 38 (February 1981): 415–422.

Haring, Norris G., and Phillips, E. Lakin. *Analysis and Modification of Classroom Behavior*. Englewood Cliffs, N.J.: Prentice-Hall, 1972.

Harter, Susan. "Pleasure Derived from Cognitive Challenge and Mastery." *Child Development* 45 (September 1974): 661–669.

Harter, Susan "A Model of Mastery Motivation in Children: Individual Differences and Developmental Change." In *Minnesota Symposia on Child Psychology*. Vol. 14. Edited by W. Andrew Collins, pp. 215–255. Hillsdale, N. J.: Lawrence Erlbaum Associates, 1981.

Hill, Kenneth. "Debilitating Motivation and Testing: A Major Educational Problem—Possible Solutions and Policy Application." In *Research on Motivation in Education, Vol. I: Student Motivation*, edited by Russell Ames and Carole Ames. New York: Academic Press, 1984.

Hunt, J. McVicker. "Toward a History of Intrinsic Motivation." In *Intrinsic Motivation: New Direction in Education*, edited by Daniel E. Berlyn and David Hunt. Toronto: Holt, 1971.

Lefcourt, Herbert. *Locus of Control: Current Trends in Theory and Research*. Hillsdale, N. J.: Lawrence Erlbaum Associates, 1976.

Lepper, Mark R.; Greene, David; and Nisbett, Richard E. "Undermining Children's Intrinsic Interest with Extrinsic Reward." *Journal of Personality and Social Psychology* 28 (October 1973): 129–137.

Levine, J. M. "Social Comparison and Education." In *Teacher and Student Perceptions: Implications for Learning*, edited by J. M. Levine and Margaret C. Wang. Hillsdale, N. J.: Lawrence Erlbaum Associates, 1983.

Maehr, Martin L. "Continuing Motivation: An Analysis of a Seldom Considered Educational Outcome." *Review of Educational Research* 46 (Summer 1976): 443–462.

Maehr, Martin, and Stallings, William. "Freedom from External Evaluation." *Child Development* 43 (March 1972): 177–85.

Morgan, Mark. "Reward-induced Decrements and Increments in Intrinsic Motivation." *Review of Educational Research* 54 (Spring 1984): 5–30.

Nicholls, J., and Miller, A. "Conceptions of Ability and Achievement Motivation." In *Research on Motivation in Education, Vol. 1: Student Motivation*, edited by Russell Ames and Carol Ames. New York: Academic Press, 1984.

Parsons, Jacquelynne; Kaczala, Caroline; and Meece, Judith L. "Socialization of Achievement Attitudes and Beliefs: Classroom Influences." *Child Development* 53 (April 1982): 322–339.

Pascarella, Ernest; Walberg, Herbert J.; Junker, Linda K.; and Haertel, Geneva D. "Continuing Motivation in Science for Early and Late Adolescents." *American Educational Research Journal* 18 (Winter 1981): 439–452.

Peterson, Penelope L., and Swing, Susan R. "Beyond Time on Task: Students' Reports of Their Thought Processes during Classroom Instruction." *Elementary School Journal* 82 (May 1982): 481–492.

Peterson, Penelope L.; Swing, Susan R.; Stark, Kevin D.; and Waas, Gregory A. "Students' Cognitions and Time on Task during Mathematics Instruction." *American Educational Research Journal* 21 (Fall 1984): 487–515.

Piaget, Jean. *The Origins of Intelligence in Children*. New York: W. W. Norton, 1952.

Rainey, Robert G. "The Effects of Directed vs. Nondirected Laboratory Work on

High School Chemistry Achievement." *Journal of Research in Science Teaching* 3: 4 (1965): 286–292.

Rholes, William; Blackwell, Janette; Jordan, Carol; and Walters, Connie. "A Developmental Study of Learned Helplessness." *Developmental Psychology* 16 (November 1980): 616–624.

Rogers, Carl. *Client-Centered Therapy*. New York: Houghton-Mifflin, 1951.

Rosenholtz, Susan J., and Simpson, Carl. "Classroom Organization and Student Stratification." *Elementary School Journal* 85 (September 1984): 21–37.

Rotter, Julian B. "Generalized Expectancies for Internal versus External Control of Reinforcement." *Psychological Monographs* 1, whole no. 609, 1966.

Schunk, Dale. "Effects of Effort Attributional Feedback on Children's Perceived Self-Efficacy and Achievement." *Journal of Educational Psychology* 74 (August 1982): 548–556.

Schunk, Dale. "Reward Contingencies and the Development of Children's Skills and Self-efficacy." *Journal of Educational Psychology* 75 (August 1983): 511–518. (a)

Schunk, Dale. "Ability versus Effort Attributional Feedback: Differential Effects on Self-efficacy and Achievement." *Journal of Educational Psychology* 75 (December 1983): 848–856. (b)

Slavin, Robert. *Cooperative Learning*. New York: Longman, 1983.

Stipek, Deborah. "Developmental Aspects of Motivation in Children." In *Research on Motivation in Education, Vol. 1: Student Motivation*. New York: Academic Press, 1984. (a)

Stipek, Deborah. "Young Children's Performance Expectations: Logical Analysis or Wishful Thinking?" In *The Development of Achievement Motivation*, edited by J. Nicholls, pp. 33–56. Greenwich, Conn.: JAI Press, 1984. (a)

Stipek, Deborah, and Weisz, John R. "Perceived Personal Control and Academic Achievement." *Review of Educational Research* 51 (Spring 1981): 101–137.

Wang, Margaret C., and Stiles, Billie. "An Investigation of Children's Concept of Self-responsibility for Their School Learning." *American Educational Research Journal* 13 (Summer 1976): 159–179.

Weiner, Bernard. "A Theory of Motivation for Some Classroom Experiences." *Journal of Educational Psychology* 71 (February 1979): 3–25.

White, Robert W. "Motivation Reconsidered: The Concept of Competence." *Psychological Review* 66 (September 1959): 297–333.

10

Alternative Conceptions of Intelligence and Their Implications for Education

Richard K. Wagner and Robert J. Sternberg

The concept of intelligence pervades our daily lives at least as much as does any other psychological concept. Notions about intelligence are particularly consequential in education. Almost without exception, students will have taken many intelligence or scholastic aptitude tests before completing their education; for many of these students, their level of performance will have had important consequences for their school and later careers. Paradoxically, although intelligence tests have been widely used in education, the concept of intelligence has not been particularly informative to educators, beyond its use in providing a rough guide to determining reasonable expectations regarding academic performance for students with different levels or patterns of intellectual skills.

The relationship between intelligence and education is of critical importance to those concerned with educational practice and to those who do research on intelligence. This relationship is important to

Reprinted, with permission, from *Review of Educational Research* 54 (Summer 1984): 179–233. © 1984 by the American Educational Research Association, Washington, D.C.

Preparation of this article was supported in part by a contract from the National Commission on Excellence in Education and in part by Contract N0001483K0013 from the Office of Naval Research and the Army Research Institute. An earlier version of this article was submitted to the National Commission on Excellence in Education.

educators because the intelligence of students constrains and informs educational practice. The magnitude of these effects may be underestimated because of the natural tendency to view students largely in terms of their grade levels, which is determined for most students by their chronological age. But it is neither chronological age nor grade level per se that requires placing say, calculus, late rather than early in the sequence of mathematics courses. Rather, it is in large part students' developed intellectual skills and knowledge. The relation between intelligence and education is important to researchers in intelligence because formal education is a major factor in the development of intelligence (Cole and Scribner 1974; Scribner and Cole 1981). Indeed, intelligence tests are to a large extent measures of achievement for grades a few years earlier than that of the students being tested on a given intelligence test.

The information-rich world to be faced by today's students will be even more demanding than before on intellectual skills. Because the field of intelligence is presently very different from that which gave rise to the technology of intelligence tests that pervades education, and because the intellectual demands of society are rapidly changing, it is important to examine alternative conceptions of intelligence from the viewpoint of their implications for today's educators.

This article is divided into two main parts. First, we consider the basic question of what intelligence is. One cannot meaningfully discuss issues pertaining to the assessment and training of intelligence without first discussing what it is that needs to be assessed or trained, and so we deal with this question in some detail. Because there is no single, universally accepted view of what intelligence is, we divide this part of our review into four sections. Three sections present alternative perspectives on the question being considered. The first section presents the standard psychometric view, which generated conventional intelligence, aptitude, and achievement tests. The second section presents the Piagetian view, as developed by the late Jean Piaget and his colleagues. The third section presents the information-processing view, which is probably the most popular one among contemporary cognitive and educational psychologists. This view perceives intelligence as a set of information-processing skills that can be identified and understood through the methods of experimental psychological research. The final section presents a comparison and evaluation of the three perspectives.

Second, we consider the implications of notions of intelligence for schooling. Our consideration deals with the training of content knowledge, which is currently emphasized in our schools, and with the training of intellectual skills, which is emphasized to a lesser degree. This part of our review is divided into five sections. The first three sections present the implications for assessment and training of the psychometric, Piagetian, and information-processing perspectives, respectively. The fourth section presents research that combines or relates aspects of these three perspectives. The final section presents a comparison and evaluation of the alternative perspectives.

We conclude by summarizing the implications of current conceptions of intelligence for education, and by making recommendations for researchers and practitioners that follow from our analysis.

WHAT IS INTELLIGENCE?

The Psychometric Perspective

The psychometric perspective on intelligence is usually traced to the work of Alfred Binet and his colleagues in France (Binet and Simon 1905) and subsequently to the work of Lewis Terman and his colleagues in the United States (Terman and Merrill 1960). Their psychometric perspective sought to understand intelligence by analysis of the increasing ability of children to solve relatively complex problems requiring skills of the sort encountered in everyday experience.

Psychometricians have sought alternative ways of conceptualizing the nature of intelligence. One such way has been through the model of factor analysis, a statistical tool that seeks out common sources of variation among people and identifies these sources as unitary psychological attributes, or factors. Different theorists have proposed different sets of factors to account for the structure of mental abilities.

The earliest view, that of Spearman (1927), is that intelligence comprises a general factor (g) common to performance on all tests that are used to measure intelligence, plus a specific factor (s) involved in performance on each individual test. The number of specific factors, therefore, is equal to the number of tests. A later view, that of Thurstone (1938), is that intelligence is best described as comprising a set of approximately seven primary mental abilities, namely, verbal comprehension, verbal fluency, number, spatial visualization, perceptual speed, memory, and reasoning. According to this view, any general factor that exists must be viewed as "second order," existing only by virtue of correlations between the primary mental abilities. A relatively more recent view, that of Guilford (1967, 1982), is that intelligence comprises at least 150 factors, each of which involves an operation, a content, and a product. There are five kinds of operations, six kinds of products, and five kinds of contents, yielding the 150 (5 × 6 × 5) factors. Examples of such factors are cognition of figural relations measured by tests such as figural (abstract) analogies, and memory for semantic relationships such as "gold is more valuable than iron." Probably the most widely accepted view among factor theorists today is a hierarchical one, which has been proposed by several theorists in somewhat different forms (for example, Burt 1940; Snow 1978; Vernon 1971). According to Vernon's view, for instance, intellectual abilities constitute a hierarchy, with a general factor (g) at the top; two major group factors, verbal-educational ability and spatial-mechanical ability at the second level; minor group factors at the third level; and specific factors at the bottom. Hierarchical models such as this one seem to account for much of the correlational data on the structure of intelligence.

The Piagetian Perspective[1]

The Piagetian perspective on intelligence is usually viewed as independent and distinct from the psychometric perspective, but in fact it in some ways arose from it. Jean Piaget first entered the field of cognitive development when, working in Binet's lab, he began studying children's *wrong* answers to Binet's test items. Through repeated observation of children's performance, particularly their errors in reasoning, Piaget concluded that there are coherent logical structures underlying children's thought, but that these structures are different from those underlying adult thought. In the six decades that followed, Piaget focused his research on delineating what those cognitive structures might be at different stages of development and how they might evolve from one stage to the next.

Piaget thought that there are two interrelated aspects of intelligence: its function and its structure. Piaget, a biologist by training, saw the function of intelligence as no different from the function of

---

1. This section represents a collaboration between Janet S. Powell and Robert J. Sternberg.

other biological activities, that is, adaptation, which includes assimilating the environment to one's cognitive structures to encompass new aspects of the environment. "A certain continuity exists . . . between intelligence and the purely biological process of morphogenesis and adaptation to the environment" (Piaget 1952, p. 1). In Piaget's theory, the function of intelligence—adaptation—provided this continuity with lower biological acts. Piaget rejected the sharp delineation proposed by others between "intelligent" acts, which were suggested to require insight or thought, and "nonintelligent" acts, which were proposed to require only habits or reflexes. Instead, he preferred to speak of a continuum in which behavior becomes more intelligent as the pathways between the subject and the objects on which it acts become progressively more complex (Piaget 1976).

Piaget further proposed that the internal organizational structure of intelligence and of how intelligence is manifested differ with age. Piaget divided the intellectual development of the child into discrete, qualitatively distinct stages. As the child progresses from one stage to the next, the cognitive structures of the preceding stage are reorganized and extended, through the child's own adaptive action, to form the underlying structures of the equilibrium characterizing the next stage. Piaget proposed three distinct stages of development: the sensorimotor stage (which lasts from birth to approximately two years of age), the period of preparation for and organization of concrete operations (which is often subdivided into a preoperational and a concrete-operational stage, lasting approximately from age two to age twelve), and the formal-operational stage (which is begun at approximately age twelve and continues through adulthood) (Piaget 1976). Because of space limitations, we will not describe Piaget's stages of intellectual development here. Instead, we refer the reader to summaries by Flavell (1963) and Ginsburg and Opper (1979); a more dense but also more complete account can be found in the original works of Piaget (1970, 1976).

Underlying Piaget's descriptions of the child's intellectual development are three core assumptions about the nature of the developmental process. First, according to Piaget, there are four factors that interact to bring about the child's development. Three of these factors are usually proposed: maturation, experience of the physical environment, and the influence of the social environment. To these three factors, Piaget added a fourth, which coordinates and guides the other three: equilibration, that is, the child's own self-regulatory processes. Thus, Piaget's theory centers on the assertion that the child is a very active participant in the construction of his or her own intelligence. Second, Piaget asserted that this intellectual development results in the appearance of developmental stages and that these stages follow an invariant sequence, with each succeeding stage incorporating and extending the accomplishments of the preceding stage. Third, although the rate of development may vary across children, the stages themselves and their sequence were considered by Piaget to be universal. In sum, Piaget's theory asserted that there is a single route of intellectual development that all humans, regardless of individual differences, follow. Individual differences result from different rates of progression along this route, or from individuals stopping along the way rather than following the route to completion.

The Information-Processing Perspective

Information-processing conceptions of intelligence have in common their view of intelligence as deriving from the ways in which people mentally represent and process information. Such conceptions have often used the computer program as a metaphor and heuristic for understanding how humans process information. Although the history of the information-processing approach is often traced to Donders (1868), who proposed that the time between a stimulus and a response could be decomposed into a sequence of successive processes, the modern history of the approach dates back only to about 1960. Two seminal works appeared in that year: Newell, Shaw, and Simon's (1960) "Report on a General Problem-Solving Program," and Miller, Galanter, and Pribram's (1960) monograph, *Plans and the Structure of Behavior*. These works each proposed theories of information processing and proposed that these theories could be implemented and tested via digital computers. Newell and his colleagues actually presented a program, the General Problem Solver (GPS), that could solve difficult reasoning problems using only a relatively small number of algorithms and heuristics.

Whereas traditional psychometric theorists of intelligence have agreed on the factor as the fundamental unit in terms of which intellectual behavior should be analyzed, many information-processing theorists have agreed on the elementary information process as the fundamental unit of behavior (Newell and Simon 1972). It is assumed that all behavior of a human information-processing system is the result of combinations of these elementary processes. The processes are elementary in the sense that they are not further

broken down into simpler processes by the theory under consideration. The level of analysis that is considered to be "elementary" will
depend on the type of behavior under consideration and the level at
which the theory attempts to account for the behavior.

The notion of an elementary information process is obviously a
general one. Some investigators have sought to specify further the
notion and the ways multiple elementary information processes might
combine in task performance.

Consider first Miller, Galanter, and Pribram's (1960) proposal of
the Test-Operate-Test-Exit (TOTE) as the unit of interest. Each unit
of behavior begins with a test of the present outcome against the
desired outcome. If the result of the test is congruent with the desired
outcome (an *Image*), an exit is made. If not, another operation is
performed to make the result of the next test conform as closely as
possible to the Image. If the result of the next test is congruent with
the Image, an exit is made. Otherwise, another operation is performed, and so on down the line until a test result corresponds to the
Image (which may have been modified along the way to make it
conform more closely to the demands of reality).

Sternberg (1980, 1984) has expanded the notion of an elementary
information process in a somewhat different way, suggesting that
processes can be viewed as being of three basic types—metacomponents,
performance components, and knowledge-acquisition components. Metacomponents are higher-order control processes that are used for
executive decision-making in problem solving. They include processes
such as deciding on the nature of the problem being confronted, deciding
on a strategy for task performance, and correctly interpreting external
feedback. Performance components are the processes actually used in
executing task performance. They include processes such as encoding
the terms of the problem, inferring relations between these terms, and
comparing alternative possible solutions. Knowledge-acquisition components are processes used in learning new and consequential information. They include processes such as selective encoding, by which one
distinguishes relevant from irrelevant information encountered in material to be learned, and selective comparison, by which one relates new
information just encoded to old information that was already part of
one's knowledge base.

Newell and Simon (1972) have proposed yet another expansion of
the notion of the elementary information process, suggesting that
information processing can be understood in terms of the operations
of "production systems" having productions as the basic constituent

units. A production is a condition-action sequence. If a certain condition is met, then a certain action is performed. Sequences of ordered productions are then called production systems. The "executive" for a production system is hypothesized to make its way down an ordered list of productions until one of the conditions is met. The action corresponding to that condition is executed, and control is returned to the top of the list. The executive then makes its way down the list again, trying to satisfy a condition. When it does so, an action is executed and control returns to the top.

In conclusion, the information-processing approach has provided a major step forward in our understanding of intelligence by specifying intelligent functioning with precision and testability unrivaled by other accounts.

Comparison and Evaluation of Perspectives

The similarities and differences among the three approaches to defining the nature of intelligence can perhaps best be pointed out by comparing how they would account for performance on a single type of problem. Consider, for example, an analogy of the form A : B :: C: (D1, D2), such as doctor : patient :: lawyer: (judge, client). Analogies have been found to be among the best single indicators of overall intelligence (Reitman 1965; Spearman 1923; Sternberg 1977; Whitely 1977), and so provide a particularly apt example.

A psychometrician would attempt to understand performance on the analogy by examining the underlying factors of intelligence that contribute to individual differences in performance. He or she would proceed by examining relations among individual differences in solving analogies and individual differences in abilities that underlie performance on psychometric tests of intelligence. In this approach, the analysis of intellectual behavior (a) employs a structural model, (b) concentrates on variation among individuals, (c) employs standard IQ tests to assess intelligence, and (d) assumes that performance on a given task is an additive function of a set of underlying abilities expressed as factors.

A Piagetian would attempt to understand performance on the analogy by understanding the logical operations underlying analogy solution and by identifying stages leading up to satisfactory analogy solution. In fact, Piaget, with Montangero and Billeter (1977), has suggested three stages in the development of analogical reasoning. In the first stage, characterizing the performance of children of ages five and six, children can understand relations between pairs of terms, but ignore higher-order relations between pairs. Thus, although these children can link A to B or C to D, they cannot link A-B to C-D. In the second stage, characterizing the performance of children from about eight to eleven years of age, children can form analogies, but when challenged with countersuggestions, they readily rescind their proposed analogies. Piaget interprets this finding as evidence of only a weak or tentative level of analogical reasoning ability. In the third stage, characterizing the performance of children age eleven and older, children form analogies, are able to state explicitly the conceptual bases of these analogies, and resist countersuggestions from the experimenter. Note that in this approach, the analysis of behavior (a) employs a model of the development of schemes for problem solving, (b) concentrates on what is common to individuals of a given age, but not common to individuals of different ages, (c) employs a clinical method (usually observation) to assess intelligence, and (d) assumes that performance on a given task can be understood in terms of the availability of logical functions for problem solving.

An information-processing psychologist would attempt to understand performance on the analogy by examining the processes that contribute to performance and that make some analogies more difficult than others. For example, in Sternberg's theory of analogical reasoning (Sternberg 1977; Sternberg and Gardner 1982), an individual's performance would be analyzed as requiring *encoding* the terms of the analogy, *inferring* the relation between the A and B terms (doctor and patient), *mapping* the higher-order relation that links the first half of the analogy to the second (the doctor half to the lawyer half) *applying* the relation previously inferred from A to B to create an ideal completion to the analogy (say, client), *comparing* the answer options to see which is closer to the ideal answer (in this case, one of the options is identical to the ideal), and *responding*. Note that in this approach, the analysis of intellectual behavior (a) employs a process model, (b) concentrates on variation in item difficulties, (c) decomposes tasks that are found on standard IQ tests, and (d) assumes that performance on a given task can be understood in terms of a set of component processes, whose component latencies add up to yield total latency.

We believe the three approaches to understanding intelligence are largely complementary rather than mutually exclusive. Indeed, it has been shown that their forms of analysis map into each other (Sternberg 1982; see also Jensen 1982). Consider first the relations between psychometric factors and information processes. Psychometric factors are derived from analysis of "between-subject" sources of variance, whereas information processes are usually derived from analysis of "between-stimulus" sources of variance. Aspects of task performance that vary only trivially across individuals yet nevertheless may be fundamental to task performance would be missed by traditional psychometric analysis, whereas such aspects would figure prominently in traditional information-processing analysis of task performance. Conversely, aspects of task performance that vary only trivially across item types yet nevertheless may be interesting sources of individual differences would be missed by traditional information-processing analysis of task performance but would figure prominently in traditional psychometric analysis. It should be noted, however, that the underlying sources of between-subject variance captured by psychometric factors presumably include individual differences in (a) elementary information processes and the efficiency with which they are executed and (b) higher-order control processes and their effectiveness in initiating and monitoring the execution of elementary information processes.

What the Piagetian perspective provides that is largely ignored by the psychometric and information-processing perspectives is an account of the *development* of intellectual competence. The Piagetian perspective provides mechanisms of cognitive development (that is, equilibrium, assimilation, accommodation) and descriptions of the nature of intellectual competence at various stages of development.

In sum, we see no need to "choose" among approaches. Rather, a better goal would be to view each as dealing with different but overlapping aspects of intelligence. The question then arises as to whether there are aspects of intelligence or its functioning that are neglected by all three approaches.

We would characterize intelligence, when applied to the everyday world in which we live, as involving purposive adaptation to, shaping of, and selection of real-world environments relevant to one's life. We wish to emphasize that we are not hereby defining what intelligence is, but rather characterizing it in terms of the real-world tasks to which it is applied. This characterization has several implications.

First, intelligence needs to be considered in relation to real-world environments. None of the three approaches has seriously dealt with tasks and task performance that are relevant to the everyday world beyond the classroom.

Second, intelligence is characterized in terms of its application to the environment as it is relevant to one's life. The manifestation of intelligence in one culture may be quite different from the manifestation of intelligence in another culture, depending on the demands of the culture and its surroundings (see, for example, Baltes, Dittmann-Kohli, and Dixon 1982; Berry 1974, 1980; Charlesworth 1979; Cole and Scribner 1974; Keating 1984; Laboratory of Comparative Human Cognition 1982). But the kinds of problems that have been studied seem to have little relevance to most persons' lives. Neisser (1976) has characterized tasks found in classrooms and on tests as (a) being devised by others, (b) often being of little or no intrinsic interest, (c) having all needed information available from the beginning , and (d) being disembedded from an individual's ordinary experience. Further, we would add that (e) academic tasks usually are well defined, (f) they often have one correct answer, and (g) there often is but one method of correct solution.

Third, intelligence is characterized in terms of its application to, adaptation to, shaping of, and selection of environments. Although the tasks and theories that have been proposed may be related to such skills, what relations exist need to be pointed out more clearly. The ability to answer analogies or to answer vocabulary questions may well be predictive of everyday functioning. But none of the tests or theories deals directly with adaptation, shaping, and selection.

Finally, we characterize intelligence as purposive. One shapes one's life according to plans, short term and long term. Although current theories and tests may assess planning skills, the plans assessed are at a much more microscopic level than the kinds of plans we believe are relevant to living in real-world environments.

Our conclusion, then, is that theorists and technologists have to get out of laboratories and into the real world, whether it is the world of the school or the world of the adult worker (see also Charlesworth 1976; Goodnow 1976; McClelland, 1973; Neisser 1976, 1979; Wagner and Sternberg, 1985). We do not believe that current theories and tests have no value. To the contrary, they seem to deal well with intelligence as it relates to the *internal environment* of the individual: The theories aptly decompose intelligence into its constituent parts. Where the theories seem inadequate is in their inattention to the relation between intelligence and the *external environment* in which intelligence functions. Intelligence does not operate in a vacuum but rather in a world that is constantly increasing in complexity. If our understanding of intelligence is to have any relevance for understanding the interface between the individual and this world rather than merely in a laboratory or on a standardized test. Studying such functioning is much more difficult than studying functioning under the highly controlled conditions of a psychologist's laboratory. But we fear that unless the leap is made, psychologists—with their theories and tests—will be left far behind in a rapidly changing world. Their notions of intelligence and intelligence testing may continue to develop, but in ways progressively more out of touch with the real world. We believe the time has come to bring the world into testing. Ideally, this day would have come before testing was brought so prominently into the world.

IMPLICATIONS OF THEORIES OF INTELLIGENCE FOR EDUCATION

What implications for intelligence can be derived from the alternative approaches we have just considered? We now turn to this central question, dealing in turn with each of the psychometric, Piagetian, and information-processing approaches. We will divide our consideration of each approach into two major sections. The first section will deal with deriving educational objectives; the second section will deal with reaching educational objectives. Each of these sections will be further divided into two subsections, one concerning the development of intellectual skills (for example, reasoning ability, vocabulary, analytical thinking), the other concerning the development of knowledge and knowledge-related skills (for example, reading, spelling, mathematics, social studies).

Educational Implications of the Psychometric Approach to Intelligence

The psychometric approach to intelligence has been closely tied to education since the turn of the century. Indeed, Alfred Binet's work began with his commission to identify children who would be unable to profit from normal instruction in the public schools of France. Since Binet's time, the testing movement has always been very closely linked to educational goals and to the educational establishment.

Deriving Educational Objectives: Intellectual Skills. Many intervention programs have been aimed at the goal of improving intellectual skills, especially programs at the preschool level whose purpose has been to prepare children for formal schooling. (See Bronfenbrenner 1975; Gordon 1975; Jensen 1969; and Palmer and Anderson 1979 for comprehensive reviews of such programs.)

Project Head Start is perhaps the most conspicuous example of such a program. The program has provided activities designed to facilitate language development and to enhance performance on a variety of tasks similar to those found on intelligence tests. The program has had other equally important goals, such as providing health services and enhancing social development. (See Zigler 1973 and Zigler and Valentine 1979 for comprehensive reviews of the program.) There is no universal Head Start curriculum (Zigler and Seitz 1982), and in fact, no one has been in a position to say just what the experiences in most of the centers were like (Miller 1979).

Although it is not possible to speak of a single Head Start curriculum, one can identify program models that were adopted by multiple Head Start centers. One such model is a program developed by Carl Bereiter and Siegfried Engelmann at the University of Illinois in 1966 (Bereiter and Engelmann 1966). The curriculum was essentially a crash program designed to build the skills that would be needed for first-grade work. The program in fact resembled a first-grade class more than did most other programs. The program's highly academic emphasis can be seen by considering just a few of the fifteen specific minimum goals it set for students (Whimbey, with L. Whimbey, 1975): (a) ability to use both affirmative and negative statements in reply to the question, What is this? (b) ability to use the prepositions *on, in, under, over,* and *between* to describe relations among objects; (c) ability to perform simple *if-then* deductions; and (d) ability to name colors. The Bereiter-Engelmann program and other highly academically oriented programs like it seemed to produce greater gains in both IQ and achievement test performance than did the less academically oriented programs.

Because of the great diversity in Head Start centers, it has been difficult to evaluate the success of the program in terms of gains in academically important intellectual competencies. Recently, Lazar and Darlington (1982) completed a longitudinal follow-up on twelve early intervention programs. These programs were not a random sample of Head Start centers but rather a clearly nonrandom sample of experimental, research-oriented programs for children from low-income families for which careful documentation was available. Long-lasting effects were reported in some areas but not others. Some of the main conclusions were the following:

1. Performance on the Stanford-Binet Intelligence Scale was higher for children in the programs than for children who served as controls and did not participate in the programs. The gains lasted for several years after the completion of the programs, but eventually disappeared. Follow-ups ten to seventeen years after the programs ended found no significant differences between program and control children.
2. Children who attended the programs were less likely to be assigned to special education classes and were less likely to be retained in grade than were control children.
3. The programs resulted in improved attitudes toward school performance on the part of students and their mothers.

Another approach to intellectual skills training is that provided by Guilford's Structure-of-Intellect (SOI) Model (Guilford 1967, 1982). The model, mentioned earlier, classifies intellectual factors according to contents (visual, auditory, symbolic, semantic, and behavioral), operations (cognition, memory, evaluation, convergent production, and divergent production), and products (units, classes, relations, systems, transformations, and implications). Guilford and his associates have devised tests purported to measure most but not all of the factors generated by crossing all possible combinations of contents, operations, and products. Meeker (1969) devised a means of describing performance on individual intelligence tests in terms of the SOI model and provided guidance on use and interpretation of the model.

An example of a longitudinal implementation of the SOI model is the Glendora Unified School District Program (Valett 1978). Norms have been determined for children five to twelve years old on numerous short tests designed to assess performance on each of the SOI factors. A profile is constructed for each child on the basis of his or her test performance, and a prescriptive educational program is then implemented. A number of games, activities, and curriculum materials have been constructed for the purpose of remediation of weaknesses. Initial results suggest that children in the program do significantly better when tested later on the SOI tests than do comparable control children.

Another program based on Guilford's model is Think (see Valett 1978). The Think curriculum is used with elementary and secondary school students who demonstrate a weakness in conceptual abilities. The program has been designed especially to develop six thinking skills: thing making (mental processes for becoming aware of and naming things), qualification (recognizing the unique sensory, emotional, or logical aspects of a thing), classification (sorting into groups on the basis of common properties), structure analysis (dividing things into parts), operation analysis (dividing events into phases or stages), and seeing analogies (recognizing similarities between relationships). Evaluation of the program suggests that students participating in it improve in language and reading skills.

It has been argued that an important reason for the popularity of the IQ as a measure of program effectiveness—and of IQ tests as the basis for program curricula—is that intervention programs commonly yielded gains in IQ of about ten points (Zigler and Seitz 1982) and occasionally more (Hunt 1971). There is doubt about how much of this gain reflects actual intellectual skill differences, however. It seems likely that the programs effected motivational changes and improvements in test-taking skills as well as improvements in cognitive skills (Seitz, Abelson, Levine, and Zigler 1975; Zigler, Abelson, Trickett, and Seitz 1982). The motivational explanation is consistent with the common finding that the gains are lost when children leave the program. This subsequent loss had led Zigler and Seitz to recommend that interventions be directed at improving family support systems, because such systems would be a necessary (although clearly not sufficient) condition for maintaining gains, at least through a child's schooling.

An example of an intellectual skills training program that included interventions directed at improving family support systems is the Milwaukee Project (Garber and Heber 1981, 1982). Low-IQ (seventy-five or below) mothers who were seriously economically disadvantaged and their newborn children (three months of age) were the targets of this intervention program. Mothers were provided a rehabilitation program that included vocational training, instruction in home management, and remedial education that took place during the first two years of the program. Children were provided a full-day, year-round preschool program from the age of three months until the age of six years or entry to first grade. The preschool program was highly structured and educationally oriented, emphasizing problem solving and language skills development. An advantage of twenty-five points on the Stanford-Binet Intelligence Test was found for children in the program compared to a control group of disadvantaged children with low-IQ mothers who did not participate in the program. A follow-up that has continued for four years after children finished the program found a significant advantage for the experimental group over the control group on a variety of academic-related measures.

However, during the follow-up period, the performance of the experimental and control groups declined relative to national norms, and the performance advantage of the experimental group over the control group diminished.

Deriving Educational Objectives: Knowledge and Knowledge-related Skills. The product of the psychometric approach as applied to knowledge and knowledge-related skills is the standardized achievement test. An example of such a test is the Stanford Achievement Test. This test, like others of its kind, is used for diagnosing strengths and weaknesses in the past learning of individual students, groups of students, and school curricula. In particular, test scores can be used to generate educational objectives for students with weaknesses in particular content areas. The areas covered by the Stanford—vocabulary, reading comprehension, wotd study skills, mathematics concepts, mathematics computation, mathematics applications, spelling, language, social science, science, and listening comprehension—are typical of such tests.

More specific tests have also been designed that provide diagnostic information in more limited academic areas. For example, the Stanford Diagnostic Reading Test provides scores for literal reading comprehension, inferential reading comprehension, vocabulary, sound discrimination, blending, and rate of reading. Although the information provided by specific diagnostic tests such as this one is more precise than information provided by more general achievement tests, the lack of emphasis on process in the psychometric approach presents a problem for prescribing educational objectives: Without an understanding of the processes that underlie say, sound blending, it can be difficult to generate a prescription regarding exactly how teaching and learning should proceed that goes beyond simple practice, which may not be sufficient to remediate deficits in a skill such as sound blending, in at least some cases.

Reaching Educational Objectives: Intellectual Skills. How can tests be used in the schools, particularly for assessing the interface between intellectual skills and schooling? Several suggestions have been made in this regard (for example, Federico 1980; McCombs and McDaniel 1981). One set of suggestions derives from Glaser (1977, 1980), who proposed that the interface between testing and schooling can proceed according to any one of five models:

1. *Selective, fixed-track model.* Tests are used to judge whether a student

has the initial competence needed to succeed in an instructional program. If the initial competence is present, the student is admitted to the program; if not, the student is designated a poor learner and is not admitted to the program. This has been the traditional approach to dealing with intellectually handicapped children. Until recently, such students would be routinely excluded from regular public school programs.

2. *Development of initial competence model.* This model includes all aspects of the first model plus an additional aspect. If, upon initial testing, the student does not demonstrate the competency required for program entry, a remedial program is instituted to improve the competency to the point where the student can enter the program. Federally funded remedial reading and mathematics programs are examples of this model: Students who do poorly on standardized reading and mathematics tests are eligible to receive remedial help. (In the pure case, students would not be allowed into regular programs until the initial required competence was fully demonstrated.)

3. *Accommodation to different styles of learning model.* This model is similar to the first model except for the fact that several programs are offered, each with its own test of competence for being admitted to the program. A student could be admitted to any program for which the required competence was demonstrated. The idea is that a learner could find a program that accommodates his or her particular style. At first glance, tracking in public schools might appear to be an example of this model. But such tracking is a poor example, because tracking generally takes into account only rate, not style, of learning.

4. *Development of initial competence and accommodation to styles of learning model.* As the name suggests, this model is the third one with the added provision that students who do not demonstrate competence for being admitted to any of the programs are given an option to receive remediation that will eventually enable their admission.

5. *Alternate terminal attainments model.* This model is the fourth with the modification that all students need not meet the same terminal criterion. This model is illustrated by high schools that award different diplomas depending on the nature and level of student accomplishments.

Another set of suggestions regarding the uses of standardized IQ tests in the schools was put forward by Resnick (1979), who suggested that three purposes could be served by standardized tests in the management of instruction:

1. *Sorting function.* Tests are used to determine who gets into which program.
2. *Grading function.* Tests are used in conjunction with grades in school to assess how well a student is learning. Often, a student is labeled an "underachiever" if high IQ test scores are accompanied by low grades or achievement test scores.
3. *Monitoring function.* Monitoring is the assessment of performance during a program for the purpose of making adjustments in the program or its implementation. According to Resnick, standardized tests do not serve this function well, because they do not provide the precise determination of what has been mastered and what should come next.

Reaching Educational Objectives: Knowledge and Knowledge-related Skills. The psychometric approach can be used for the purpose of reaching educational objectives related to the development of knowledge and knowledge-related skills when it provides information (often in the form of test scores) that can be used to describe the instructional program that would best suit a particular learner.

A substantial body of research on aptitude x treatment interactions (ATIs) addresses the issue of matching instruction to learner characteristics. A thorough review of the ATI approach and studies done under this approach can be found in Cronbach and Snow (1977). We provide only two examples here.

The first is a recent study by Peterson, Terence, and Swing (1981) on interactions between intellectual ability and large- versus small-group instruction in fourth- and fifth-grade students. Students were taught a two-week geometry unit in either a large- or a small-group situation. A significant curvilinear aptitude x treatment interaction was reported, with high- and low-ability students doing better in the small-group condition than in the large-group condition. Medium-ability students did slightly better in the large-group condition. This result is explained in terms of high- and low-ability students benefiting relatively more from the peer tutoring processes that occur in small-group instruction.

A second study (Janicki and Peterson 1981) examined the interaction of either direct instruction (as in a classroom) or a small-group variation of direct instruction with learner attitudes and locus of control. Locus of control refers to beliefs about the extent to which important life events are under one's own control. An ATI was reported in which students with more positive attitudes and an internal locus of control were better in the small-group variation of direct instruction than in the classroom variant. The explanation offered was that the small-group setting offered more opportunity for choosing activities and exerting control over learning.

Comprehensive reviews of the ATI literature suggest several limitations on what, in theory, would be an ideal approach for relating intellectual characteristics of the learner to instructional treatments (see Cronbach and Snow 1977; Snow 1976, 1977; Tobias 1981, 1982). First, although support for the existence of ATIs between general mental ability and various educational treatments is provided by the ATI literature, little support can be found for ATIs between treatments and more specific aptitudes. Second, there is some question concerning the generality of ATIs. Cronbach (1975) suggested that they may be specific to time and place. Third, an ATI study requires a tremendous amount of statistical power (that is, ability to reject the null hypothesis if it is false), and few of the studies that have been done have had the statistical power they ideally should have had. Fourth, there is often a gap between the theory generating the study and the experimental operations used to test the theory. As a result, the studies are often only minimal tests of the hypotheses they set out to investigate.

Dissatisfaction with the results of many ATI studies led to at least two relatively recent developments: (a) an increased interest in learner control of instruction (Merrill 1975; Snow 1980) and (b) attempts to identify the underlying information processes common to performance on aptitude tests and instructional settings. The interest in learner control of instruction stems from the belief that the learner, rather than the teacher, knows best the learner's specific strengths and weaknesses and therefore is better able to design an optimal educational environment or treatment. The attempts to identify the underlying information processes common to performance on aptitude tests and instructional settings are motivated by the belief that ATIs can be understood accurately only at the level of information processes. These two developments may well result in a set of more positive and more replicable results. But we believe that at present the gap between what is tested in IQ tests and what is taught in schools—both in terms of knowledge and skills—is sufficiently large that it will be difficult indeed to bring the two together.

Summary. To summarize, the psychometric approach to intelligence has been closely linked to the schooling process ever since Binet's original development of his test for identifying retarded individuals who would not profit from normal instruction. The links between the psychometric approach and schooling have taken a number of forms, many of which we have considered here. To the extent that the linkage has not always succeeded, we believe that several problems can be identified as hindering the flow of information from tests to schools and back again. First, the tests do not provide the kinds of information about process that seem to be necessary for an effective training program that seeks, in fact, to train students in the processes (or products) of learning. Second, a large gap exists between the kinds of microprocesses required on IQ tests and the macroprocesses required for school learning. Although the tests may well be predictive of such learning, it would be difficult to argue that IQ tests directly tap the skills involved, say, in writing a paper. Third, motivational and situational limitations intervene between test and school performance to reduce further the relationship between the two. Until a theory and measurement of motivation can be brought into the assessment process, tests of purely cognitive functioning will remain highly limited predictors of school accomplishment. Fourth, there has been a notable gap between theory and practice. The links between psychometric theories of intelligence on the one hand and tests and training programs based on these theories on the other have been tenuous at best. Fifth and finally, much of the research that has been done that has sought to link theory to practice has been flawed (see, for example, the review in Cronbach and Snow 1977). Even if strong links existed, it is not clear that they would regularly be found, if only because of inadequacies in the designs of existing studies. As a result, the fruitfulness of linking psychometric theory to educational practice is still in need of stronger demonstration.

Educational Implications of the Piagetian Approach to Intelligence

Piaget and his Genevan collaborators have not been interested primarily in the implications of his theory for educational practice (Duckworth 1979a, 1979b; Elkind 1974; McNally 1974). Rather, their interest has been primarily in epistemology, the area of philosophy concerned with the nature and origin of knowledge. American educators and psychologists have been largely responsible for bringing

Piagetian theory into the educational arena, and they have done so in a manner that has resulted in a considerable amount of tension between what can be regarded as Genevan and American views.

American educators and psychologists have been interested particularly in how to speed up the development of Piagetian "intellectual structures," which typically develop slowly. The Genevan position was originally that such acceleration is not possible. This position was later modified slightly to the new position that some, but very limited, learning of intellectual structures can take place. The issue of whether Piagetian structures can be trained has stimulated a considerable body of research (see Beilin 1971, 1977 for reviews of this literature), but the issue remains unresolved at present.

One of the reasons the issue may have remained unresolved is that it has been difficult not only to derive prescriptions for educational practice from the theory but also to derive proscriptions (Klausmeier 1979). The first large-scale attempt to apply Piagetian theory to education can probably be traced to the Woods Hole Conference of 1959 (see Bruner 1961), which was seminal for a number of the sweeping educational reforms of the 1960s. Examples of curricula based at least in part on Piagetian ideas of intellectual development have included the New Math, Minimath, Science Curriculum Improvement Study Guide, Project Physics, and Man: A Course of Study (see Klausmeier 1979).

Deriving Educational Objectives: Intellectual Skills.. Piagetian theory has often been interpreted as implying that a goal of education should be to propel children into subsequent developmental periods of intellectual growth earlier than they would normally enter these periods on their own. Piagetian theory can thus be seen as providing a sense of what kinds of skills should be taught to a child at each level of development. Efforts to improve intellectual skills have generally focused on either the concrete-operational period or the formal-operational period and have been "American" in their emphasis on acceleration.

A number of programs have sought to have children reach the period of concrete operations in the preschool, and thus before the usual age of six or so when concrete operations typically begin (Bingham-Newman, Saunders, and Hooper 1976; Kamii and DeVries 1977; Lavatelli 1970a, 1970b; Silverman and Weikart 1973). In the concrete-operational period, mental operations are designated as concrete because they are tied to concrete objects. The capacity for abstract thought is not yet fully developed, although the ability to reason inductively is fairly well established. Children during this period have acquired *reversibility* and *seriation*. Reversibility is shown by the children's abilities to add and subtract (which are reverses of each other), their abilities to multiply and divide (again reverses), and their ability to conserve. Conservation of quantity (or volume) is demonstrated by a child's ability to recognize that a fat, short glass holds the same amount of water as a tall, thin glass from which the water was poured. Similarly, children will realize that regardless of the shape into which a ball of clay is twisted, the amount of clay remains invariant over the various shapes. Children during this period of intellectual development also acquire the abilities to seriate and to make transitive inferences. The ability to seriate allows children to order objects along various dimensions—from short to tall, from light to dark, from fat to thin, and so forth. The ability to make transitive inferences enables a child to infer, for example, that if John is taller than Pete, and Pete is taller than Bill, then John is taller than Bill.

Training programs directed at having preschool children reach the period of concrete operations have in common the goal of providing children with activities appropriate to their developmental levels. Activities appropriate to children's developmental levels are defined as activities that challenge children's thinking but at the same time are not so difficult as to lead to repeated failure. The nature of these activities has varied from program to program. For example, a program by Furth and Wachs (1974) is based on a set of thinking games that are designed to engage children in creative, independent thinking. Alternatively, a program by Kamii and DeVries (1977) is based on more traditional child development activities, including listening to stories, painting, puzzles, block building, and sand and water play. There has been a shift in Piagetian preschool programs away from highly structured curricula to the view that children should be left alone to direct their own thinking in a rich and supporting environment (Kuhn 1979a). Evaluation of Piagetian preschool programs indicates that children in the programs do indeed reach the period of concrete operations, but it is not clear they actually do so *earlier* than do children who are not in the programs (Kuhn 1979a). Moreover, there is no evidence at all that earlier attainment of the concrete-operational period results in earlier attainment of the subsequent period of formal operations, which we consider next.

In the formal-operational period, usually beginning at the age of eleven or twelve, children acquire the ability to reason abstractly without reference to concrete objects or events. Children become more able to reason from the general to the specific (deductively), and thus to use the peculiar blend of inductive and deductive reasoning that characterizes scientific inquiry. During this period, children acquire the ability to comprehend second-order relations of the kind used in reasoning by analogy (that is, relations between relations). This period is often characterized as the first one to enable children to contemplate not only what is, but what might be (Kuhn 1979b). Examples of formal-operational reasoning include constructing an argument for a position you may not support, using proportional relationships to determine whether the economy size box of cereal is really more economical than the regular size, and determining what time you are likely to reach your destination on an automobile trip by taking into account your present rate of travel.

Formal-operational thinking is of particular interest to educators for two reasons. First, formal-operational thinking is required for a full understanding of academic disciplines, such as physics, mathematics, and literature (Chiapetta 1976; Collis 1971; Griffiths 1976; Peel 1976), as well as for many examples of everyday reasoning (Capon and Kuhn 1979; Kuhn and Brannock 1977). Second, there are data to suggest that less than half of all high school students, college students, and adults are fully capable of formal-operational reasoning (Chiapetta 1976), although this percentage may vary somewhat as a function of the individual's familiarity with particular tasks (Dasen 1977; Sinnott 1975). It is also interesting that whereas there is a correlation between formal-operational reasoning ability and traditional measures of intelligence (Kuhn 1976), a substantial number of individuals who do well on standardized tests may not yet be fully capable of formal-operational reasoning (Nucci and Gordon 1979). What makes the attainment of formal-operational reasoning a seemingly inherently more worthwhile educational goal than the early attainment of concrete operations is that whereas all normal individuals eventually attain full concrete-operational reasoning, the same does not appear to be true for formal-operational reasoning.

An example of a program designed with the goals of attainment of formal operations and teaching science concepts is Karplus's (1974) Science Curriculum Improvement Study (SCIS) (see also Lawson 1975; Lawson, Blake and Norland 1975; Lawson and Renner 1975; Lawson and Wollman 1975.) This curriculum and its derivatives have been developed for students from elementary to high school levels. Science concepts are taught by activities provided in three phases. In an exploration phase, students manipulate materials and observe results. Next, in an invention phase, the teacher introduces symbols and words that help students label what they have observed. Finally, in a discovery phase, students apply what they have learned in more general and abstract contexts. The desired results of the program are the development of formal-operational thinking and mastery of science concepts. Efforts to train formal-operational thinking are in their early stages, so it is difficult as yet to evaluate their effectiveness.

Deriving Educational Objectives: Knowledge and Knowledge-Based Skills. As difficult as it was to use Piagetian theory to derive educational objectives for the purposes of developing intellectual skills, it is even more difficult to use the theory when one's purpose is to develop knowledge and knowledge-based skills. Piagetian theory is fundamentally a developmental theory of intelligence. The theory views learning in the educational sense as being limited to specific tasks and of only secondary importance to the learning of generalized skills (Lawton and Hooper 1978).

Piagetian theory as manifested in educational settings has typically involved a program of thinking activities along the lines of those described in the previous section that are included in addition to the usual reading, writing, and arithmetic (Furth and Wachs 1974; Kuhn 1979a). As yet, there is little integration of Piagetian thinking activities with traditional academic disciplines with the possible exception of several science-oriented programs (for example, Karplus 1974; Lawson 1975). Even in these programs, the links between the theory and program are often somewhat tenuous.

Reaching Educational Objectives: Intellectual Skills. With what has been described as the Genevan position on the futility of developing intelligence as an educational objective, it should come as no surprise that implications of the Piagetian approach for reaching educational objectives are not easily found.

One approach would be to attempt to diagnose intellectual level with tasks that measure a variety of Piagetian concepts and then to tailor remedial instruction accordingly. Tuddenham (1975), for example, has constructed a battery of Piagetian tasks to measure intellectual level. This approach has been largely rejected by adherents of Piaget's theory as being (a) impractical, especially if the preferred practice of individualized clinical assessment is used; (b) unwise, because it is doubtful that training of intellectual structures is possible; and (c) against good educational practice, because learning is inhibited when externally imposed tasks are used, as would be the case in most training programs (Duckworth 1979a; Furth 1970; McNally 1974; Piaget 1970). Moreover, it is probably a mistake to infuse Piagetian tasks into the school curriculum because such tasks are simply *indicators* of the level of cognitive functioning; there is no reason to expect simple practice on the tasks to enhance cognitive development. Klausmeier (1979) proposed the analogy that teaching Piagetian tasks is like teaching specific items on an intelligence test for the purpose of developing intelligence.

Reaching Educational Objectives: Knowledge and Knowledge-based Skills. The theory does serve as a useful source of educational implications for reaching objectives in the development of knowledge and knowledge-based skills. Consider four general implications of the theory.

1. *Active discovery is preferable to passive, receptive learning.* Piaget (1970) made a distinction between two types of schools. Traditional schools are characterized by work being imposed on students from external sources, usually the teacher. For Piaget (and John Dewey), work imposed by others is the antithesis of intrinsic interest and therefore of learning (McNally 1974). Some have charged American educators and psychologists with being preoccupied with the study of the effects of the environment on an individual who is conceived of as being nothing more than a passive recipient of information (for example, Reid 1979). "Activity schools," on the other hand, are characterized by active-discovery learning. Students learn in situations by actively working on something—by attempting to obtain a practical result that they can then understand (Athey and Rubadeau 1970; Duckworth 1979a; Reid 1979).

   Overall, Piaget's view of education is quite similar to the experimentalist position of John Dewey (1968). This position holds that knowledge develops from activity and, more specifically, from applying the scientific method to whatever problems the environment has to offer. The steps of learning involve (a) becoming aware of the problem, (b) clarifying the problem, (c) proposing hypotheses for solving the problem, (d) reasoning out the implications of each hypothesis, and (e) testing each hypothesis (McNally 1974).

The sharp distinction made between traditional schools and activity schools is perhaps overly simplistic, but the point being made is an important one. The Piagetian view seems clearly to lead to a preference for the kinds of programs found today in open, rather than in traditional, schools (Lawton and Hooper 1978).

2. *Motivation is fundamentally important.* This implication follows from the view that in any learning situation, it is the learner who is doing most of the work, not the teacher. What is of particular interest is that the concept of motivation is deeply embedded in the functioning of cognitive structures. Motivation derives directly from the operations of the intellectual structures (Furth 1970). According to Piaget, those things are most interesting that pose moderate novelty to the individual, and thus to which the individual's cognitive structures can be accommodated: Too little novelty is a bore; too much novelty passes the individual by.

This view suggests the great importance of matching the task to the child's cognitive structures; but the question remains as to how best to go about doing this. Because one cannot know precisely the cognitive structures that an individual brings to a situation, it is usually recommended that a wide variety of tasks be made available and that the children given the tasks then be watched to determine what grabs their interest. The tasks that interest particular children are those most likely to be well matched to their existing cognitive structures (Farnham-Diggory 1972; McNally 1974).

3. *Learning situations must be practical.* Practical situations are those that correspond to an individual's natural activity (Duckworth 1979a). Learning in schools should not be different from an individual's natural form of learning about the world. The most important thing schools can do is to encourage students to think about things they might not have thought to think about on their own. A closely related point is that what is practical is also that which is concrete, at least until the stage of formal operations. Manipulative activities with concrete materials are therefore to be recommended, at least until the stage of formal operations (Ginsburg and Opper 1979).

4. *Flexibility is essential.* The best learning situations are those that permit the learner to establish plans for reaching a distant goal,

where wide latitude is given as to permissible approaches or paths to reach the goal (Athey and Rubadeau 1970; Duckworth 1979a).

Summary. The educational implications of Piagetian theory have been difficult to come by, because Piaget's theory is a theory of intellectual development rather than of learning in the educational sense of the word. Thus, if the theory does not have clear implications for education, neither was it meant to. We will conclude with a discussion of four reasons why we believe the theory is probably not optimally suited for widespread use in education, while expressing our sympathy with the four implications just discussed.

1. *The theory is of competence rather than of performance.* Competence refers to all that a person is capable of, regardless of internal or external constraints that interfere with the application of this full competence. Performance refers to demonstrated competence. Any number of factors act to limit competence—motivation, external resources, attention, and the like. Educators must deal with manifest performance as well as underlying competence. Otherwise, they will create unrealistic expectations for students. Indeed, Piagetian-based programs seem, if anything, to involve setting expectations that are simply too high for students to reach. The same result could be expected from any educational program based on a theory of competence rather than of performance (Davidson and Sternberg, 1985). Duckworth (1979b) suggested that educators stop trying to develop intellectual structures and instead be concerned with developing individuals' use of their structures to learn new things about the world. In other words, Duckworth is arguing that educators should pay attention to performance rather than to competence.

2. *The long time covered by each period limits the usefulness of the periods for sequencing instruction.* The periods may provide general guidelines for, but certainly do not provide specific sequencing of, educational objectives. The time ranges covered by the periods and even the subperiods are simply too great. Although further subdivision on the bases of identified lags in development (so-called horizontal decalages) is possible, these lags are treated by the theory as anomalies and therefore are of little use in sequencing instruction (Klausmeier 1979).

3. *The theory emphasizes maturation rather than learning.* The emphasis in Piaget's theory is clearly on the unfolding of a preprogrammed set of skills over time. Short shrift is given to learning and environmental influences on learning. Piaget does not ignore the environment: To the contrary, he emphasizes the individual's interaction with the environment. But the development of cognitive structures is believed to be primarily maturational, and, as noted earlier, Piagetians have, if anything, scoffed at attempts to teach these structures.

4. *The theory lacks sufficient empirical support to serve, at present, as a basis for educational interventions.* As noted earlier, the empirical support for Piaget's theory is mixed at best (see especially, Brainerd 1978; Brown and Desforges 1979; Siegel and Brainerd 1978). As time goes on, successively larger chunks of the theory are being undermined by new data. One therefore must be reluctant to apply the theory to education, lest the interventions fail in part because the theory on which they are based is incorrect.

In sum, then, educators seeking to apply Piaget's theory to educational interventions would do well to pause before jumping in. At the same time, some of the implications that follow from the theory, particularly those applying to active learning, motivation, practicality, and flexibility, would seem to be well worth heeding. Perhaps the lesson to be learned is that if one is selective in the aspects of the theory used rather than trying to apply it wholesale, one is much more likely to design a successful, practically feasible educational program.

Educational Implications of the Information-processing Approach

Compared to our attempt to derive educational objectives from the Piagetian perspective, an attempt to derive such objectives from an information-processing perspective is easy. The attempt is nontrivial, however, especially because the gap between cognitive psychology and education has been and continues to be quite substantial.

Deriving Educational Objectives: Intellectual Skills. Information-processing theories of intelligence can be used for the purpose of deriving educational objectives by virtue of their providing a means of decomposing task performance into its underlying mental processes.

Educational objectives can then be developed to improve the efficiency with which the identified information-processing components are executed.

An example of this approach is provided by the work of Whitely and Dawis (1974). Inner-city high school students were trained to solve verbal analogies, problems such as the doctor : patient :: lawyer : (judge, client) problem given earlier. Students were given training that consisted of various combinations of (a) practice on verbal analogies, (b) feedback about the correct answers, (c) instruction on topics such as types of analogy relationships (for example, opposites, functional relations, and the like), and (d) instructions regarding the formal structure of an analogy. Earlier information-processing analyses of analogy performance were used to provide a theoretical basis for the training. Improvement was found on a subsequent test of analogical reasoning for the group that received instruction on relationships, feedback, and structure. Other studies similar to the Whitely and Dawis study have also reported success in improving children's performance on various kinds of reasoning problems (for example, Holzman, Glaser, and Pellegrino 1976; Sternberg and Weil 1980).

A similar approach has been applied to the task of improving memory performance in mildly retarded individuals. For example, Engle and Nagle (1979) trained mildly retarded fifth- and sixth-grade students on three strategies for remembering a series of pictures of common objects. A semantic encoding strategy group was instructed to think of the meaning of each item, of a personal experience with it, of its function, and of other items in the list of objects that were in the same category. An acoustic encoding strategy group was instructed to think of the sound of the word and to repeat the verbal label of the pictures. The choice of strategies to be trained followed from information-processing theories of memory performance. Subsequent performance was best for the semantic encoding strategy group up to seven days after training. A follow-up seven months later found no evidence for the retention of the strategies, although when the strategies were prompted, performance again was superior for the semantic encoding strategy group.

Similar results have been reported by others (for example, Brown and Barclay 1976; Butterfield, Wambold, and Belmont 1973), but demonstrations of durability and transfer of training remain skimpy. When transfer has been tested in retarded individuals, almost none has been found, even for highly similar items and tasks (Resnick 1981). Whether individuals of normal intelligence would show significantly more transfer than is shown by the retarded remains unanswered. Concern over the problem of transfer has prompted a shift in emphasis to the metacognitive level, that is, the level of executive planning and decision processes rather than of lower-order task-performance components. Evidence is becoming available that emphasis on metacognitive training does result in some degree of durability and transfer.

Kendall, Borkowski, and Cavanaugh (1980), for example, studied the maintenance and generalization of an interrogative strategy for remembering pairs of pictures of common objects. The strategy consisted of having the child covertly perform four steps for each pair of to-be-remembered items: (a) state a relationship between the items of the pair, (b) ask a "why" question about the relationship, (c) analyze the items semantically (that is, think about their meaning), and (d) apply the semantic analysis to answer the "why" question. To enhance strategy maintenance and transfer, the training was characterized by (a) active student participation, (b) extended strategy training, (c) semantic processing of item pairs, (d) provision of feedback about the value of using the strategy, (e) use of many examples provided by the experimenter as a means of explaining the parts of the strategy, (f) systematic introduction of the parts of the strategy, and (g) fading of experimenter involvement over the course of the training. The outcome of the study was that strategy maintenance was obtained (at least for a week or so) and that generalization was obtained to a new task in which the student was required to remember sets of three pictures. Although it would have been desirable to use a transfer task less similar to the original task than this one was, given past results, a finding of any transfer at all was impressive. Success with similar approaches to training intellectual skills has been reported by others as well (see, for example, Belmont, Butterfield and Borkowski 1978; Borkowski and Cavanaugh 1979; Brown and Campione 1977; 1981; Lipman, Sharp, and Oscanyan 1979, 1980; Ross and Ross 1978).

By far the largest training program based on information-processing analysis is Feuerstein's (1980) Instrumenal Enrichment (IE) program. This extensive program for retarded learners has been employed in many countries, with at least tentative indications of success. Feuerstein proposes three major phases of information-processing: the input phase, the elaboration phase, and the output phase. The input phase concerns gathering data as an individual begins to consider a problem. The elaboration phase concerns using the data gathered in the input phase for solving a problem. The output phase concerns communicating the outcome of the elaboration phase. Within each phase, Feuerstein has identified specific impairments in information processing that are targets of the training program. Examples of specific impairments include (a) lack of, or impaired, capacity for considering two sources of information at once, which results in dealing with data in a piecemeal fashion rather than as a unit of organized facts; (b) blurred and sweeping perception characterized by viewing stimuli with a lack of precision and the completeness necessary for proper distinction among and description of stimuli; and (c) lack of, or deficient need for, precision and accuracy in data gathering. Although the program concentrates on training performance on IQ-like tasks, it also involves motivational components that encourage retarded performers to work to their full capacity. Because of the range of the program, a full discussion of it would be beyond the scope of this paper (see, however, Sternberg, 1985, for a lengthy discussion and evaluation).

In sum, information-processing theories of intelligence permit the decomposition of intelligent behavior into components, each of which can serve as a locus for a training intervention. Transfer of training seems to depend at least in part on training at the metacognitive as well as the cognitive level.

Deriving Educational Objectives: Knowledge and Knowledge-based Skills. Just as it is possible to decompose tasks that are believed to measure intellectual skills, it is possible to use information-processing techniques to decompose tasks that are involved in the acquisition of academic knowledge and skills. The trend toward focusing on metacognitive processes that we observed for intellectual tasks is also evident in the literature on academic tasks.

Support for the importance of metacognitive skills to learning in school settings comes from a series of studies of fifth-grade students conducted by Bransford, Franks, Stein, and their colleagues (Bransford et al. 1982; Franks et al. 1982; Stein, Bransford, Franks, Owings, Vye, and McGraw 1982; Stein, Bransford, Franks, Vye, and Perfetto 1982). Space restriction precludes a detailed review of these studies, but one result will be briefly described. Compared to academically unsuccessful fifth graders, academically successful fifth graders were (a) more accurate in their initial judgments about the relative difficulty of remembering sentences expressing nonarbitrary relations (for example, "The strong man helped his friend move the piano") compared to remembering sentences expressing arbitrary relations (for example, "The strong man read the paper during breakfast"), which were more difficult to remember, and (b) better at revising their initial difficulty judgments after being given practice at remembering both types of sentences. Academically unsuccessful fifth graders were trained to (a) evaluate the relative arbitrariness of sets of sentences and (b) activate knowledge that would make relations less arbitrary. After training, these students were better able to judge the difficulty of remembering sentences expressing arbitrary and non-arbitrary relations and, more important, showed better memory performance.

Rigney (1980) proposed that the learner is continually seeking answers to six questions: (a) What is it? (b) What should I do about it? (c) How can I do it? (d) Can I do it? (e) How am I doing it? (f) Am I through? For routine events, these questions are asked automatically without the learner's conscious attention. For other than routine events, answers may not be apparent, which will necessitate applying conscious cognitive resources. Self-monitoring skills identified by Rigney as being necessary for successful performance on academic tasks include keeping one's place in a long sequence of operations, knowing that a subgoal has been obtained, detecting errors, and recovering from errors either by making a quick fix or by retreating to the last known correct operation. Such monitoring involves both "looking ahead" and "looking back." Looking ahead includes learning the structure of a sequence of operations, identifying areas where errors are likely, choosing a strategy that will reduce the possibility of error and that will provide easy recovery, identifying the kinds of feedback that will be available at various points, and evaluating the usefulness of these various kinds of feedback. Looking back includes detecting errors previously made, keeping a history of what has been done to the present and thereby what should come next, and assessing the reasonableness of the present immediate outcome of task performance.

Collins and Smith's (1982) program for directly teaching reading comprehension shares Rigney's emphasis on metacognitive aspects of task performance. Four basic types of comprehension failures are proposed: (a) failure to understand particular words, (b) failure to understand particular sentences, (c) failure to understand relations between sentences, and (d) failure to understand how the text fits together as a whole. Varieties of comprehension failures within the four basic types are described. For example, failure to understand a sentence includes failing to find any interpretation at all, finding an interpretation that is too abstract to be useful, finding several conflicting interpretations, or finding an interpretation that conflicts with prior knowledge. Six remedies for comprehension failures are taught: (a) ignore and read on, (b) suspend judgment (that is, wait to see if the failure is resolved in the next few sentences), (c) form a tentative hypothesis, (d) reread the current sentence(s), (e) reread the previous context, and (f) go to an expert source. This program for directly teaching reading comprehension is only now being implemented, so the effectiveness of the program has yet to be demonstrated.

Greeno (1980) has formalized an information-processing analysis of task performance by developing a computer simulation model called Perdix that represents the knowledge required to solve problems in geometry. The program was developed largely by observing ninth-grade students solving geometry problems and thinking aloud as they solved the problems. Greeno identified three domains of knowledge that he believed are required for solving geometry problems: propositions used in making inferences, perceptual concepts used in recognizing patterns, and strategic principles used in setting goals and planning. It is this third domain of strategic principles that is of particular interest to us here. Included in this domain is knowledge of general plans that can lead to a desired outcome. For example, the knowledge that there are three alternative approaches available for demonstrating that two triangles are congruent would be an instance of knowledge that can be used for deciding on a problem-solving strategy.

The views of Rigney, Collins and Smith, and Greeno are representative of a growing number of views that emphasize metacognitive skills in academic performance (see, for example, Brown 1978, 1980; Carroll 1980; Flavell 1976; Snow 1980). Metacognitive theorists have in common their belief that teaching specific strategies just won't work in the long run: One must teach general principles and how to apply them over a variety of task domains.

Reaching Educational Objectives: Intellectual Skills. An implication of recent information-processing work for reaching educational objectives is that metacognitive as well as cognitive skills should be trained. An example of a program that follows this implication is one designed to develop general learning ability in university undergraduates (Dansereau et al. 1979). The program stresses six executive-level steps to learning that have the interesting, if macabre, acronym of MURDER.

The M corresponds to setting the mood to study; the U to reading for understanding; the R to recalling material without referring to the text; the D to digesting the material by amplifying it; the E to expanding knowledge by self-inquiry; and the R to reviewing mistakes made on tests and practice exercises. Each executive step is associated with a family of substrategies. Students who completed the program performed significantly better on comprehension tests on textbook passages than did students who did not complete the program. This testing took place one week after training, indicating at least short-term durability. Students in the program also reported significant changes in self-report measures of study practices.

Belmont and Butterfield (1977) reviewed a total of 114 studies on the use of cognitive instruction. None of the 114 studies involved training metacognitive skills, and none of these studies reported generalization of training. Conversely, Belmont, Butterfield, and Ferretti (1982) reviewed seven studies that directly taught metacognitive skills. Generalization of training was reported in six of seven studies. Belmont and his colleagues (1982) proposed training the following metacognitive steps for problem solving: (a) decide on a goal; (b) make a plan to reach the goal; (c) try the plan; (d) ask whether the plan worked; if the answer is *yes*, you are done; if it is *no*, proceed to the next step; (e) ask whether the plan was actually followed; if the answer is *no*, go back to step 3; if it is *yes*, proceed to the next step; and (f) ask what was wrong with the plan and then return to step 2. An example of a study involving training of metacognitive skills included in several of these steps is provided by Bornstein and Quevillon (1976), who instructed four-year-old children with impulsive behavior to ask themselves questions about solving items found on intelligence tests. The questions induced the children to set goals (step 1), helped them to make a plan for solving the problem (step 2), and encouraged them to ask whether or not the plan worked (step 4) by having the children reinforce themselves when a plan worked. Although training was carried out in a laboratory setting, transfer of training was reported for performance on academic problems in a classroom.

Another program designed to develop metacognitive skills needed for solving problems similar to those found on intelligence tests is the "Problem Solving and Comprehension: A Short Course in Analytical Reasoning" (Whimbey and Lochhead 1980). This program pairs up students, with one student describing to his or her partner the steps being tried to solve the problem. The partner points out errors but does not correct them. The exercises provided by the program are designed to reduce four common errors made in problem solving: (a) failing to use all relevant facts; (b) failing to use a systematic, step-by-step approach; (c) jumping to conclusions; and (d) using an inadequate or incorrect representation of the problem. A possible limitation of this program is that for many problems, the student partner may be unable to point out errors because he or she knows as little about how to solve the problem as does the student who is attempting to solve the problem.

Although almost all of the studies have focused on the role of schooling in the development of intellectual skills, some have centered on the role of the parents as well as of the school. In particular, it has been proposed that the parent serves a key role in a child's intellectual development by modeling self-control strategies that are gradually learned by the child over the course of the years of parent-child interaction (Brown and Campione 1981; Feuerstein 1980; Wertsch 1978). Feuerstein suggested that mediation of learning experiences by the parent is perhaps *the* critical way in which young children learn.

Reaching Educational Objectives; Knowledge and Knowledge-based Skills. The importance of considering metacognitive performance when one's purpose is to develop knowledge and knowledge-based skills is highlighted by the accumulating evidence that students, especially young students, are not very adept at monitoring what they do when learning. Generally speaking, students blindly follow instructions and do not question themselves in a manner that would lead to efficient task performance (Brown 1980). We will mention four areas of metacognitive performance that have been found to be problematic for students. (See Brown 1978, 1980, for comprehensive reviews.)

1. *Task difficulty.* Students have been shown to be relatively unskilled in predicting the difficulty of a task and in recognizing when task difficulty changes markedly. For example, Moynahan (1973) found that young children would predict that a noncategorized set of items would be as easy to remember as a categorized set, even though the category structure actually improved their recall performance markedly. Similarly, Tenney (1975) asked kindergarten, third- and sixth-grade students to compose lists of words that would be easy to recall. Developmental differences were found whereby the older students were more likely to demonstrate the insight that organization by taxonomic category made lists easier

to remember (see also Brown 1975, 1978; Brown, Campione, and Murphy 1977; Flavell, Friedrichs, and Hoyt 1970; Salatas and Flavell 1976; Smirnov 1973).

2. *Comprehension monitoring.* Students have been shown to be insensitive to incomprehensibility and incompleteness of task directions, textual information, and verbal communications. For example, Markmam (1977) asked first- through third-grade students to help in finding a way to teach children a magical trick. The directions for the trick as presented to the students were incomprehensible. After the directions were presented, the students were asked ten probing questions that measured the extent to which the students were aware of the incomprehensibility of the directions. The older students demonstrated their awareness of the incomprehensibility of the directions with only minimal probing. The younger students often did not realize that they did not comprehend until they attempted to use the directions for actually performing the magic trick. In a different paradigm, Ironsmith and Whitehurst (1978) had kindergarten, second-, fourth-, and sixth-grade students listen to a speaker and then select one of four sets of pictures on the basis of the speaker's message. The students were told to ask questions if they needed more information. The speaker's messages were either informative as to the set of pictures to choose or ambiguous in that two of the four sets of pictures satisfied the speaker's directives. Kindergarten students responded identically to the informative and ambiguous messages. Second-grade students sometimes made general requests for more information, and fourth- and sixth-grade students often asked specifically for the relevant missing information. Similar results have been obtained in a variety of paradigms (for example, Asher 1978; Cosgrove and Patterson 1977; Karabenick and Miller 1977; Patterson, Massad, and Cosgrove 1978; Shatz 1977).

3. *Study-time apportionment.* Students have been shown to have difficulty in planning ahead, especially in terms of study-time apportionment. Study-time apportionment refers to how one studies in anticipating a future test, including such things as determining what is important to remember and what is not, choosing a strategy or tactic to improve learning, determining how successful the chosen strategy appears to be, and determining whether or not another strategy should be employed (Brown 1980). An experimental analogue has been developed to study a simple case of study-time utilization in young children (see, for example, Brown

and Campione 1977; Masur, McIntyre, and Flavell 1973). Children are presented the task of remembering a series of pictures over several study trials. After each succeeding trial, the children are allowed to pick only half of the items for further study. Young children and slow learners were found to pick items for further study at random. Children above third grade were found to select those items that they had missed previously as the target ones for further study. Clearly, their strategy is the wiser one.

4. *Predicting one's own performance.* Students have been shown to have difficulty in monitoring the success of their performance and in determining when they have studied enough to have mastered the material confronting them. For example, Brown and Barclay (1976; see also Brown, Campione, and Barclay 1978) investigated the accuracy children exhibit when predicting at what point they could recall without error a series of pictures of common objects. Subjects in their study consisted of educable mentally retarded children with mental ages of six and eight. The students were trained in mnemonic memory strategies and were instructed to continue with such strategies until they had mastered the entire set of pictures. Few of the subjects were able to estimate accurately when they had learned the items.

The picture that emerges from these and other lines of research is that young children and retarded children show little metacognitive awareness. There is some evidence to suggest that older students may also be deficient in at least some metacognitive skills. In a survey study, Anderson (1980) found university students to be more likely to use the study strategy of reading and rereading with some underlining and note taking than to engage in questioning and surveying activities prior to reading, or to engage in recitation, reflection, and review afterwards. Yet the latter study strategies have been found to be superior (Pauk 1962; Robinson 1970; Thomas and Robinson 1972). Students did not report frequent use of commonly recommended strategies such as skimming, summarizing, working practice problems, and self-testing. In a related vein, Greeno (1980) reported that high school students are typically unable to explain their strategies in solving geometry problems.

An example of a training program that is directed at improving metacognitive skills needed for acquisition of knowledge and knowledge-related skills is "The Productive Thinking Program: A Course in Learning to Think" (Covington, Crutchfield, Davies, and

Olton 1974). Students are taken through the solutions of complex problems step by step, and are asked at various points to state the problem in their own words, generate and test possible hypotheses, and evaluate alternative approaches to solving the problem. A second example of a metacognitive training program is the CoRT Thinking Program (de Bono 1983, 1985). Students are taught thinking strategies for solving problems of everyday life such as changing jobs or deciding how to spend a vacation. A tool for thinking about practical problems taught by the program has the acronym "PMI." The thinker first looks in the Plus direction, or considers the good points of a given solution to a problem. The thinker then looks in the Minus direction, or considers the bad points of the solution. Finally, the thinker looks in the Interesting direction, or considers interesting consequences of the solution that may be neither good nor bad. This program has recently been implemented experimentally in Venezuela, England, and elsewhere, but results about the effectiveness of the program are not yet available. Similar training programs and guides also have been devised for training metacognitive skills needed for solving mathematical and scientific problems (see, for example, Hayes 1981; Newell and Simon 1972; Polya 1957; Rubenstein 1975; Wickelgren 1974).

Summary. Everything considered, the main implication of recent information-processing research would seem to be the advisability of teaching metacognitive as well as cognitive skills in a skills-instructional curriculum. The argument in favor of explicit teaching of metacognitive skills is an easy one to make: (a) metacognitive skills are important in cognitive performance; (b) students have what seem to be inadequately developed metacognitive skills; and (c) metacognitive skills are not now being taught in most curricula. But there are reasons for being wary of drastic revisions of current educational practices. It is not clear that massive doses of instruction in metacognitive skills is truly what is called for. Consider some reasons why.

1. *Large-scale metacognitive training may be impractical.* For one thing, we are only beginning to get a glimpse of what metacognitive skills go hand in hand with the development of intelligence. For another, those individuals who demonstrate the greatest deficiencies in metacognitive skills (young children and novices of any age at various tasks) seem to have virtually no idea of what they are doing when performing a task. Even when appropriate metacogni-

tive strategies are known, therefore, students may not have the necessary internal referents for the tasks they are working on optimally to take advantage of the metacognitive instruction they receive. Teaching a student to plan is of no help if the student does not know what to plan for, that is, the kinds of strategies that can be used in a task.

2. *Effects of metacognitive activities may be reduced when they are externally imposed rather than spontaneously generated by students.* There is at least some suggestion that the performance of students using a spontaneously adopted strategy is superior to that of students using a strategy imposed by a teacher or experimenter (Brown, Campione, and Barclay 1978; Brown and Smiley 1978).

3. *Being aware that a certain strategy is beneficial is not enough to result in students actually using the strategy.* It is one thing to teach students generalized strategies for dealing with problems; it is another to get them to use the strategies. Often, students seem not to use what they are taught (Flavell 1976; Kreutzer, Leonard, and Flavell 1975; Moynahan 1973; Salatas and Flavell 1976).

4. *To be effective, strategies must be so well learned and performed that they do not interfere with actual learning.* Rigney (1980) pointed out that new strategies can actually interfere with performance by taking up resources that otherwise would go to other aspects of problem solving. One characteristic commonly attributed to the superior performance of experts over novices is the experts' automatization of control of processing (de Groot 1966; Rumelhart and Norman 1978; Simon 1976). Automatization is the transfer of information-processing operations from a limited-capacity, working memory to a virtually unlimited-capacity system that operates without the need for conscious attention. If a new strategy is not automatized, it may take up more mental resources than a student can afford to expend on the strategy.

5. *Recent work questions the effectiveness of general metacognitive strategies.* Programs that have trained general metacognitive strategies have typically used abstract tasks and problems (Glaser 1983). The question that arises is whether these strategies actually work well in thinking and problem solving in specific domains of knowledge. When individuals face novel situations, they rely on general methods; in more familiar situations, individuals appear to rely more on domain-specific knowledge than on general all-purpose strategies (Chase and Simon 1973; Chi, Feltovich, and Glaser 1981; Chi, Glaser, and Rees 1982; de Groot 1966; Jeffries, Turner,

Polson, and Atwood 1981; Larkin 1981; Larkin, McDermott, Simon, and Simon 1980; Simon and Simon 1978).

If metacognitive skills are not now being directly taught, then one might wonder how they ever could be learned. It is probable that induction from examples plays an important role. Such inductions are simulated by a computer program developed by Williams (1972), the Aptitude Test Taker. This program decides how to solve different types of problems of the sort found on aptitude tests, given only examples of solved problems as a basis for its decisions. A major underlying principle of the program is that the ability to solve a task is largely dependent on one's ability to induce a solution-strategy from worked-out examples (Simon 1976). Similarly, induction of general properties from examples was proposed as the means by which strategies for doing geometry problems are learned (Greeno 1980). An implication of the importance of induction from examples in the development of metacognitive skills is that one might expect an interaction between mental ability and the need to be explicitly taught metacognitive skills. Less able students may not be able to induce effective strategies on their own (see, for example, Resnick and Glaser 1976). Others have, in fact, suggested that less able students do better in highly structured learning situations where direct help is given than do more able students (Cronbach and Snow 1977), for whom less structured situations seem preferable.

In conclusion, the information-processing approach to instruction seems to possess many fertile implications for the improvement of intellectual and knowledge-based skills as well as for improving direct instruction of curriculum content. But at present there is a wide gap between theory and practice, and this gap will not be narrowed until some of the problematical issues discussed earlier are dealt with. We are optimistic that the information-processing approach will result in improved instruction, but the fruits of the approach will emerge, we believe, only after extended periods whose duration is unknown.

"Transperspective" Perspectives

To this point we have considered what we believe to be the educational implications of the psychometric, Piagetian, and information-processing perspectives, respectively. But the picture we have presented is perhaps oversimplified and surely incomplete, because we have neglected research that has attempted to combine aspects of more than a single perspective. In this section, we consider research that combines or relates (a) the psychometric and Piagetian perspectives, (b) the psychometric and information-processing perspectives, and (c) the Piagetian and information-processing perspectives.

An issue that has motivated research at the interface of the Piagetian and psychometric perspectives is that of the extent to which Piagetian tasks and traditional psychometric intelligence tests overlap in what they measure. For example, Stephens, McLaughlin, Miller, and Glass (1972) used factor analysis to determine relations between twenty-seven Piagetian reasoning assessments and standard measures of intelligence and achievement for 150 normal and mentally retarded children ages six to eighteen (see also DeVries 1974; Dudek, Lester, Goldberg, and Dyer 1969; Elkind 1969; Freyberg 1966; Green, Ford, and Flamer 1971; Tuddenham 1975). The authors concluded that the Piagetian reasoning tasks measured abilities separate from abilities measured by standard tests of intelligence and achievement: The Piagetian tasks and the traditional ability tests loaded on different factors. However, a reanalysis of the same data using a different method of factor analysis led Humphreys and Parsons (1979) to conclude that the communalities far outweighted the differences between Piagetian tasks and intelligence tests. The sensible conclusion to be drawn at the present is that Piagetian tasks and traditional intelligence tests overlap in what they measure, but that the extent of overlap has yet to be determined.

An example of combining aspects of the psychometric and information-processing approaches is provided by Carroll (1976; see also Carroll 1981), who has used information-processing theories of cognitive processes to classify the twenty-four cognitive factors derived from the seventy-four tests of the *Kit of Reference Tests for Cognitive Factors* (French, Ekstrom, and Price 1963). Classification of cognitive factors was accomplished by classifying the tests from which a factor is derived on the basis of differences in (a) stimulus materials, (b) overt response to be made at end of task, (c) task structure (for example, whether or not there is a temporal separation between stimulus presentation and response), (d) operations and strategies (for example, store item in memory, mentally rotate spatial configuration), (e) temporal aspects of the operation or strategy (for example, average duration ranging from very short—less than two hundred milliseconds—to longer—greater than five seconds), and (f) memory store involved, which includes type of memory store (that is, sensory buffer, short-term memory, intermediate-term memory, long-term memory) and contents (for example, lines, geometric patterns and shapes, pictures of three-dimensional situations, faces, letters, words). Although the validity and usefulness of this coding system has yet to be empirically established, it is a good example of combining aspects of two perspectives.

A second example of combining aspects of psychometric and information-processing perspectives is provided by Snow (1980), who argued that traditional ATI studies need to be followed up by information-processing analyses of the psychological processes that underlie observed ATI (see also Calfee and Hedges 1980). Snow proposed four categories of information processes as sources of individual differences in task performance: (a) parameter differences (p-variables), which are quantitative differences in steps or components used in task performance (for example, time needed to encode a stimulus); (b) sequence differences (q-variables), which are differences in sequencing of step or component execution; (c) route differences (r-variables), which involve the use of qualitatively different steps or components in task performance; and (d) summation or strategic differences (s-variables), which are differences in summative, strategic, and other molar properties of information-processing performance. The goal of information-processing analyses of psychological processes underlying ATIs is to understand how the four information-processing sources of individual differences combine to produce observed differences in task performance.

A third example of combining aspects from psychometric and information-processing perspectives comes from a training study by Sternberg and Weil (1980), in which information-processing analyses were combined with psychometrically measured aptitudes in training college students [in] strategies for solving linear syllogisms— reasoning problems of the form, John is taller than Jim, Bill is taller than John, who is tallest? Sternberg and Weil used mathematical modeling of information-processing strategies to classify subjects into four homogeneous strategy groups on the basis of whether a linguistic, spatial, mixed spatial-linguistic, or simple algorithmic model better fit a given subject's response pattern. Performance in solving linear syllogisms was related to psychometric measures of verbal and spatial aptitude. Striking relations were found between psychometric aptitudes and performance in solving linear syllogisms as a function of task strategy: Task performance using the linguistic strategy was related to verbal ability but not to spatial ability; task performance using the spatial strategy was related to spatial ability but not to verbal ability; task performance using the mixed strategy was related to both abilities; and finally, task performance using the algorithmic strategy was less related to verbal ability than was task performance for subjects using the linguistic strategy. The implication of these results is that there can be more than one information-processing strategy for performing a task, and that the best strategy for a given individual depends in part on his or her pattern of abilities.

An example of combining aspects of information-processing and Piagetian perspectives is provided by the "neo-Piagetian" approach proposed by Pascual-Leone (1970) and elaborated by Case (1974, 1978). Pascual-Leone and Case proposed a view of cognitive development that differs from the Piagetian perspective from which it derives in two major ways. First, developmental structures conceptualized by Piaget in terms of logicomathematical systems and modeled by symbolic logic are conceptualized here as groups of executive strategies that can be modeled by computer simulation. Second, a fundamental basis for development in the theories of Pascual-Leone and Case is the amount of working memory available. For example, Case (1978) analyzed Noelting's (1975) task, in which a child must decide which of two pitchers of orange juice will taste more strongly of orange juice on the basis of the number of tumblers of orange juice and water that have been poured into each pitcher. Children have been found to use increasingly sophisticated strategies with increasing age. For example, children of ages three to four seem to use a two-step strategy: (a) look for the color of orange juice in the first pitcher; if found, say it will taste of orange juice; and (b) perform the same action for the second pitcher. Note that this strategy identifies which pitcher will taste more strongly of orange juice only when there is at least some orange juice in one pitcher and pure water in the other. Children of ages nine to ten seem to use a more complicated seven-step strategy: (a) count tumblers of orange juice added to first pitcher; (b) count tumblers of water added to first pitcher; (c) notice how many more tumblers of the greater liquid (either orange juice or water) were added relative to the lesser liquid; (d), (e), and (f) are repetitions of the first three steps for the second pitcher; and (g) pick the pitcher with relatively more orange juice than water. The memory demand of these and other strategies is based on the number of items that must be attended to in working memory to accomplish the strategy. The greater working memory demand of more complex strategies is proposed as the factor that limits the use of complex strategies to older children. One limitation of this approach is the lack of specificity of the procedures used for determining exactly how many items must be attended to in working memory to accomplish a given strategy.

A second example of combining aspects of information-processing and Piagetian perspectives is provided by Siegler's rule-assessment account of developmental differences in performance on a balance scale task similar to that studied by Inhelder and Piaget (Siegler and Klahr 1982; Siegler and Richards 1982). There are five major assumptions of the rule-assessment approach. First, children's conceptual understanding follows a sequence of qualitatively discrete rules. Second, the rules are ordered in terms of increasing correspondence to the correct rule in a given situation, and children adopt new rules only if they correspond more closely to the correct rule. Third, the effectiveness of a learning experience is determined by the extent to which the learning experience distinguishes the child's existing rule from the correct rule. Fourth, children are prevented from immediately adopting the correct rule because of limited encoding of the correct rule's component dimensions. Fifth, failure to encode a dimension is caused by lack of knowledge of the importance of the dimension to the situation or by the dimension's lack of perceptual salience for a child in a given situation. Siegler and his colleagues performed information-processing task analysis to determine the rule and cue knowledge associated with different levels of performance on the balance scale task. They discovered that children of age five had difficulty with the balance problems because rather than encoding distance information, the children relied exclusively on weight information. After training in encoding distance information, children used a more correct rule (taking both distance and weight information into account), which resulted in improved performance on the task.

Comparison and Evaluation of Perspectives

The similarities and differences among the three approaches to training intellectual and achievement-related skills as well as content knowledge can perhaps best be pointed out by comparing how they would address the problem of training students on a single type of problem. For comparability to our previous section on comparison and evaluation, the type of problem we will consider is the analogy of the form $A : B :: C : (D_1, D_2)$.

Psychometric Approach. An educator adhering to the psychometric approach would first seek to determine what factors of intellect enter into analogy solution and then devise a training program around exercises that might raise the individual's standing on these factors. The form the training would take would depend on the theory.

Spearman's (1927) theory would account for the solution of analogies almost entirely in terms of the g (general) factor, which in itself is not particularly helpful in suggesting a training program. Spearman (1923) also proposed an information-processing theory, however, according to which solution of analogies was proposed to require apprehension of experience (encoding the analogy terms), eduction of relations (inferring the A to B relation), and eduction of correlates (applying the inferred relationship from C to an ideal solution). Thurstone's (1938) theory would probably account for verbal analogy solution in terms of individual differences in the verbal comprehension and reasoning factors but would not have clear process implications for what should be trained. Guilford's (1967) theory would attempt to train specific cubes of Guilford's model relevant to analogy solution, such as cognition of semantic units, cognition of semantic relations, convergent production of semantic relations, and so on. Note that Guilford's theory handles the process, content, and product with considerable explicitness.

Several general points should be made about the psychometric approach to training. First, unless the theory has a set of process factors (for which Guilford's theory is unique) or is accompanied by a separate information-processing theory (for which Spearman's theory is unique), it is not clear just what one is to train. Second, the decision as to what to train is made on the basis of factors that are derived from individual diferences data. If there are processes in item solution that are not sources of individual diferences, they will not be identified as involved in solution. Third, in most cases the lack of explicit process specification in psychometric theories will result in a rather loose connection between theory and training. As a result, neither success nor failure will necessarily be particularly informative about the value of the theory, if indeed there is an explicit theory underlying the training. Finally, the choice of the analogy in the first place as worthwhile for training will be determined by its centrality in the psychometric theory of intelligence as a marker for one or more factors of intelligence. For example, the analogy would be a good choice of problem to train in Spearman's theory because of its high loading (correlation with) the g factor.

Piagetian Approach. An educator adhering to the Piagetian approach would probably first attempt to determine the child's cognitive level and whether the child's cognitive structures are ready to accommodate analogy solution. If not, the attempt at training might be aborted before it even starts. If the child does appear ready, then the educator might work with the child individually, guiding him or her through the kinds of relations needed to solve the problem. First, the educator would concentrate on pair relations, and once the child seemed to understand these, the educator might increasingly play the critic's role, challenging the child in his or her construction or solution of analogies. The point of such criticism would be to bring the child to the point where he or she could solve the item with assurance and lack of hesitation.

Again, several general points should be made about this approach to training. First, the training would almost certainly be preceded by a diagnosis of the child's cognitive state to see whether he or she is ready for training; if not, training would be aborted. In Piagetian theory, there is simply no sense to training a child in skills for which he or she is not yet ready. Second, emphasis in training would be on logical relations of the kinds specified by Piagetian theory. The goal would be not to train particular processes, but rather to induce understanding of the structural relations that constitute an analogy. Third, the mode of training probably would be individualized, with considerable emphasis on challenge and questioning. The educator wishes to assure that the child truly understands what he or she is doing and is not just mimicking an algorithm picked up from the trainer. Finally, choice of the analogy item as worthwhile for training would be determined by the centrality of the underlying relations in Piaget's theory. In this case, second-order relations are often used to mark the transition from concrete to formal operations, and thus are viewed as of considerable importance.

Information-processing Approach. An educator adhering to the information-processing approach would first attempt a task analysis of the analogy problem, or use a previously performed task analysis, and only then attempt training on the basis of the task analysis. Depending on the educator, training might emphasize only the cognitive components involved in analogy solution (for example, encoding, inference, mapping, application, justification, and response, according to Sternberg's [1977] theory); only the metacognitive components involved in analogy solution (for example, selection of a set of cognitive components, selection of a strategy into which to combine the components, deciding how best to represent information about the analogy terms, monitoring one's place in the solution strategy); or both the cognitive and metacognitive components involved. The educator might attempt to maximize the probability of generalization by concentrating on information-processing components rather than on the particular task, and by giving the student practice in solving other kinds of induction problems that involve the same metacognitive or cognitive components.

Here, as before, several general points should be made about this approach to training. First, the training is preceded by a task analysis, in this case, of an analogy. Note that there is probably a greater emphasis on the task and a lesser emphasis on the subject than in the other two approaches. Second, emphasis in the training is on processing components, whether at the cognitive or metacognitive level or at both levels. Third, the mode of training will be to emphasize how a set of processes can be combined to solve a problem, of which an analogy is only one example. Good training programs would almost certainly try to show how the same components can be applied to other, related problems as well, so that the student learns to emphasize process generality rather than task specificity in problem solving. Finally, choice of the task will be motivated by the task's centrality in a process-theoretic account of some domain of task performance, in this case, perhaps inductive reasoning. Because analogies are seen as prototypical of induction tasks, their choice would be easily justified.

CONCLUSIONS

We have shown that the three major conceptions of intelligence—the psychometric, Piagetian, and information-processing—are largely complementary and can be used in conjunction to study different but overlapping aspects of intelligence. Nevertheless, proponents of all three approaches have failed to deal adequately with intelligence as it occurs in the real world, focusing instead on testlike and laboratory tasks.

Although the psychometric approach to intelligence has been closely linked to schooling since the time of Binet, and the links between this approach and schooling have taken many forms, the implications of the psychometric approach for education have been surprisingly difficult to derive. The probable reasons for this include the following: (a) the tests do not provide the kinds of information about process necessary for effective training; (b) the processes required for test performance are not necessarily those required for school training; (c) motivational and situational factors are not assessed by the tests; (d) there has been a notable gap between theory and practice; and (e) much of the research that has sought to link theory to practice has been flawed, especially by a lack of statistical power.

The difficulty in deriving educational objectives from Piagetian theory is due in large part to the theory being one of intellectual development through maturation rather than of learning in the educational sense of the word. The theory was not intended to have clear implications for education. The general implications of the theory (that is, active discovery is preferable to passive learning, motivation is fundamentally important, learning situations must be practical, flexibility is essential) support but do not add much to sound educational practice. Four major limitations in the theory must be overcome by those who would insist on deriving educational implications: (a) the theory is of competence rather than of performance; (b) the stages cover periods too long to be useful in sequencing instruction; (c) the theory emphasizes maturation rather than learning; and (d) empirical support for key parts of the theory is being eroded.

The information-processing approach to instruction appears to us to be a promising one for improving intellectual and knowledge-based skills and for improving direct instruction of curriculum content. Information-processing analyses can uncover, with a precision unrivaled by other approaches, underlying processes and skills that are potential targets of training programs. Paradoxically, whereas the imprecision of the psychometric and Piagetian approaches has limited their generation of implications for education, the traditional information-processing approach may be too microscopic to be maximally useful for educators. It is not clear how educational programs affect task performance at the level of information processes, because so little is known about how individuals acquire and manage their information processes. The difficulty in getting transfer of training in recent information-processing research argues for training at the metacognitive as well as cognitive levels. There are, however, several reasons to be cautious about the advisability of immediate large-scale training of metacognitive skills: (a) we are only beginning to identify metacognitive skills to be trained; (b) those who demonstrate the greatest deficiencies in metacognitive skills (young children and novices) may lack the internal referents of task performance required to profit from direct metacognitive instruction; (c) effects of metacognitive activities may be reduced when they are externally imposed rather than being spontaneously generated by students, especially for highly able students; and (d) to be effective, metacognitive strategies must be so well learned and performed that they do not interfere with actual learning.

We agree with Snow's (1982) assessment that attempts to train intellectual skills and knowledge and knowledge-related skills must go beyond simple manipulations of practice, feedback, and coaching. We conclude from our review that maximally successful programs for training intellectual skills and knowledge and knowledge-related skills should be based on task analyses common to the information-processing approach, but should go beyond the traditional information-processing approach in several important ways.

First, successful programs must be based on tasks characteristic of intelligent behavior in the everyday world, including, but not limited to, the world of the school. It is unlikely that training programs based solely on testlike and laboratory tasks will provide effects that generalize to everyday intellectual performance in and out of the school. The growing body of evidence in support of the role of domain-specific knowledge in skilled performance undermines approaches to training that rely almost exclusively on abstract, all-purpose strategies and skills.

Second, successful programs must be directed toward the metacognitive and cognitive levels, as well as toward their interaction. There is ample evidence that training programs that omit metacognitive skills training have effects highly specific to the training task and situation.

Third, successful training programs will incorporate aspects of the psychometric perspective so as to be maximally responsive to individual differences, and will incorporate aspects of the Piagetian perspective so as to provide a framework for the development of skilled performance. In short, successful training programs will require selective application of aspects of the three major perspectives, as opposed to wholesale application of any one.

Although we cannot guarantee, especially in the short run, that recent conceptions of intelligence will be any more consequential to education than past conceptions, the work reviewed has informed our understanding about what limits the ease with which implications for education can be derived. Further, comparison of the alternative conceptions of intelligence, and of the effectiveness of training programs based on them, provides us with an account of at least some of the characteristics a training program would require that goes beyond simple manipulations of practice, feedback, and coaching.

REFERENCES

Anderson, Thomas H. "Study Strategies and Adjunct Aids." In *Theoretical Issues in Reading Comprehension*, edited by Rand Spiro, Bertram Bruce, and William F. Brewer. Hillsdale, N.J.: Lawrence Erlbaum Associates, 1980.

Asher, S. R. "Referential Communication." In *The Functions of Language and Cognition*, edited by Grover Whitehurst and Barry J. Zimmerman. New York: Academic Press, 1978.

Athey, Irene J., and Rubadeau, Duane O., eds. *Educational Implications of Piaget's Theory*. Waltham, Mass.: Ginn-Blaisdell, 1970.

Baltes, Paul B.; Dittmann-Kohli, F.; and Dixon, R. A. "Intellectual Development during Adulthood: General Propositions towards Theory and a Dual-Process Conception." Unpublished manuscript, 1982.

Beilin, Harry. "The Training and Acquisition of Logical Operation." In *Piagetian Cognitive Development Research and Mathematics Education*, edited by Myron F. Rosskopf, Leslie P. Steffe, and Stanley Taback. Washington, D.C.: National Council of Teachers of Mathematics, 1971.

Beilin, Harry. "Inducing Conservation Through Training." In *Psychology of the 20th Century*. Vol. 7. Edited by G. Steiner. Bern: Kinder, 1977.

Belmont, John M., and Butterfield, Earl C. "The Instructional Approach to Developmental Cognitive Research." In *Perspectives on the Development of Memory and Cognition*, edited by Robert Kail and John W. Hagen. Hillsdale, N.J.: Lawrence Erlbaum Associates, 1977.

Belmont, John M.; Butterfield, Earl C.; and Borkowski, John G. "Training Retarded People to Generalize across Memory Tasks." In *Practical Aspects of Memory*, edited by Michael Gruneberg, Peter Morris, and R. N. Sykes. London: Academic Press, 1978.

Belmont, John M.; Butterfield, Earl C.; and Ferretti, Ralph P. "To Secure Transfer of Training Instruct in Self-Management Skills." In *How and How Much Can Intelligence Be Increased?* edited by Douglas Detterman and Robert Sternberg. Norwood, N.J.: Ablex, 1982.

Bereiter, Carl., and Engelmann, Siegfried. *Teaching Disadvantaged Children in the Preschool*. Englewood Cliffs, N.J.: Prentice-Hall, 1966.

Berry, John W. "Radical Cultural Relativism and the Concept of Intelligence." In *Culture and Cognition: Readings in Cross-Cultural Psychology*, edited by John W. Berry and Pierre Dasen. London: Methuen, 1974.

Berry, John W. "Ecological Analyses for Cross-Cultural Psychology." In *Studies in Cross-Cultural Psychology*, edited by Neil Warren. London: Academic Press, 1980.

Binet, Alfred, and Simon, Theophile. "Methodes nouvelles pour le diagnostic du niveau intellectuel des anormaux." *L'Annee Psychologique* 11 (1905): 191–244.

Bingham-Newman, Ann; Saunders, Ruth A.; and Hooper, Frank H. *Logical Operations in the Preschool: The Contribution of Piagetian Theory to Early Childhood Education*. Tech. Report No. 354. Madison: Wisconsin Research and Development Center for Cognitive Learning, 1976.

Borkowski, John G., and Cavanaugh, John C. "Maintenance and Generalization of Skills and Strategies by the Retarded." In *Handbook of Mental Deficiency*, edited by Norman Ellis. Hillsdale, N.J.: Lawrence Erlbaum Associates, 1979.

Bornstein, Phillip H., and Quevillon, Randal P. "The Effects of a Self-Instructional

Package on Overactive Preschool Boys." *Journal of Applied Behavioral Analysis* 9 (1976): 179–188.

Brainerd, Charles J. "The Stage Question in Cognitive-Developmental Theory." *Behavioral and Brain Sciences* 1 (1978): 173–182.

Bransford, John D.; Stein, Barry S.; Vye, Nancy J.; Franks, Jeffrey J.; Auble, Pamela M.; Mezynski, Karen J.; and Perfetto, Greg A. "Differences in Approaches to Learning: An Overview." *Journal of Experimental Psychology: General* III (1982): 390–398.

Bronfenbrenner, Urie. "Is Early Intervention Effective?" In *Handbook of Evaluation Research*, vol. 2, edited by Marcia Guttentag and Elmer L. Struening. Beverly Hills, Calif.: Sage Publications, 1975.

Brown, Ann L. "The Development of Memory: Knowing, Knowing about Knowing, and Knowing How to Know." In *Advances in Child Development and Behavior*, vol. 10, edited by H. W. Reese. New York: Academic Press, 1975.

Brown, Ann L. "Knowing When, Where, Where, and How to Remember: A Problem of Metacognition." In *Advances in Instructional Psychology*, vol. 1, edited by Robert Glaser. Hillsdale, N.J.: Lawrence Erlbaum Associates, 1978.

Brown, Ann L. "Metacognitive Development and Reading." In *Theoretical Issues in Reading Comprehension*, edited by Rand J. Spiro, Bertram Bruce, and William Brewer. Hillsdale, N.J.: Lawrence Erlbaum Associates, 1980.

Brown, Ann L., and Barclay, Craig R. "The Effects of Training Specific Mnemonics on the Metamnemonic Efficiency of Retarded Children." *Child Development* 47 (1976): 70–80.

Brown, Ann L., and Campione, Joseph. "Training Strategic Study Time Apportionment in Educable Retarded Children." *Intelligence* 1 (1977): 94–107.

Brown, Ann L., and Campione, Joseph. "Inducing Flexible Thinking: The Problem of Access." In *Intelligence and Learning*, edited by Morton Friedman, J. P. Das, and Neil O'Connor. New York: Plenum, 1981.

Brown, Ann L.; Campione, Joseph; and Barclay, Craig. R. "Training Self-checking Routines for Estimating Test Readiness: Generalization from List Learning to Prose Recall." Unpublished manuscript, University of Illinois, 1978.

Brown, Ann L.; Campione, Joseph; and Murphy, Martin. "Maintenance and Generalization of Trained Metamnemonic Awareness in Educable Retarded Children." *Journal of Experimental Child Psychology* 24 (1977): 191–211.

Brown, Ann L., and Smiley, Sandra. "The Development of Strategies for Studying Texts." *Child Development* 49 (1978): 1076–1088.

Brown, Geoffrey, and Desforges, Charles. *Piaget's Theory: A Psychological Critique.* Boston: Routledge and Kegan Paul, 1979.

Bruner, Jerome S. *The Process of Education.* Cambridge, Mass.: Harvard University Press, 1961.

Burt, Cyril. *The Factors of the Mind.* London: University of London Press, 1940.

Butterfield, Earl C.; Wambold, Clark L.; and Belmont, John M. "On the Theory and Practice of Improving Short-term Memory." *American Journal of Mental Deficiency* 77 (1973): 654–669.

Calfee, Robert C., and Hedges, Larry V. "Independent Process Analyses of Aptitude-Treatment Interactions." In *Aptitude, Learning, and Instruction*, vol. 1, edited by Richard Snow, Pat-Anthony Federico, and William Montague. Hillsdale, N.J.: Lawrence Erlbaum Associates, 1980.

Capon, Noel, and Kuhn, Deanna. "Logical Reasoning in the Supermarket: Adult Females' Use of a Proportional Reasoning Strategy in an Everyday Context." *Developmental Psychology* 4 (1979): 450–452.

Carroll, John B. "Psychometric Tests as Cognitive Tasks: A New 'Structure of Intellect'." In *The Nature of Intelligence*, edited by Lauren Resnick, Hillsdale, N.J.: Lawrence Erlbaum Associates, 1976.

Carroll, John B. "Aptitude Processes, Theory, and the Real World." In *Aptitude, Learning, and Instruction*, vol. 1, edited by Richard Snow, Pat-Anthony Federico, and William Montague. Hillsdale, N.J.: Lawrence Erlbaum Associates, 1980.

Carroll, John B. "Ability and Task Difficulty in Cognitive Psychology." *Educational Researcher* 10:1 (1981): 11–21.

Case, Robbie. "Mental Strategies, Mental Capacity, and Instruction: A Neo-Piagetian Investigation." *Journal of Experimental Child Psychology* 18 (1974): 372–397.

Case, Robbie. "Intellectual Development from Birth to Adulthood: A Neo-Piagetian Interpretation." In *Children's Thinking: What Develops?* edited by Robert Siegler. Hillsdale, N.J.: Lawrence Erlbaum Associates, 1978.

Charlesworth, William R. "Human Intelligence as Adaptation: An Ethological Approach." In *The Nature of Intelligence*, edited by Lauren Resnick. Hillsdale, N.J.: Lawrence Erlbaum Associates, 1976.

Charlesworth, William R. "An Ethological Approach to Studying Intelligence." *Human Development* 22 (1979): 212–216.

Chase, William G., and Simon, Herbert A. "Perception in Chess." *Cognitive Psychology* 4 (1973): 55–81.

Chi, Michelene T. H.; Feltovich, Paul; and Glaser, Robert. "Categorization and Representation of Physics Problems by Experts and Novices." *Cognitive Science* 5 (1981): 121–152.

Chi, Michelene T. H.; Glaser, Robert; and Rees, Ernest. "Expertise in Problem Solving." In *Advances in the Psychology of Human Intelligence*, vol. 1, edited by Robert Sternberg. Hillsdale, N.J.: Lawrence Erlbaum Associates, 1982.

Chiapetta, Eugene L. "A Review of Piagetian Studies Relevant to Science Instruction at the Secondary and College Level." *Science Education* 60 (1976): 253–261.

Cole, Michael, and Scribner, Sylvia. *Culture and Thought*. New York: Wiley, 1974.

Collins, Allan, and Smith, Edward E. "Teaching the Process of Reading Comprehension." In *How and How Much Can Intelligence Be Increased?* edited by Douglas Detterman and Robert Sternberg. Norwood, N.J.: Ablex, 1982.

Collis, Kevin. "A Study of Concrete and Formal Reasoning in School Mathematics." *Australian Journal of Psychology* 23 (1971): 289–296.

Cosgrove, J. Michael, and Patterson, Charlotte. "Plans and the Development of Listener Skills." *Developmental Psychology* 13 (1977): 557–564.

Covington, Martin V.; Crutchfield, Richard S.; Davies, L.; and Olton, R.M., Jr. *The Productive Thinking Program: A Course in Learning to Think*. Columbus, Ohio: Charles E. Merrill, 1974.

Cronbach, Lee J. "Beyond the Two Disciplines of Scientific Psychology." *American Psychologist* 30 (1975): 116–127.

Cronbach, Lee J., and Snow, Richard E. *Aptitudes and Instructional Methods*. New York: Irvington, 1977.

Dansereau, Donald F.; Collins, Karen W.; McDonald, Barbara A.; Holley, Charles

D.; Garland, John; Diekhoff, George; and Evans, Selby H. "Development and Evaluation of a Learning Strategy Training Program." *Journal of Educational Psychology* 71 (1979): 64–73.

Dasen, Pierre. *Piagetian Psychology: Cross-Cultural Contributions.* New York: Gardner Press, 1977.

Davidson, Janet E., and Sternberg, Robert J. "Competence and Performance in Intellectual Development." In *Moderators of Competence,* edited by Edith Neimark, Richard DeLisi, and Judith Newman. Hillsdale, N.J.: Lawrence Erlbaum Associates, 1985.

De Bono, Edward. "The Direct Teaching of Thinking as a Skill." *Phi Delta Kappan* 64 (1983): 703–708.

De Bono, Edward. "The CoRT Thinking Program." In *Thinking and Learning Skills: Relating Instruction to Basic Research,* vol. 1, edited by J. W. Segal, S. F. Chipman, and Robert Glaser. Hillsdale, N.J.: Lawrence Erlbaum Associates, 1985.

De Groot, A. D. "Perception and Memory versus Thought: Some Old Ideas and Recent Findings." In *Problem Solving: Research, Method, and Theory,* edited by Benjamin Kleinmuntz. New York: Wiley, 1966.

De Vries, Rheta. "Relationships among Piagetian, IQ, and Achievement Assessments." *Child Development* 45 (1974): 746–756.

Dewey, John. *Democracy and Education.* New York: Free Press, 1968. Originally published 1916.

Donders, F. C. "Over de snelheid van psychoische processen. Onderzoekingen gedaan in het Physiologisch Laboratorium der Utrechtsche Hoogeschool, 1868–1869." *Tweede reeks* 2 (1868): 92–120.

Duckworth, Eleanor. "Either We're Too Early and They Can't Learn It or We're Too Late and They Know It Already: The Dilemma of 'Applying Piaget'." *Harvard Educational Review* 49 (1979): 297–312. (a)

Duckworth, Eleanor. "An Introductory Note about Piaget." *Journal of Education* 161 (1979): 5–12. (b)

Dudek, S. Z.; Lester, E. P.; Goldberg, J. S.; and Dyer, G. B. "Relationship of Piagetian Measures to Standard Intelligence and Motor Scales." *Perceptual and Motor Skills* 28 (1969): 351–362.

Elkind, David. "Piagetian and Psychometric Conceptions of Intelligence." *Harvard Educational Review* 39 (1969): 319–337.

Elkind, David. *Children and Adolescents: Interpretative Essays on Jean Piaget.* 2d ed. New York: Oxford University Press, 1974.

Engle, Randall W., and Nagle, Richard J. "Strategy Training and Semantic Encoding in Mildly Retarded Children." *Intelligence* 3 (1979): 17–30.

Farnham-Diggory, Sylvia. *Cognitive Processes in Education: A Psychological Preparation for Teaching and Curriculum Development.* New York: Harper and Row, 1972.

Federico, Pat-Anthony. "Adaptive Instruction: Trends and Issues." In *Aptitude, Learning, and Instruction,* vol. 1, edited by Richard Snow, Pat-Anthony Federico, and William Montague. Hillsdale, N.J.: Lawrence Erlbaum Associates, 1980.

Feuerstein, Reuven. *Instrumental Enrichment: An Intervention Program for Cognitive Modifiability.* Baltimore: University Park Press, 1980.

Flavell, John H. *The Developmental Psychology of Jean Piaget.* New York: D. Van Nostrand, 1963.

Flavell, John H. "Metacognitive Aspects of Problem Solving." In *The Nature of*

Intelligence, edited by Lauren Resnick. Hillsdale, N.J.: Lawrence Erlbaum Associates, 1976.

Flavell, John H.; Friedrichs, Ann; and Hoyt, Jane D. "Developmental Changes in Memorization Processes." *Cognitive Psychology* 1 (1970): 324–340.

Franks, Jeffrey J.; Vye, Nancy J.; Auble, Pamela M.; Mezynski, Karen J.; Perfetto, Greg A.; Bransford, John D.; Stein, Barry, S.; and Littlefield, Joan. "Learning from Explicit versus Implicit Texts." *Journal of Experimental Psychology: General* 111 (1982); 414–422.

French, J. W.; Ekstrom, R. B.; and Price, L. A. *Kit of Reference Tests for Cognitive Factors*. Princeton, N.J.: Educational Testing Service, 1963.

Freyberg, P. S. "Concept Development in Piagetian Terms in Relation to School Attainment." *Journal of Educational Psychology* 57 (1966): 164–168.

Furth, Hans G. *Piaget for Teachers*. Englewood Cliffs, N.J.: Prentice-Hall, 1970.

Furth, Hans G., and Wachs, Harry. *Thinking Goes to School: Piaget's Theory and Practice*. London: Oxford University Press, 1974.

Garber, Howard L., and Heber, Rick. "The Efficacy of Early Intervention with Family Rehabilitation." In *Psychosocial Influences in Retarded Performance, Vol. 2: Strategies for Improving Competence*, edited by Michael Begab, H. Carl Haywood, and Howard L. Garber. Baltimore: University Park Press, 1981.

Garber, Howard L., and Heber, Rick. "Modification of Predicted Cognitive Development in High-risk Children through Early Intervention." In *How and How Much Can Intelligence Be Increased?* edited by Douglas Detterman and Robert Sternberg. Norwood, N.J.: Ablex, 1982.

Ginsburg, Herbert, and Opper, Sylvia. *Piaget's Theory of Intellectual Development: An Introduction*. 2d ed. Englewood Cliffs, N.J.: Prentice-Hall, 1979.

Glaser, Robert. *Adaptive Education: Individual Diversity and Learning*. New York: Holt, Rinehart and Winston, 1977.

Glaser, Robert. "Relationships between Aptitude, Learning, and Instruction." In *Aptitude, Learning, and Instruction*, vol. 2, edited by Richard Snow, Pat-Anthony Federico, and William Montague. Hillsdale, N.J.: Lawrence Erlbaum Associates, 1980.

Glaser, Robert. *Education and Thinking: The Role of Knowledge*. Tech. Report PDS-6. Pittsburgh, Penn.: University of Pittsburgh, 1983.

Goodnow, Jacqueline J. "The Nature of Intelligent Behavior: Questions Raised by Cross-Cultural Studies." In *The Nature of Intelligence*, edited by Lauren Resnick. Hillsdale, N.J.: Lawrence Erlbaum Associates, 1976.

Gordon, Ira J. *The Infant Experience*. Columbus, Ohio: Charles E. Merrill, 1975.

Green, Donald R.; Ford Marguerite P.; and Flamer, George B. *Measurement and Piaget*. New York: McGraw-Hill, 1971.

Greeno, James G. "Some Examples of Cognitive Task Analysis with Instructional Implications." In *Aptitude, Learning, and Instruction*, vol. 2, edited by Richard Snow, Pat-Anthony Federico, and William Montague. Hillsdale, N.J.: Lawrence Erlbaum Associates, 1980.

Griffiths, David H. "Physics Teaching: Does It Hinder Intellectual Development?" *American Journal of Physics* 44 (1976): 81–86.

Guilford, J. P. *The Nature of Human Intelligence*. New York: McGraw-Hill, 1967.

Guilford, J. P. "Cognitive Psychology's Ambiguities: Some Suggested Remedies." *Psychological Review* 89 (1982): 48–49.

Hayes, J. R. *The Complete Problem Solver*. Philadelphia: Franklin Institute Press, 1981.

Holzman, Thomas G.; Glaser, Robert; and Pellegrino, James W. "Process Training Derived from a Computer Simulation Theory." *Memory and Cognition* 4 (1976): 349–356.

Humphreys, Lloyd G., and Parsons, Charles K. "Piagetian Tasks Measure Intelligence and Intelligence Tests Assess Cognitive Development: A Reanalysis." *Intelligence* 3 (1979): 369–382.

Hunt, J. McVicker. "Parent and Child Centers: Their Basis in the Behavioral and Educational Sciences." *American Journal of Orthopsychiatry* 41 (1971): 13–38.

Ironsmith, Marsha, and Whitehurst, Grover. "The Development of Listener Abilities in Communication: How Children Deal with Ambiguous Information." *Child Development* 49 (1978): 348–352.

Janicki, Terence C., and Peterson, Penelope. "Aptitude-Treatment Interaction Effects of Variations in Direct Instruction." *American Educational Research Journal* 1 (1981): 63–82.

Jeffries, Robin; Turner, Althea T.; Polson, Peter G.; and Atwood, Michael E. "Processes Involved in Designing Software." In *Cognitive Skills and Their Acquisition*, edited by John R. Anderson. Hillsdale, N.J.: Lawrence Erlbaum Associates, 1981.

Jensen, Arthur R. "How Much Can We Boost IQ and Scholastic Achievement?" *Harvard Educational Review* 39 (1969): 1–123.

Jensen, Arthur R. "The Chronometry of Intelligence." In *Advances in the Psychology of Human Intelligence*. Vol. 1. Edited by Robert Sternberg. Hillsdale, N.J.: Lawrence Erlbaum Associates, 1982.

Kamii, Constance, and DeVries, Rheta. "Piaget for Early Education." In *The Preschool in Action*, 2d ed, edited by Mary Day and Ronald Parker. Boston: Allyn and Bacon, 1977.

Karabenick, Julie D., and Miller, Scott A. "The Effects of Age, Sex, and Listener Feedback on Grade School Children's Referential Communication." *Child Development* 48 (1977): 678–684.

Karplus, Robert. *Science Curriculum Improvement Study: Teacher's Handbook*. Berkeley: Lawrence Hall of Science, University of California, 1974.

Keating, D. P. "The Emperor's New Clothes: The 'New Look' in Intelligence Research." In *Advances in the Psychology of Human Intelligence*, vol. 2, edited by Robert Sternberg. Hillsdale, N.J.: Lawrence Erlbaum Associates, 1984.

Kendall, Constance R.; Borkowski, John G.; and Cavanaugh, John C. "Metamemory and the Transfer of an Interrogative Strategy by EMR Children." *Intelligence* 4 (1980): 255–270.

Klausmeier, Herbert J. *Cognitive Learning and Development: Information Processing and Piagetian Perspectives*. Cambridge, Mass.: Ballinger, 1979.

Kreutzer, Mary Anne; Leonard, Catherine; and Flavell, John H. "An Interview Study of Children's Knowledge about Memory." *Monographs of the Society for Research in Child Development* 40 (1975): 1, Serial No. 159.

Kuhn, Deanna. "The Relation of Two Piagetian Stage Transitions to IQ." *Developmental Psychology* 12 (1976): 157–161.

Kuhn, Deanna. "The Application of Piaget's Theory of Cognitive Development to Education." *Harvard Educational Review* 49 (1979): 340–360. (a)

Kuhn, Deanna. "The Significance of Piaget's Formal Operations Stage in Education." *Journal of Education* 161 (1979): 34–50. (b)

Kuhn, Deanna, and Brannock, Joann. "Development of the Isolation of Variables Scheme in Experimental and 'Natural Experiment' Contexts." *Developmental Psychology* 13 (1977): 9–14.

Laboratory of Comparative Human Cognition. "Culture and Intelligence." In *Handbook of Human Intelligence*, edited by Robert Sternberg. New York: Cambridge University Press, 1982.

Larkin, Jill H. "Enriching Formal Knowledge: A Model for Learning to Solve Textbook Physics Problems." In *Cognitive Skills and Their Acquisition*, edited by John R. Anderson. Hillsdale N.J.: Lawrence Erlbaum Associates, 1981.

Larkin, Jill H.; McDermott, John; Simon, Dorthea P.; and Simon, Herbert A. "Models of Competence in Solving Physics Problems." *Cognitive Science* 4 (1980): 317–345.

Lavatelli, Celia. *Early Childhood Education—A Piaget Program*. Boston: American Science and Engineering, 1970.(a)

Lavatelli, Celia. *Teacher's Guide to Accompany Early Childhood Curriculum—A Piaget Program*. Boston: American Science and Engineering, 1970. (b)

Lawson, Anton. "Developing Formal Thought through Biology Teaching." *American Biology Teacher* 37 (1975): 411–429.

Lawson, Anton; Blake, Anthony; and Norland, Floyd H. "Training Effects and Generalization of the Ability to Control Variables in High School Biology Students." *Science Education* 59 (1975): 387–396.

Lawson, Anton, and Renner, John W. "Relationships of Science Subject Matter and Developmental Levels of Learners." *Journal of Research in Science Teaching* 10 (1975): 1–12.

Lawson, Anton, and Wollman, Warren T. *Encouraging the Transition from Concrete to Formal Cognitive Functioning—An Experiment*. Advancing Education through Science-Oriented Programs, Report ID-15. Berkeley: Lawrence Hall of Science, University of California, 1975.

Lawton, J. T., and Hooper, F. H. "Piagetian Theory and Early Childhood Education: A Critical Analysis." In *Alternatives to Piaget: Critical Essays on the Theory*, edited by Linda Siegel and Charles Brainerd. New York: Academic Press, 1978.

Lazar, Irving, and Darlington, Richard. "Lasting Effects of Early Education: A Report from the Consortium for Longitudinal Studies." *Monographs of the Society for Research in Child Development* 47 (1982): 2–3, Serial No. 195.

Lipman, Matthew; Sharp, Ann M.; and Oscanyan, Frederick S. *Philosophical Inquiry: Instructional Manual to Accompany Harry Stottlemeier's Discovery*, 2d ed. Upper Montclair, N.J.: Institute for the Advancement of Philosophy for Children, 1979.

Lipman, Matthew; Sharp, Ann M.; and Oscanyan, Frederick S. *Philosophy in the Classroom*. 2d ed. Philadelphia: Temple University Press, 1980.

Markmam, Ellen. "Realizing That You Don't Understand." *Child Development* 48 (1977): 986–992.

Masur, Elise F.; McIntyre, Curtis W.; and Flavell, John H. "Developmental Changes in Apportionment of Study Time among Items in a Multitrial Free Recall Task." *Journal of Experimental Child Psychology* 15 (1973): 237–246.

McClelland, David. "Testing for Competence Rather than for 'Intelligence'." *American Psychologist* 28 (1973): 1–14.

McCombs, Barbara, and McDaniel, Mark A. "On the Design of Adaptive Treatments for Individualized Instructional Systems." *Educational Psychologist* 16 (1981): 11–22.

McNally, Douglas W. *Piaget, Education, and Teaching.* Sussex, England: New Education Press, 1974.

Meeker, Mary N. *The Structure of Intellect: Its Interpretation and Uses.* Columbus, Ohio: Charles E. Merrill, 1969.

Merrill, M. David. "Learner Control: Beyond Aptitude-Treatment Interactions." *AV Communication Review* 23 (1975): 217–226.

Miller, George A.; Galanter, Eugene; and Pribram, Karl H. *Plans and the Structure of Behavior.* New York: Holt, Rinehart and Winston, 1960.

Miller, L. B. "Development of Curriculum Models in Head Start." In *Project Head Start: A Legacy of the War on Poverty,* edited by Edward Zigler and Jeanette Valentine. New York: Free Press, 1979.

Moynahan, Eileen. "The Development of Knowledge Concerning the Effect of Categorization upon Free Recall." *Child Development* 44 (1973): 238–246.

Neisser, Ulric. "General, Academic, and Artificial Intelligence." In *The Nature of Intelligence,* edited by Lauren Resnick. Hillsdale, N.J.: Lawrence Erlbaum Associates, 1976.

Neisser, Ulric. "The Concept of Intelligence." In *Human Intelligence: Perspectives on Its Theory and Measurement,* edited by Robert Sternberg and Douglas Detterman. Norwood, N.J.: Ablex, 1979.

Newell, Allen; Shaw, J. C.; and Simon, Herbert A. "Report on a General Problem-Solving Program." *Proceedings of the International Conference on Information Processing.* Paris: UNESCO, 1960.

Newell, Allen, and Simon, Herbert A. *Human Problem Solving.* Englewood Cliffs, N.J.: Prentice-Hall, 1972.

Noelting, Gerald. "Stages and Mechanisms in the Development of the Concept of Proportion in the Child and Adolescent." Paper presented at the Fifth Interdisciplinary Seminar on Piagetian Theory and Its Implications for the Helping Professions, University of Southern California, Los Angeles, 1975.

Nucci, Larry P., and Gordon, Neal J. "Educating Adolescents from a Piagetian Perspective." *Journal of Education* 161 (1979): 87–101.

Palmer, F. H., and Anderson, L. W. "Long-term Gains from Early Intervention: Findings from Longitudinal Studies." In *Project Head Start: A Legacy of the War on Poverty,* edited by Edward Zigler and Jeanette Valentine. New York: Free Press, 1979.

Pascual-Leone, Juan. "A Mathematical Model for the Transition Rule in Piaget's Development Stages." *Acta Psychologica* 63 (1970): 301–345.

Patterson, Charlotte J.; Massad, Christopher M.; and Cosgrove, J. Michael. "Children's Referential Communication: Components of Plans for Effective Listening." *Developmental Psychology* 14 (1978): 401–406.

Pauk, Walter. *How to Study in College.* Boston: Houghton-Mifflin, 1962.

Peel, E. A. "The Thinking and Education of the Adolescent." In *Piaget, Psychology, and Education,* edited by Ved Varma and Phillip Williams. Itasca, Ill.: F. E. Peacock, 1976.

Peterson, Penelope; Janicki, Terence C.; and Swing, Susan R. "Ability x Treatment Interaction Effects on Children's Learning in Large-group and Small-group

Approaches." *American Educational Research Journal* 18 (1981): 453–473.

Piaget, Jean. *The Origins of Intelligence in Children.* New York: International Universities Press, 1952.

Piaget, Jean. *Science of Education and the Psychology of the Child.* New York: Orion Press, 1970.

Piaget, Jean. *The Psychology of Intelligence.* Totowa, N. J.: Littlefield, Adams, and Co., 1976.

Piaget, Jean (with Montangero, J., and Billeter, J.). "Les Correlâts." *L'Abstraction Refléchissante.* Paris: Presses Universitaires de France, 1977.

Polya, George. *How To Solve It: A New Aspect of Mathematical Method.* 2d ed. Princeton, N.J.: Princeton University Press, 1957.

Reid, D. Kim. "Equilibration and Learning." *Journal of Education* 161 (1979): 51–70.

Reitman, Walter. *Cognition and Thought.* New York: Wiley, 1965.

Resnick, Lauren B. "The Future of IQ Testing in Educaton." In *Human Intelligence: Perspectives on Its Theory and Measurement*, edited by Robert Sternberg and Douglas Detterman. Norwood, N.J.: Ablex, 1979.

Resnick, Lauren B. "Instructional Psychology." *Annual Review of Psychology* 32 (1981): 659–704.

Resnick, Lauren B., and Glaser, Robert. "Problem Solving and Intelligence." In *The Nature of Intelligence*, edited by Lauren B. Resnick. Hillsdale, N.J.: Lawrence Erlbaum Associates, 1976.

Rigney, J. W. "Cognitive Learning Strategies and Dualities in Information Processing." In *Aptitude, Learning, and Instruction*, vol. 1, edited by Richard Snow, Pat-Anthony Federico, and William Montague. Hillsdale, N.J.: Lawrence Erlbaum Associates, 1980.

Robinson, Frances, P. *Effective Study.* New York: Harper and Row, 1970. Originally published 1941.

Ross, Dorothea M., and Ross, Sheila A. "Facilitative Effect of Mnemonic Strategies on Multiple Associate Learning in EMR Children." *American Journal of Mental Deficiency* 82 (1978): 460–466.

Rubenstein, M. F. *Patterns of Problem Solving.* Englewood Cliffs, N.J.: Prentice-Hall, 1975.

Rumelhart, David D., and Norman, D. A. "Accretion, Tuning, and Restructuring: Three Modes of Learning." In *Semantic Factors in Cognition*, edited by John Cotton and Roberta Klatzky. Hillsdale N.J.: Lawrence Erlbaum Associates, 1978.

Salatas, Harriet, and Flavell, John H. "Behavioral and Metamnemonic Indicators of Strategic Behaviors under Remember Instructions in First Grade." *Child Development* 47 (1976): 80–89.

Scribner, Sylvia, and Cole, Michael. *The Psychology of Literary.* Cambridge, Mass.: Harvard University Press, 1981.

Seitz, Victoria; Abelson, Willa D.; Levine, Elizabeth; and Zigler, Edward. "Effects of Place of Testing on the Peabody Picture Vocabulary Test Scores of Disadvantaged Head Start and Non-Head Start Children." *Child Development* 46 (1975): 481–486.

Shatz, Marilyn. "The Relationship Between Cognitive Processes and the Development of Communication Skills." In *Nebraska Symposium on Motivation*, edited by B. Keasy. Lincoln: University of Nebraska Press, 1977.

Siegel, Linda, and Brainerd, Charles J., eds. *Alternatives to Piaget: Critical Essays on the Theory*. New York: Academic Press, 1978.

Siegler, Robert S., and Klahr, David. "When Do Children Learn? The Relationship between Existing Knowledge and the Acquisition of New Knowledge." In *Advances in Instructional Psychology*, vol. 2, edited by Robert Glaser. Hillsdale, N.J.: Lawrence Erlbaum Associates, 1982.

Siegler, Robert S., and Richards, D. D. "The Development of Intelligence." In *Handbook of Human Intelligence*, edited by Robert Sternberg. New York: Cambridge University Press, 1982.

Silverman, Charles, and Weikart, David. *Open Framework: Evolution of a Concept in Preschool Education*. Ypsilanti, Mich.: High Scope Educational Research Foundation Report, 1973.

Simon, D. P., and Simon, Herbert A. "Individual Differences in Solving Physics Problems." In *Children's Thinking: What Develops?* edited by Robert Siegler. Hillsdale, N.J.: Lawrence Erlbaum Associates, 1978.

Simon, Herbert A. "Identifying Basic Abilities Underlying Intelligent Performance in Complex Tasks." In *The Nature of Intelligence*, edited by Lauren B. Resnick. Hillsdale, N.J.: Lawrence Erlbaum Associates, 1976.

Sinnott, Joy. "Everyday Thinking and Piagetian Operativity in Adults." *Human Development* 18 (1975): 430–443.

Smirnov, Anatole A. *Problems of the Psychology of Memory*. New York: Plenum Press, 1973.

Snow, Richard E. "Research on Aptitude for Learning: A Progress Report." In *Review of Research in Education*, vol. 4, edited by Lee Shulman. Itasca, Ill.: F. E. Peacock, 1976.

Snow, Richard E. "Individual Differences and Instructional Theory." *Educational Researcher* 6: 10 (1977): 11–15.

Snow, Richard E. "Theory and Method for Research on Aptitude Processes." *Intelligence* 2 (1978): 225–278.

Snow, Richard E. "Aptitude Processes." In *Aptitude, Learning, and Instruction*, vol. 1, edited by Richard E. Snow, Pat-Anthony Federico, and William Montague. Hillsdale, N.J.: Lawrence Erlbaum Associates, 1980.

Snow, Richard E. "The Training of Intellectual Aptitude." In *How and How Much Can Intelligence Be Increased?* edited by Douglas Detterman and Robert Sternberg. Norwood, N.J.: Ablex, 1982.

Spearman, Charles. *The Nature of "Intelligence" and the Principles of Cognition*. London: Macmillan, 1923.

Spearman, Charles. *The Abilities of Man*. New York: Macmillan, 1927.

Stein, Barry, S.; Bransford, John D; Franks, Jeffrey J.; Owings, Richard A.; Vye, Nancy J.; and McGraw, William. "Differences in the Precision of Self-Generated Elaborations." *Journal of Experimental Psychology: General* III (1982): 399–405.

Stein, Barry S.; Bransford, John D.; Franks, Jeffrey J.; Vye, Nancy J.; and Perfetto, G. A. "Differences in Judgments of Learning Difficulty." *Journal of Experimental Psychology: General* III (1982): 406–413.

Stephens, Beth; McLaughlin, John A.; Miller, Charles K.; and Glass, Gene V. "Factorial Structure of Selected Psycho-educational Measures and Piagetian Reasoning Assessments." *Developmental Psychology* 6 (1972): 343–348.

Sternberg, Robert J. *Intelligence, Information Processing, and Analogical Reasoning: The Componential Analysis of Human Abilities.* Hillsdale, N.J.: Lawrence Erlbaum Associates, 1977.

Sternberg, Robert J. "Sketch of a Componential Theory of Human Intelligence." *Behavioral and Brain Sciences* 3 (1980): 573–584.

Sternberg, Robert J. "A Componential Approach to Intellectual Development." In *Advances in the Psychology of Human Intelligence*, vol. 1, edited by Robert J. Sternberg. Hillsdale, N.J.: Lawrence Erlbaum Associates, 1982.

Sternberg, Robert J. "Mechanisms of Cognitive Development." In *Mechanisms of Cognitive Development*, edited by Robert J. Sternberg. San Francisco: Freeman, 1984.

Sternberg, Robert J. "Instrumental and Componential Approaches to the Training of Intelligence." In *Thinking and Learning Skills: Current Research and Open Questions*, vol. 2, edited by Judith W. Segal, Susan F. Chipman, and Robert Glaser. Hillsdale, N.J.: Lawrence Erlbaum Associates, 1985.

Sternberg, Robert J., and Gardner, M. K. "A Componential Interpretation of the General Factor in Human Intelligence." In *A Model for Intelligence*, edited by Hans J. Eysenck. Heidelberg: Springer-Verlag, 1982.

Sternberg, Robert J., and Weil, Evelyn M. "An Aptitude-Strategy Interaction in Linear Syllogistic Reasoning." *Journal of Educational Psychology* 72 (1980): 226–234.

Tenney, Yvette J. "The Child's Conception of Organization and Recall." *Journal of Experimental Child Psychology* 19 (1975): 100–114.

Terman, Lewis M., and Merrill, Maud A. *Stanford-Binet Intelligence Scale.* Boston: Houghton Mifflin, 1960.

Thomas, Ellen, and Robinson, H. Alan. *Improving Reading in Every Class: A Source-Book for Teachers.* Boston: Allyn and Bacon, 1972.

Thurstone, Louis L. *Primary Mental Abilities.* Chicago: University of Chicago Press, 1938.

Tobias, Sigmund. "Adapting Instruction to Individual Differences among Students." *Educational Psychologist* 16 (1981): 111–120.

Tobias, Sigmund. "When Do Instructional Methods Make a Difference?" *Educational Researcher* 11:7 (1982): 4–9.

Tuddenham, Read D. "A 'Piagetian' Test of Cognitive Development." In *On Intelligence*, edited by W. B. Dockrell. Toronto: Ontario Institute for Studies in Education, 1975.

Valett, Robert E. *Developing Cognitive Abilities: Teaching Children to Think.* St. Louis: C. V. Mosby, 1978.

Vernon, Philip E. *The Structure of Human Abilities.* London: Methuen, 1971.

Wagner, Richard K., and Sternberg, Robert J. "Practical Intelligence in Real-World Pursuits: The Role of Tacit Knowledge." *Journal of Personality and Social Psychology* 49 (1985): 436–458.

Wertsch, James V. "Adult-Child Interaction and the Roots of Metacognition." *Quarterly Newsletter of the Institutes of Comparative Human Development* 2 (1978): 15–18.

Whimbey, Arthur, and Lochhead, J. *Problem Solving and Comprehension: A Short Course in Analytical Reasoning.* 2d ed. Philadelphia: Franklin Institute Press, 1980.

Whimbey, Arthur, with Whimbey, L. S. *Intelligence Can Be Taught*. New York: Dutton, 1975.

Whitely, Susan E. "Information-Processing on Intelligence Test Items: Some Response Components." *Applied Psychological Measurement* 1 (1977): 465–476.

Whitely, Susan E., and Dawis, Rene V. "Effects of Cognitive Intervention on Latent Ability Measured from Analogy Items." *Journal of Educational Psychology* 66 (1974): 710–717.

Wickelgren, Wayne A. *How to Solve Problems: Elements of a Theory of Problems and Problem Solving*. San Francisco: W. H. Freeman, 1974.

Williams, D. S. "Computer Program Organization Induced from Problem Examples." In *Representation and Meaning*, edited by Herbert A. Simon and Laurent Siklossy. Englewood Cliffs, N.J.: Prentice-Hall, 1972.

Zigler, Edward. "Project Head Start: Success or Failure?" *Learning* 1 (1973): 43–47.

Zigler, Edward; Abelson, Willa D.; Trickett, Penelope; and Seitz, Victoria. "Is an Intervention Program Really Necessary to Raise Disadvantaged Children's IQ Scores?" *Child Development* 53 (1982): 340–348.

Zigler, Edward, and Seitz, Victoria. "Social Policy and Intelligence." In *Handbook of Human Intelligence*, edited by Robert J. Sternberg. New York: Cambridge University Press, 1982.

Zigler, Edward, and Valentine, Jeanette, eds. *Project Head Start: A Legacy on the War on Poverty*. New York: Free Press, 1979.

11

Achievement and the Quality of Student Effort

C. Robert Pace

"If students expect to benefit from what this college or university has to offer, they have to take the initiative." More than 95 percent of undergraduates from all over the country agree with that statement. Students know that what they get out of college will depend, to a considerable degree, on what they put into it. They are right. Exactly how right they are, and what it means more specifically for the achievement of important educational goals, are the subjects of this chapter.

What is quality of effort? How is it measured? Having measured it, what do we know about its importance in accounting for quality of results? Then, although our current data come from research on higher education, what relevance might be projected for the quality of education at all levels?

All learning and development require an investment of time and effort by the student. Time is a frequency dimension. Effort is a quality dimension in the sense that some kinds of effort are potentially more educative than others. Effort at what? The college experience consists of the events that occur in a college environment. The relevant experiences are those that stem from the events and conditions and facilities that the college makes possible and are intended to facilitate student learning and development. Obvious examples of major facilities in a college or university are classrooms, libraries, laboratories, cultural facilities, student unions, athletic and recreational facilities, and residence units. Then there are other events and experiences that are not necessarily connected with a specific facility but are nevertheless important opportunities for the personal and social development of students. Obvious examples are contacts with faculty members, involvement in clubs and organizations, experiences in writing, the breadth and depth of student acquaintances, opportunities that lead to self-understanding, and the general nature and level of conversations among students. We selected the facilities and opportunities just mentioned for use in measuring the quality of effort students expend during their college experience.

How does one measure the quality of effort in the use of such facilities and opportunities? We devised brief activity checklists for each facility or opportunity and we asked students to indicate how often they had engaged in each activity during the current school year. The activities range from relatively common ones that require little effort to ones that require a greater investment of effort and that have a greater potential for influencing learning and development. Some examples will clarify the concept of quality of effort and the measurement of the quality of effort expended in the use of facilities and opportunities.

Consider the library as a facility. A library has certain purposes and certain properties as a repository of information and as a resource. To what extent do students use the facility to capitalize on those properties? Some students may use the library building simply as a convenient and quiet place to study materials they have brought with them; this use of the facility has no basic connection with its purposes as a library. Others may use the library to read something available in the library that was explicitly assigned; this makes some use of the library as a repository. Still other students may discover that the library is a resource offering exciting avenues for exploration—they might examine indexes and guides, follow up on various references, look for materials under different headings, browse in the stacks, or take out something because it looks interesting, which might then lead their interest into something else. The quality-of-effort dimension with regard to library experiences is that of using the library's potential; the experiences include exploring that potential independently, learning how to find information one needs, and thereby increasing one's competence for independent learning.

With respect to course learning, such activities as making outlines from class notes and readings or trying to explain the material to another person are higher-level cognitive activities than merely taking notes or underlining points in a textbook. The quality dimension is the level of cognitive effort, and the higher levels contribute more solidly to the acquisition of knowledge and understanding.

Each scale has a similar type of underlying quality dimension. Overall, the scales are intended to provide a systematic, structured, and reliable inventory of the amount, scope, and quality of effort students put into capitalizing on their college experience. The student's score on a particular scale reflects how often the student has engaged in the activities; and since a high score can be obtained only by engaging in the higher-level activities, the score reflects the quality of effort and experience and not merely its frequency.

The fourteen quality-of-effort scales (seven are concerned with the use of college facilities and seven are concerned with personal and social opportunities) form the major part of a questionnaire called "College Student Experiences." The other parts of the questionnaire include items that enable one to determine relationships between quality of effort and achievement, and these parts also include many elements that might help to explain those relationships. For example, there are (1) questions about the students' background and their status in college; (2) rating scales intended to characterize important qualities of the college environment such as its emphasis on intellectual, creative, and vocational objectives and on the nature, quality, and particularly the supportiveness of personal relationships in the college environment; (3) items to measure students' satisfaction with college; and (4) a list of eighteen important general objectives or goals of undergraduate education. The students respond to these objectives by indicating how much gain or progress they feel they have made on each since entering college. The statements of goals fall into four major categories: (1) objectives related to personal and social development, such as self-understanding and clarifying values; (2) objectives related to general education, literature, and arts; (3) objectives related to development of intellectual skills such as logic, synthesis, and independent learning; and (4) understanding science.

By the end of spring 1982, approximately 18,000 undergraduates from seventy different colleges and universities had responded to the "College Student Experiences" questionnaire. With the exception of a few places where the questionnaire was given to a special group (for example, freshmen only or seniors only) the sample of student responses came from a good cross section of undergraduates.

The first set of results, based on an analysis made in 1979 of responses from some 3,000 students from eleven colleges and universities, is in many respects the most dramatic. Subsequent analyses based on larger samples have merely confirmed these results. The question to be answered is this: Given all the elements in the questionnaire (students' background characteristics, their status in college, their satisfaction with college, their assessment of the college environment, and their scores on the various quality-of-effort scales) what best predicts their achivement with respect to each of the four categories of goals of higher education?

In analyzing the data we used stepwise regression, a procedure that first identifies the variable that has the largest relationship to achievement, then identifies the variable that has the next largest relationship, and so forth until adding more variables contributes little or nothing more toward accounting for the performance. The results clearly showed that quality of effort was the best predictor of achievement. In relation to every one of the four main categories of achievement, one or more of the quality-of-effort scales made the greatest contribution toward explaining that achievement.

Another way to highlight the contribution that quality of effort makes in predicting achievement is to put all the variables into the computer in a predetermined sequence: first, put in all the students' background or status variables; second, put in all the college status variables; third, put in all the environment ratings; and, finally, after all of these commonly utilized variables have contributed as much as they can to explaining achievement, put in the quality-of-effort variables to see whether they add anything to explaining achievement.

Those data show that before considering the quality-of-effort measures, the other variables account for somewhere between 24 percent and 36 percent of the result on the criterion. This is almost exactly what many past studies have shown. But, when the quality-of-effort measures are added, one can now explain from 39 percent to 47 percent of the performance on the criterion—a substantial increase in our understanding, from 10 to 15 percentage points better than past research has typically been able to explain.

Whereas prior research has held that student characteristics and family background are the most important determinants of achievement, our results lead to a very significant and different conclusion: *Granted the importance of all the elements that influence which students go to what colleges, once the students are enrolled in college what is most important to achievement is not who the students are or where they are; rather it is what they do.* Prior research has not included what turns out to be the most influential variable—the quality of effort that students themselves invest in using the facilities and opportunities for learning and development that exist in the college setting. Now that quality of effort has been included as a variable in determining achievement, better explanations and new conclusions emerge. In addition to the above general relationship between effort and attainment, some analyses show the special diagnostic significance of quality of effort and lead to further refinements in prior conclusions.

It is true, for example, that gains in intellectual skills are related to students' grades—the better the grades, the larger the gains. But that is not the whole truth. The whole truth is that students who have high scores on the quality-of-effort scales related to academic and intellectual experiences (course learning, library, writing, and contacts with faculty) make much greater gains than students whose quality-of-effort scores are low, regardless of their grades. In fact, B minus students with high quality-of-effort scores make more progress than B plus students with low quality-of-effort scores.

It is true that living on campus, rather than living at home or elsewhere, is positively related to students' satisfaction with college. But it is not the whole truth. The whole truth is that freshmen who live in the dormitory or in fraternity or sorority houses but who put a low quality of effort into using the residence facility might as well have stayed at home as far as their satisfaction with college is concerned.

It is true that students who expect to continue their education in graduate or professional school have higher gain scores on intellectual skills and higher effort scores on academic/intellectual experiences than do students who do not plan to continue their education beyond the bachelor's degree; it is also true that outcome scores and effort scores are typically higher as students move from their freshman to their senior year. But again, this is not the whole truth. The whole truth is that, for every year in college, students who do not plan to continue but have high quality-of-effort scores make higher scores on the outcome measures than do students who plan to continue but have low quality-of-effort scores.

It is true that time-on-task has been shown in many research studies to be a very important factor in explaining achievement. But compared to quality of effort, time-on-task is a weak explanation. In our study, two variables are similar to the idea of time on task. One is how long the students have been in college; the other is how many hours a week the students usually spend on activities related to their schoolwork. Our analyses confirm the importance of time, but also the greater importance of effort. It is true, for example, that gains on the outcome measures related to intellectual skills and to general education are related to how long one has been in college—the gains reported by seniors are significantly greater than the gains reported by freshmen. But the whole truth is that freshmen whose quality-of-effort scores for intellectual and academic experiences are high (above average) report greater gains in intellectual skills and in general education than do juniors or seniors whose quality-of-effort scores are low (below average). It is also true that sheer time spent on academic work (number of hours a week) is related to progress toward objectives related to general education, to intellectual skills, and to grades. But the whole truth is that students who spend a lot of time at a low level of quality make less progress than do students who spend fewer hours at a high level of quality; students who spend about forty hours a week of high-quality effort get better grades than do students who spend fifty or more hours of low-quality effort.

Not only does quality of effort have a general predictive value and a special diagnostic value, as the results thus far presented have shown, but it also has what one might call a pervasive value. By this we mean that the range or scope of high-quality effort is related to the range or scope of high achievement. Breadth of involvement and breadth of attainments go hand in hand.

Of the fourteen quality-of-effort scales in the questionnaire, twelve are answered by everyone (not all students live in a campus residence facility and so do not respond to the Residence scale, and not all students have had a science course and so do not respond to the Science Laboratory scale). Of the twelve scales answered by everyone, four are mainly concerned with academic and intellectual activities (course learning, library, contacts with faculty, and writing), four are primarily personal and interpersonal (personal experiences, student acquaintances, conversation topics, and conversation level), and four are primarily centered around group facilities and associations (student unions, clubs and organizations, athletic and recreational facilities, and cultural facilities related to art, music, and theater). We devised a "breadth index," which is defined as the number of scales (different aspects of campus life) on which a student's score is above the median of some baseline group. This baseline could be the median at one's own institution or the median of all student responses at all institutions. Of the thirty colleges and universities from which data had been obtained by spring 1980, twenty-four were selected to form a multi-institutional baseline; they were chosen because each had obtained replies from a good cross section of students. Students' scores on the breadth index could, and did, range from 0 to 12. Some students invested above-average quality of effort on all twelve of the topics, and some students invested above-average quality of effort on none of the twelve topics. The distribution of breadth scores for 7,800 students at these twenty-four colleges and universities was a normal distribution—one-fourth (25 percent) of the students had a breadth score of 9 or higher; about the same proportion (27 percent) had a breadth score of 3 or lower; and the median breadth score (6.4) was almost exactly halfway between 0 and 12.

Using a breadth score of 9 or higher (the upper fourth) as a definition of "high breadth," we found large differences between one college and another. For example, at one college only 10 percent of the student body had a breadth score of 9 or higher; whereas at another college 61 percent of the students had a breadth score of 9 or higher. Clearly at some colleges the vigor and vitality of what students put into the college experience cover a much wider range of college activities, and the effort is much more pervasive than at other colleges.

Indeed, the breadth index for a college may be a good indicator of the quality of its undergraduate education program or at least of the quality of undergraduate student experience at the college. This association is suggested by the relationship between breadth scores and outcomes. In the twenty-four institutions studied the rank order correlation between breadth of effort and breadth of outcomes is .80. Breadth of outcomes is the number of outcomes or objectives in which the institution's score (percentage of its students reporting very much or quite a bit of progress) was equal to or higher than the score for the composite of all institutions in the study. The breadth of above-average effort was clearly associated with the breadth of above-average attainments—the broader the scope of effort, the broader the range of outcomes.

Other evidence of the relation between breadth scores and attainment is found in comparing the percentage of students with low breadth scores and the percentage of students with high breadth scores with respect to the students' reported progress toward each of the objectives. On *all* objectives the percentage of students reporting very much or quite a bit of progress is much greater among the students with high breadth scores. On *many* objectives the percentage for the high-breadth group is more than twice the percentage for the low-breadth group. This again suggests the pervasive value of the concept of quality of effort, for it has an influence on every one of the objectives.

In a local study, based on the responses of a good cross section of undergraduates at the University of California at Los Angeles, interrelationships among environment, effort, satisfaction, and attainment were explored. These interrelationships further illustrate both the predictive and the pervasive value of quality of effort. For this study we used students' satisfaction with college as the criterion. It seems reasonable to expect that people who do not like what they are doing and do not like where they are probably are not putting much effort into the activity nor are they getting much out of it.

We divided the students into three groups: very satisfied, satisfied, and neutral to negative; then we compared the responses of these three groups with respect to their quality-of-effort scores on all fourteen aspects of the college experience, their characterizations of the college environment on all of the environment ratings, and their ratings of their progress toward all of the objectives. On every quality-of-effort scale, on every characterization of the environment, and on reported progress toward every objective, the highest (most favorable) mean scores were made by the students who were "very satisfied" with UCLA, the next best scores were made by students who were "satisfied," and the lowest scores were made by those who were "neutral to negative." There were no exceptions to this pattern.

Students who are most satisfied with college put the most effort into it and get the most out of it. Using satisfaction with college as the criterion, and then determining which variables of all the ones included in the questionnaire have the highest relationship to that criterion (best predict or best explain it), we found that the two most influential variables were (1) students' gains in the group of objectives we have described as intellectual competence and (2) an environment in which relationships among students were characterized as friendly and supportive. So, when students are very satisfied they believe they are developing their intellectual skills and consider the environment friendly and supportive. Since we do not really know if satisfaction promotes development of intellectual skills and leads to a friendly environment or vice versa, we can also state the generalization another way: When students are making progress in the development of their intellectual powers and when their experience in the environment is characterized by friendly and supportive relationships with other students, they are very satisfied with college.

These results, together with those presented earlier in this chapter, reveal a circle of influence on what can surely be called excellence: High-quality effort is the best predictor of high achievement; high achievement in intellectual skills is the best predictor of high satisfaction with college; and satisfaction as well as achievement is further enhanced in an atmosphere that is friendly and supportive.

Another study at UCLA of transfer students from community colleges included some comparisons between the quality of effort of UCLA transfer students who had persisted and those who had dropped out and also the quality of effort of these two groups when they were enrolled in community college. The academic quality-of-effort scales were used in this study—course learning, library, writing, and contacts with faculty. The population included all community college transfers to UCLA in fall 1977. We located 61 percent of the transfers, who responded to a questionnaire in spring 1979; 824 respondents were still enrolled at UCLA, and 312 had dropped out. The students indicated how often they had engaged in the various activities at UCLA and also how often they had engaged in those same activities when they were in community college. Other parts of the questionnaire asked about some characteristics of the environment at community colleges and at UCLA, and some parts dealt with students' progress toward certain objectives at their community colleges and at UCLA. On the quality-of-effort scales for library, writing, and course learning, the scores of both the dropouts and the students who remained in school were higher at UCLA than they had been at the community college, but the difference was much greater for those who remained in school than for dropouts. In other words, the dropouts had increased their quality of effort somewhat, but not nearly enough and not nearly as much as those who persisted. For example, on the Course Learning scale 55 percent of the dropouts from UCLA scored 26 or higher, whereas 37 percent of the transfers scored over 26 when they were enrolled in community college. In contrast, the corresponding percentages for those who persisted at UCLA and scored over 26 was 50 percent when they were in community college, which increased to 80 percent after their enrollment in UCLA. On the Library scale 65 percent of the students who persisted in school scored 21 points or above at UCLA, compared with 31 percent for the dropouts. For both groups, the percentage represented an increase over what their quality of effort in library use had been at the community college—the dropouts who scored over 21 points increased from 16 percent to 31 percent, and the students who persisted increased from 28 percent to 65 percent.

These differences between community college and the university are also reflected in students' ratings of progress toward important objectives. While in community college, about one-third (34 percent) of the students who later transferred and persisted at UCLA felt they had made very much or quite a bit of progress toward the objective of the ability to think analytically and logically. Only 27 percent of those who transferred and subsequently dropped out of UCLA felt they had made much progress toward that objective. Among those students who persisted at UCLA, 85 percent claimed very much or quite a bit of gain, compared with 46 percent among those who had dropped out.

From these examples, and from many others like them in the complete study, two generalizations can be made: First, the quality of academic effort needed to persist at the university was much higher than the quality of effort needed at the community college to become eligible for transfer; and second, compared with the students who later dropped out, the students who were successful at the university not only had made a much larger increase in their prior quality of effort but also had reached a much higher absolute level of effort. One of the successful transfer students put it this way: "I think it's up to the individual to realize that UCLA is not a joke. If he or she bears down and pushes himself or herself they will get the most out of what UCLA has to offer. I enjoyed it, and I am not that smart, but I worked hard. And that's what counts."

This student's comment brings us back to where we started this paper: "If students expect to benefit from what this college or university has to offer they have to take the initiative ." The quality-of-effort scales are, in a sense, measures of initiative. With a few inadvertent exceptions, nearly all of the activities in the quality-of-effort scales are essentially voluntary. They are not assigned or required, and it may be this very feature that accounts for their significant relation to high achievement and their significant value in higher education. College is basically a voluntary activity. A person does not have to go to college. An undergraduate college education is necessary in order to become a dentist, but there are no requirements that an individual become a dentist. After students begin college, they do not have to browse in the library, they do not have to make appointments to talk with faculty members, and they do not have to go to class. Students do not have to make outlines from their class notes and readings, go to concerts, or work on a committee. Students do not have to ask other people to read something they have written to see whether it is clear, nor do they have to have serious discussions with students whose personal values are very different from their own. By the words "do not have to" I mean that no one requires students to do the activities, nor are other persons checking up on students to make sure they have. This is why the quality of effort, which one might also think of as the quality of initiative, is so important at the college level—is so highly predictive of achievement, diagnostic for understanding various relationships, and pervasive in the college experience.

How useful it may be to measure "quality of effort" in high school and in elementary school may depend on how much opportunity there is for "pupil initiative" in those settings. Pupil behavior in the elementary school classroom, and the elementary school setting in general, is primarily planned and controlled by the teacher. It is the teacher who decides what activities will be done, and when, and who helps them along the way. But surely there are also opportunities for pupil initiative, for independence, and for accepting responsibility. Observers and researchers who are familiar with elementary schools could devise ways to record pupil activities that reflect quality of effort in using elementary school facilities. The evidence revealed by such measurement may well be predictive of achievement at the next level of education, where the opportunities for initiative are greater and where the connection between effort and attainment is probably stronger. In high schools more independence and adaptation are required for success. Students have different teachers for different subjects; they move from one location to another; surveillance of whether they are doing their work is not as close as it was in elementary school where they were in the same classroom with the same teacher throughout the day.

It may well be true that whenever education is compulsory, teachers feel compelled to plan and manage and monitor the activities of pupils in considerable detail. The goal is often to have as many pupils as possible master explicitly described tasks.

In higher education such detailed determination of how students spend their time is rarely found. The developmental and educative process from childhood to adolescence to adulthood, which is to say from elementary school to secondary school to college, not only is one of acquiring more and more knowledge but also is one that requires more and more initiative. It may be useful to think of the results (success) at each level as signaling readiness to take the next step.

From evidence at the college level that quality of student effort predicts progress toward the attainment of important objectives better than any other activity or characteristic, and from evidence that the quality of effort exerted in community college is not enough for persistence and success at the university, readiness to take the step from one educational level to the next may be viewed as the individual's readiness to invest time and effort in the events and experiences that are intended to facilitate learning and development.

Whatever applicability the concept of quality of effort may have in other educational settings, its value for higher education is buttressed by the evidence given in this chapter. The gist of that evidence is really quite simple: College cannot *give* persons an education; but if they go to college and make good use of the facilities and opportunities it provides, they can *get* a very good education.

POSTSCRIPT

The material in this chapter was initially presented in 1982 in my report to the National Commission on Excellence in Education. Since that time many more data have been obtained and many more analyses have been made. A second edition of the College Student Experiences questionnaire, slightly revised, was printed in 1983 and was used by forty-four colleges and universities during 1983–84. Some colleges have continued to use the initial 1979 edition. The total accumulation of questionnaires completed in fall 1984 includes approximately 40,000 undergraduates from about 130 colleges and universities.

Many of the basic analyses reported in this chapter have been repeated. The major conclusions about the predictive power of quality of effort, about its diagnostic utility, and about its pervasive nature in understanding undergraduate student learning and development have all been reconfirmed in these more recent analyses.

Many of the analyses reported in this chapter, and all the more recent analyses, are included in my monograph entitled *Measuring the Quality of College Student Experiences* (Los Angeles: UCLA Higher Education Research Institute, 1984). That monograph recounts the full story of the development, results, and significance of this line of inquiry to date.

Some of the data reported in this chapter came from work done by research assistants who were, at the time, graduate students at UCLA or who completed doctoral dissertations that analyzed data from the questionnaire. These individuals are Jon Shaver, Jack Friedlander, Mary Beth Snyder, Juan Lara, Daniel Brown, Oscar Porter, and Karen Lefever.

PART V

Conclusion

12

A Nation At Risk: Retrospect and Prospect

Herbert J. Walberg

As Tomlinson's chapter in this book demonstrates, the report of the National Commission on Excellence in Education, *A Nation At Risk*, hit a responsive chord among the American public, professional educators, and policymakers. Not only was it widely reprinted and discussed, but it also stimulated a dozen or so other national reports (see reviews by Peterson [1983] and by Westbury (1984]) and considerable legislative activity, which continues to this day.

The foregoing chapters, selected from the position papers prepared originally for the commission, provide the scholarly basis for several of the main themes of its report. In particular, as reflected in the title of this book, they illustrate the importance of academic work and educational excellence. We might ask, however, why current interest in these educational matters is so widespread and why so much legislative attention is being given to them.

Education in the Economy

Perhaps a review of the economic conditions in the United States prior to the report will help to answer these questions. These conditions included inflation, recession, stagnation of older industries, and industrial competition from abroad. As was the case in England, a country that was the "workshop of the world" a century ago, it appeared that the United States could have difficulty in competing economically with other nations not only in the new "high" technologies but also in such basic industries as iron, steel, and automotive manufacturing.

Two centuries ago Adam Smith held that the wealth of nations depends on the abilities of their people and, further, that education is not idle consumption but a useful investment for nations and for the individuals who acquire it. Though difficult to prove decisively, his ideas may be still more believable in an era of increased economic competition among nations; the continuing rise in "knowledge industries" may mean that a variety of abilities may be in greater demand (Walberg 1983).

Education, moreover, may be our largest enterprise in terms of the number of people involved, the value of human time required, and the capital and operating expenditures budgeted. The value of education invested in the American labor force, for example, rose from $65 billion to $815 billion since 1900 (Walberg 1983).

In the past few decades, spending on schools and colleges has accelerated, rising from $11 billion to $200 billion per year, and its percentage share of the gross national product rose from 3.4 percent to 6.8 percent. In addition, the inflation-adjusted annual costs of public school education rose about five-fold, from $490 to $2,500 per student from about 1930 to 1980 (Walberg 1984).

EDUCATION: A DECLINING INDUSTRY?

Even though costs have risen, the National Commission on Excellence in Education and other groups report that the products of the educational system—students—have apparently declined in the quality of their learning or in the amount they learn. Studies from the past two decades, moreover, showed that American students did poorly compared to students in other countries. Although comparisons of test results of students from countries that have consensus on national goals, ministries of education, and centralized control with those of students in the United States can be misleading, the differences are striking enough to compel attention to our assumptions about education and our practices.

Recent studies provide a grim picture of the achievement of children in even the elementary grades in the United States. In mathematics, for example, Stevenson (1983) found that students in the United States fall further behind Japanese and Taiwanese children at each grade level; and by fifth grade the worst Asian classes in his large sample exceeded the best American class. Research and observations in elementary science classes in Japan corroborate his findings. Recent achievement comparisons in high school mathematics also showed that American high school students score on average at the first or second percentile of Japanese norms (Walberg 1983; Walberg, Harnisch, and Tsai,in press).

Thus, although costs of education have risen much faster than those of other industries, it can hardly be argued that the results have risen accordingly. By what can be measured, educational productivity has not even kept up with that of the smokestack industries such as steel, automobile, and consumer electronics that are no longer world-class competitors in quality and costs.

It is difficult, of course, to arrive at definitive conclusions about the causal relation of educational investments, services, and values beyond the narrow areas indicated by objective achievement tests. Neither the costs of educational inputs (which include human effort) nor the value of immediate outputs (such as scoring well on a test) relevant to immediate and long-term values are well measured.

Nor are educational costs and the values of achievement well understood; thus they are not systematically considered in formulating policy. Better measurement of these costs and values, nonetheless, may mean that considerable improvement may be made. *A Nation At Risk* and the related scholarly papers in this volume open this problem to critical questioning and give hope that we may more effectively attain educational goals that are in our society's interest. To this end, both students and teachers must make more efficient use of school time to promote the welfare of individual students as well as the welfare of the nation.

The productivity and availability of scarce financial and human resources must also be considered if the competing goals of other national reports on educational problems are to be met. One report urges more mathematics and science; another, more English-language mastery; and still others, more foreign languages, history, civics, art, and music. Some national reports call for expanding the curriculum core of fundamental subjects and removing electives; but many educators wish to preserve the diversity of curriculum offerings. A greater consensus on national goals for education may sacrifice local autonomy and individual initiative. Achieving excellence may diminish equality of opportunity.

How can we accomplish all these goals? To avoid undesirable

trade-offs—to create a rising tide that lifts all boats—educators, parents, and students can work longer and harder (National Commission on Excellence in Education 1983); and they can also work more productively using techniques proven effective in research, many of which were revealed in the previous chapters. Educational excellence requires not a choice between effort and effectiveness but both.

TIME AND LEARNING

The commission and the authors of the chapters in this book remind us of an old and seemingly forgotten truth: Practice makes perfect. As Tomlinson states in chapter 1, hard work in school is the great equalizer; it can substitute for talent. The Greeks said there is no royal road to geometry; even nobles had to sweat over the Pythagorean theorem. And to this day, there are no magic bullets in education. Superior teaching and some educational technologies have proved reasonably and even substantially helpful; but learning still requires effort by students.

World-class accomplishments that truly deserve to be called excellent no doubt require both talent and effort; consequently, perhaps we can realistically hope only to raise generally the level of learning in a whole society. In this respect, the commission report cited the outstanding performance of Japanese students; for example, graduation rates from Japan's secondary schools of about 95 percent (in comparison to 75 percent in the United States) and outstanding performance by students on objective tests of mathematics and science are well known. Japanese students also do very well in foreign languages, geography, music, and traditional Western and Japanese arts and crafts (Schiller and Walberg 1982).

Their success seems to have less to do with culture and heredity than with diligence, which is a key ingredient in high accomplishments. In the United States, we are likely to attribute failure to a lack of talent or to poor teaching. But the Japanese often say, if you do not understand it, read it a hundred times, and you will understand it; and Japanese high school students engage in up to forty hours of extramural tutoring and study per week, in addition to regular school on Saturday and only brief summer vacations.

Research published since the commission's report also supports its conclusions about the need for more lesson and study time. Csikszentmihalyi and Larsen (1984), for example, found that American teenagers spend surprisingly small amounts of time on average attending to their teachers and studies. They transmitted signals at random intervals to electronic beepers carried for seven days by seventy-five high school students from a suburban high school in the Chicago area. On receiving the signals, these students filled out a short questionnaire to describe their current activities.

Over a nine-month period, the teenagers in the sample spent on average only thirty-eight hours a week in school classes or studying. By comparison, Japanese students, according to the investigators' estimates, spend an estimated fifty-nine hours a week in classes and at their academic studies. Of the twenty hours a week the American students spent in classes, they listened to their teachers for only four hours.

National surveys also corroborate the comparatively light academic efforts of American students and show that students have considerable discretionary time that is currently wasted. The High School and Beyond study of 1981 on more than fifty-five thousand American high school students showed, by the students' own reports, that they spent an average of four to five hours per week doing homework and about twenty-eight hours per week watching television (Peng, Fetters, Kolstad 1981; Walberg and Shanahan 1983).

If typical American students add four hours of homework per week to thirty nominal hours of schoolwork (six hours per day for five days a week) they have added 13 percent to their learning time in school. If typical Japanese adolescents add about sixteen hours of homework to thirty-six hours of schooling (they attend school on Saturdays also [Rohlen 1983]), this extra homework raises the amount of time spent learning by 44 percent. By Rohlen's estimates, the average total time spent on academic work by students in Japan, which is about fifty-two hours per week, is thus 53 percent higher than the thirty-four hours per week spent by students in the United States. If we also consider after-school tutoring, more extensive study time for special examinations, and a longer school year in Japan, then we may estimate that Japanese students spend twice as much time each year studying as students in the United States do.

In round numbers, since the Japanese spend double the time studying that students in the United States spend, they may compress eight years of American high school and college work into four years. The Japanese high school diploma, by this comparison, may be equivalent to an American baccalaureate degree. Considering the rigor of Japanese high school courses in calculus, physics, chemistry, foreign languages, geography, and other subjects, this crude comparison may not be far from accurate. Considering the very high secondary-shool completion rates in Japan, the human capital accumulated by the Japanese population by age 18 is indeed impressive.

It is difficult to estimate the extent to which this educational rigor benefits Japan as a nation. I think Adam Smith was indeed right: the wealth of a nation depends on the abilities of its people. Accumulated knowledge and skills in the Japanese population may account for Japan's unprecedented economic growth. It is also possible that habits of hard work acquired in school may carry over into adult work life.

AMERICAN FAMILIES

How much time is spent within and outside school? The twelve years of school, each year made up of 180 six-hour days, add up to 12,960 hours, which is the equivalent of 6.2 years of full-time work. This time amounts to only about 13 percent of the students' waking hours in the first eighteen years of life, leaving 87 percent of children's time under the control or influence of parents.

But this parental influence may be tenuous because the traditional American family may not be in very good shape, at least by statistical indicators. And without community and parental support, teachers by themselves may not be able to encourage children to do academic work.

Two recent trends may possibly affect children's academic achievement: an increase in the divorce rate and an increase in the number of mothers who work. Between 1860 and 1960, the divorce rate in the United States fluctuated between thirty and thirty-five per thousand marriages. Since 1960, the number of divorces has increased to unprecedented levels; at current rates, about one-third of all American children will witness the dissolution of their parents' marriage. At the same time, the percentage of working wives rose from 32 percent in 1960 to 56 percent in 1981 (Walberg 1984).

Recent evidence suggests that the "curriculum of the home," which partly overlaps the school curriculum, is decisive in children's learning, and these changes in family life may affect the ability of the child to learn at home. The home curriculum includes informed parent-child conversations about everyday events, encouragement and discussion of leisure reading, monitoring and joint analysis of televiewing, deferral of immediate gratification to accomplish long-term goals, expressions of affection and interest in the child's academic and personal growth, and serendipity. This curriculum, like the one in the school, may be indexed by amount as well as quality; both the school and home curriculum are important and multiply one another's effects.

HOMEWORK

Aside from parent-initiated, academically stimulating experience, there seems little doubt that teacher-assigned academic work to be completed at home has substantial effects on students' learning. There is even less doubt that American students, on average, allocate comparatively little time to it—perhaps about one-sixth of the amount of time they spend watching television.

Homework increases learning by increasing the length of study time. But it may have other less obvious benefits. It encourages academic pursuits independent of the teacher, which is perhaps more important than directly supervised work, and this independence is an ultimate aim of education. In an other-directed society, it may encourage solitary reflection and insight; but it need not be done alone, and teams of students may be assigned homework projects to foster cooperative skills. The amount, quality, and usefulness of homework is jointly determined by teachers, parents, and students. If one of the three legs of the homework stool is unsupportive, little may be accomplished academically in the large amount of time students spend outside school.

CONCLUSION

A Nation At Risk and other national reports have given citizens and educators a greater grasp of the facts about learning, their meaning, and their significance to our nation. Educators can profit from past successes and failures in using scarce resources, especially human time, to meet competing goals. Educational and psychological research in ordinary schools shows that improving the amount and quality of instruction can result in vastly more effective and efficient academic learning.

Recent national reports may rightly call for a rebalancing of the subject matter that constitutes the curriculum; and the commission seems right in emphasizing that children need to spend more time in school. Students should also be employing more time in academic pursuits outside school and using both in-school and out-of-school time more efficiently. Although research indicates that greater amounts and higher standards of academic work would benefit our students' learning, it is by no means clear that the spirit of our times; the structure, technology, and incentives in our schools; and the state of our families' support of learning are consistent with the changes that seem in order.

Finally, educational costs and goals beyond immediate measurement are worth remembering. But great accomplishments also result from sustained hard work, supportive parents, and world-class standards and instruction. Psychological studies of the lives of eminent painters, writers, musicians, philosophers, scientists, and religious and political leaders of past centuries as well as of the highly accomplished American adolescents of today reveal early, intense, and sustained concentration in addition to help from parents and teachers (Walberg 1983; Bloom 1985). World-class performance may require seventy hours of effective instruction and practice per week for a decade, although the possibility that it may take considerably more or less time shows how much more we need to know about investing in students and how much more seriously educators and their allies might take the potential of their own contribution to improving the prospects of a nation that remains at risk.

REFERENCES

Bloom, Benjamin S., ed. *Developing Talent in Young People.* New York: Ballentine, 1985.

Csikszentmihalyi, Mihaly, and Larsen, Richard. *Being Adolescent: Conflict and Growth in the Teen-Age Years* New York: Basic Books, 1984.

National Commission on Excellence in Education. *A Nation At Risk: The Imperative for Educational Reform.* Washington, D.C.: U.S. Government Printing Office, 1983.

Peng, Samuel S.; Fetters, William B.; and Kolstad, Andrew J. *High School and Beyond: A National Longitudinal Study for the 1980s.* Washington, D.C.: National Center for Education Statistics, 1981.

Peterson, Penelope E. "Did the Commission Say Anything?" *Brookings Review* 2 (Winter 1983): 3–11.

Rohlen, T.P. *Japan's High Schools.* Berkeley: University of California Press, 1983.

Schiller, Diane P., and Walberg, Herbert J. "Japan: The Learning Society." *Educational Leadership* 39 (March 1982): 411–413.

Stevenson, H. *Comparisons of Japanese, Taiwanese, and American Mathematics Achievement.* Stanford, Calif.: Center for Advanced Study in the Behavioral Sciences, 1983.

Walberg, Herbert J. "Families as Partners in Educational Productivity." *Phi Delta Kappan* 65 (February 1984): 397–400.

Walberg, Herbert J. "Scientific Literacy and Economic Productivity in International Perspective." *Daedalus* 112 (Spring 1983): 1–28.

Walberg, Herbert J.; Harnisch, D.; and Tsai, Shiow-Ling. "High School Productivity in Twelve Countries." *Journal of Educational Research*, in press.

Walberg, Herbert J., and Shanahan, Timothy. "High School Effects on Individual Students." *Educational Researcher* 12:7 (1983): 4–9.

Westbury, Ian. "Essay Review: A Nation At Risk." *Journal of Curriculum Studies* 16 (1984): 431–445.